HARROW

◄ FAMILY TREE ►

COUNTY™

HARROW
◆ FAMILY TREE ◆
COUNTY ™

Script
CULLEN BUNN

Art and Lettering
TYLER CROOK

DARK HORSE BOOKS

Designer
KEITH WOOD

Digital Art Technician
CHRISTIANNE GOUDREAU

NEIL HANKERSON *Executive Vice President* · **TOM WEDDLE** *Chief Financial Officer* · **RANDY STRADLEY** *Vice President of Publishing*
MATT PARKINSON *Vice President of Marketing* · **DAVID SCROGGY** *Vice President of Product Development* · **DALE LAFOUNTAIN** *Vice Preside*
of Information Technology · **CARA NIECE** *Vice President of Production and Scheduling* · **NICK McWHORTER** *Vice President of Media Licensing*
MARK BERNARDI *Vice President of Digital and Book Trade Sales* · **KEN LIZZI** *General Counsel* · **DAVE MARSHALL** *Editor in Chief*
DAVEY ESTRADA *Editorial Director* · **SCOTT ALLIE** *Executive Senior Editor* · **CHRIS WARNER** *Senior Books Editor* · **CARY GRAZZINI** *Directo*
of Specialty Projects · **LIA RIBACCHI** *Art Director* · **VANESSA TODD** *Director of Print Purchasing* · **MATT DRYER** *Director of Digital Art and Prep*
SARAH ROBERTSON *Director of Product Sales* · **MICHAEL GOMBOS** *Director of International Publishing and Licensing*

Published by Dark Horse Books
A division of Dark Horse Comics, Inc.
10956 SE Main Street
Milwaukie, OR 97222

First edition: January 2017
ISBN 978-1-50670-141-7

International Licensing: (503) 905-2377 · Comic Shop Locator Service: (888) 266-4226

Harrow County Volume 4: Family Tree

This volume collects *Harrow County* #13–#16.

10 9 8 7 6 5 4 3 2 1
Printed in China

DarkHorse.com

Library of Congress Cataloging-in-Publication Data

Names: Bunn, Cullen, author. | Crook, Tyler, artist.
Title: Harrow County. Volume 4, Family tree / script, Cullen Bunn ; art &
 lettering, Tyler Crook.
 Other titles: Family tree
Description: First edition. | Milwaukie, OR : Dark Horse Books, 2017.
Identifiers: LCCN 2016034855 | ISBN 9781506701417 (paperback)
Subjects: LCSH: Comic books, strips, etc. | BISAC: COMICS & GRAPHIC NOVELS /
 Horror. | COMICS & GRAPHIC NOVELS / Fantasy. | COMICS & GRAPHIC NOVELS /
 General.

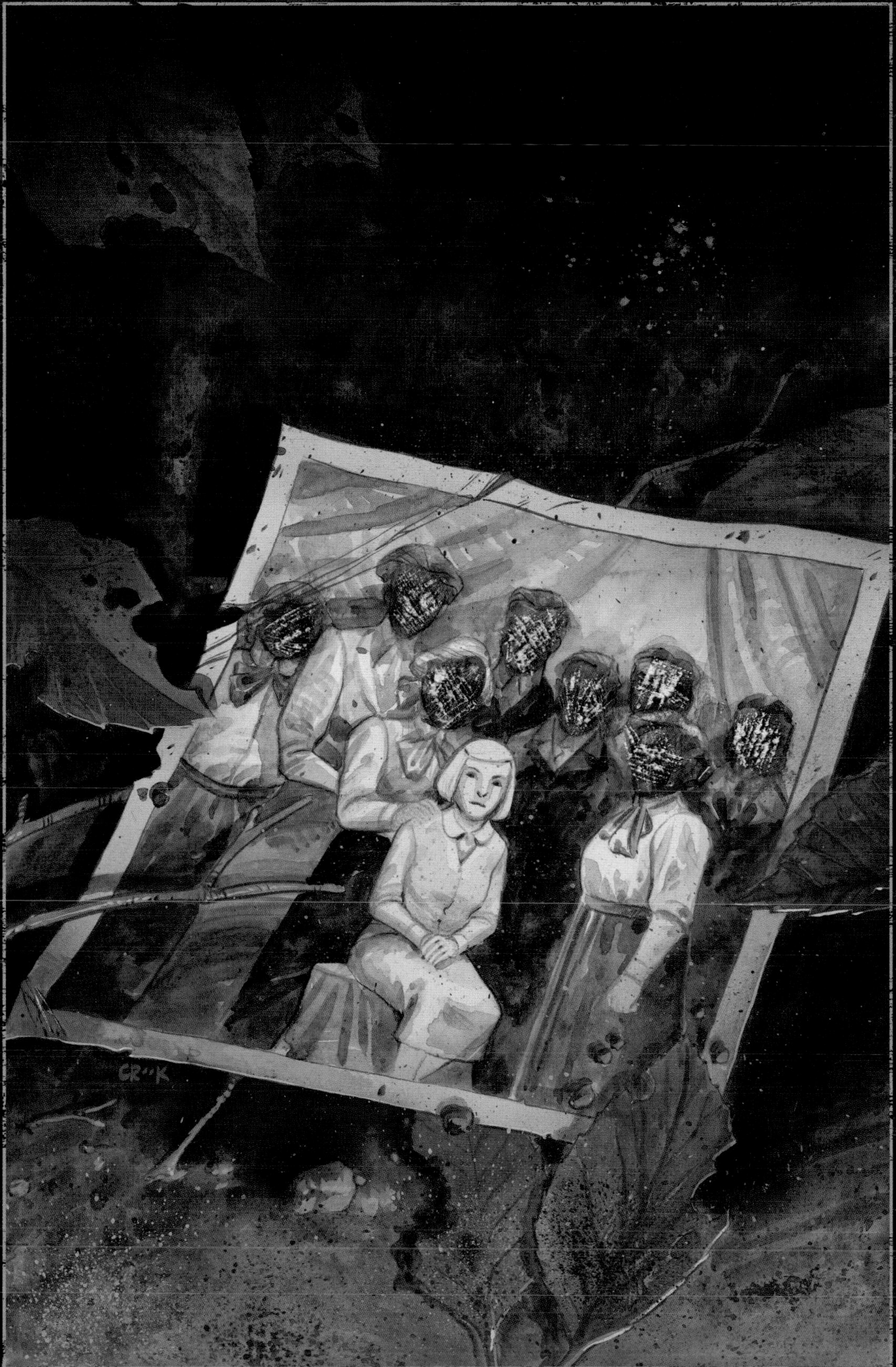

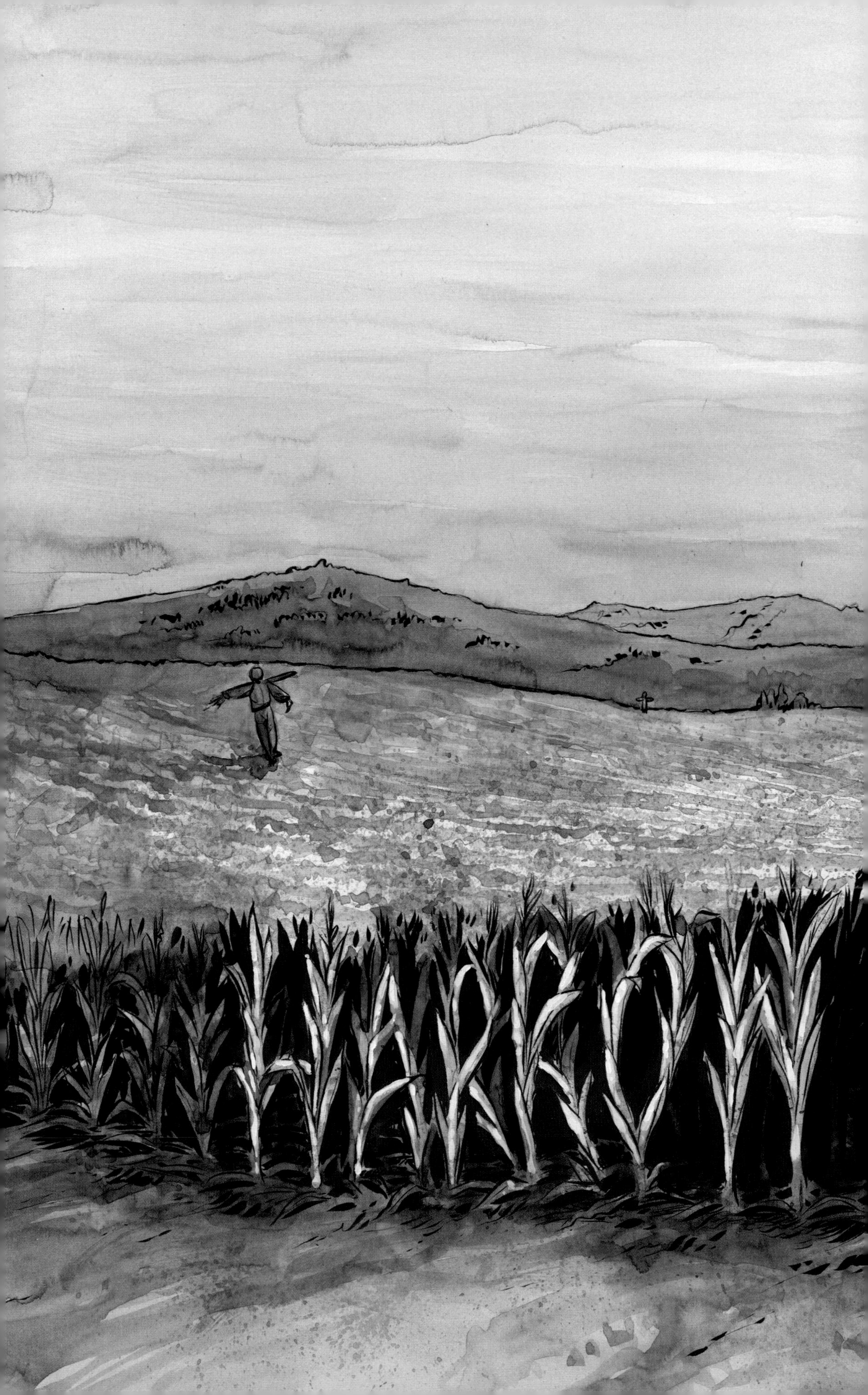

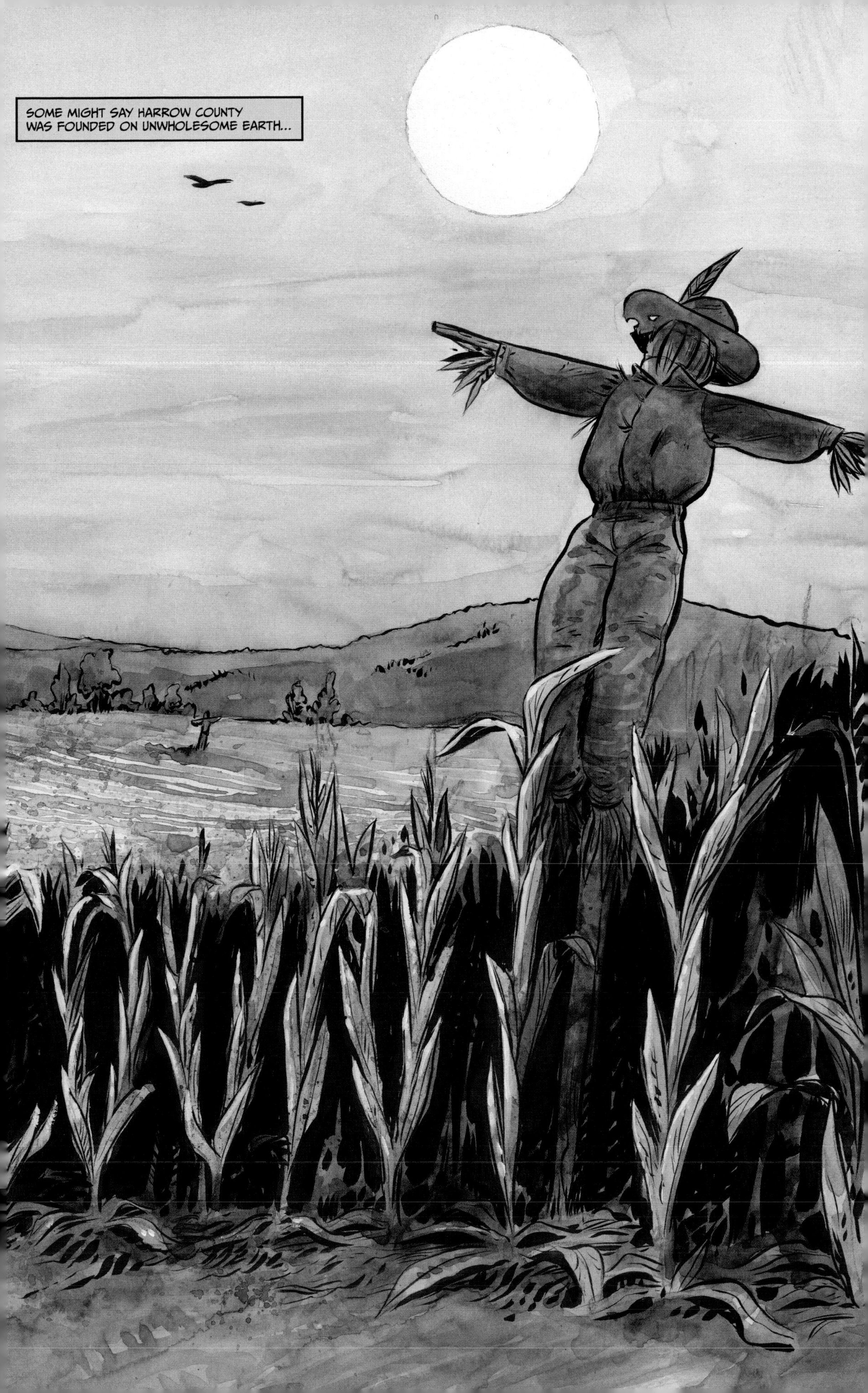
SOME MIGHT SAY HARROW COUNTY WAS FOUNDED ON UNWHOLESOME EARTH...

...THAT THE SOIL ITSELF HAD *SPOILED* LONG AGO...

...LONG BEFORE ANY *NATURAL* CREATURE HAD EVER SET FOOT THEREABOUTS.

H-HELLO?

HELLO? IS SOMEBODY OUT THERE?

WHO'S OUT THERE *A-WHISTLING?*

WHAT DO YOU WANT?

YOU *ALL RIGHT* OUT THERE?

IT WAS THIS UNDERSTANDING...

...THAT THE DIRT BENEATH YOUR FEET WAS *TAINTED*...

...THAT CAUSED FOLKS TO STEP A LITTLE MORE *CAREFULLY*...

...TO GLANCE OVER THEIR SHOULDERS, CERTAIN SOMEONE-- OR *SOMETHING*-- WAS FOLLOWING THEM...

...AND TO WATCH THE SHADOWS WITH *MOUNTING DREAD.*

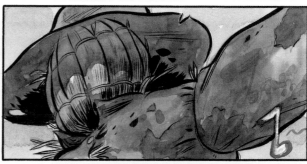

WHOEVER YOU ARE...

...WHOEVER'S OUT THERE...

...I'M SORRY, BUT I CAN'T STAY.

I'M EXPECTED BACK--

FOR IF THE VERY EARTH HAD BEEN *POISONED* BY ABNORMAL THINGS...

...WHAT STRANGE LIFE MIGHT TAKE *ROOT* THEREIN?

...HOME...
HNF
HNF
...WHICH WAY...
...WHERE AM I?
I CAME THIS WAY...
...DIDN'T I?
H-HELLO?
HELLO?
WHO'S CALLING TO ME?

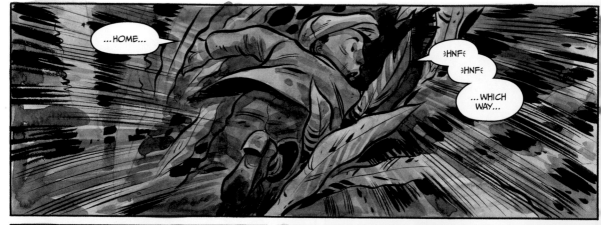

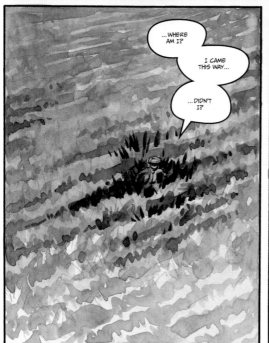

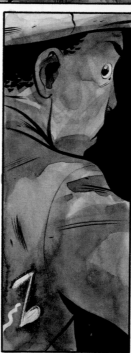

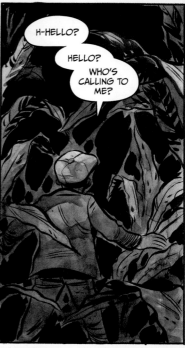

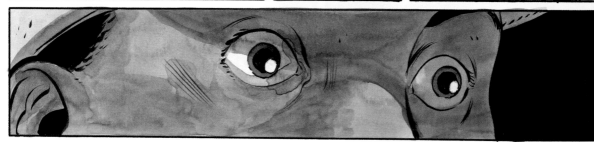

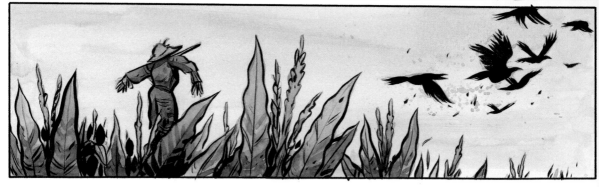

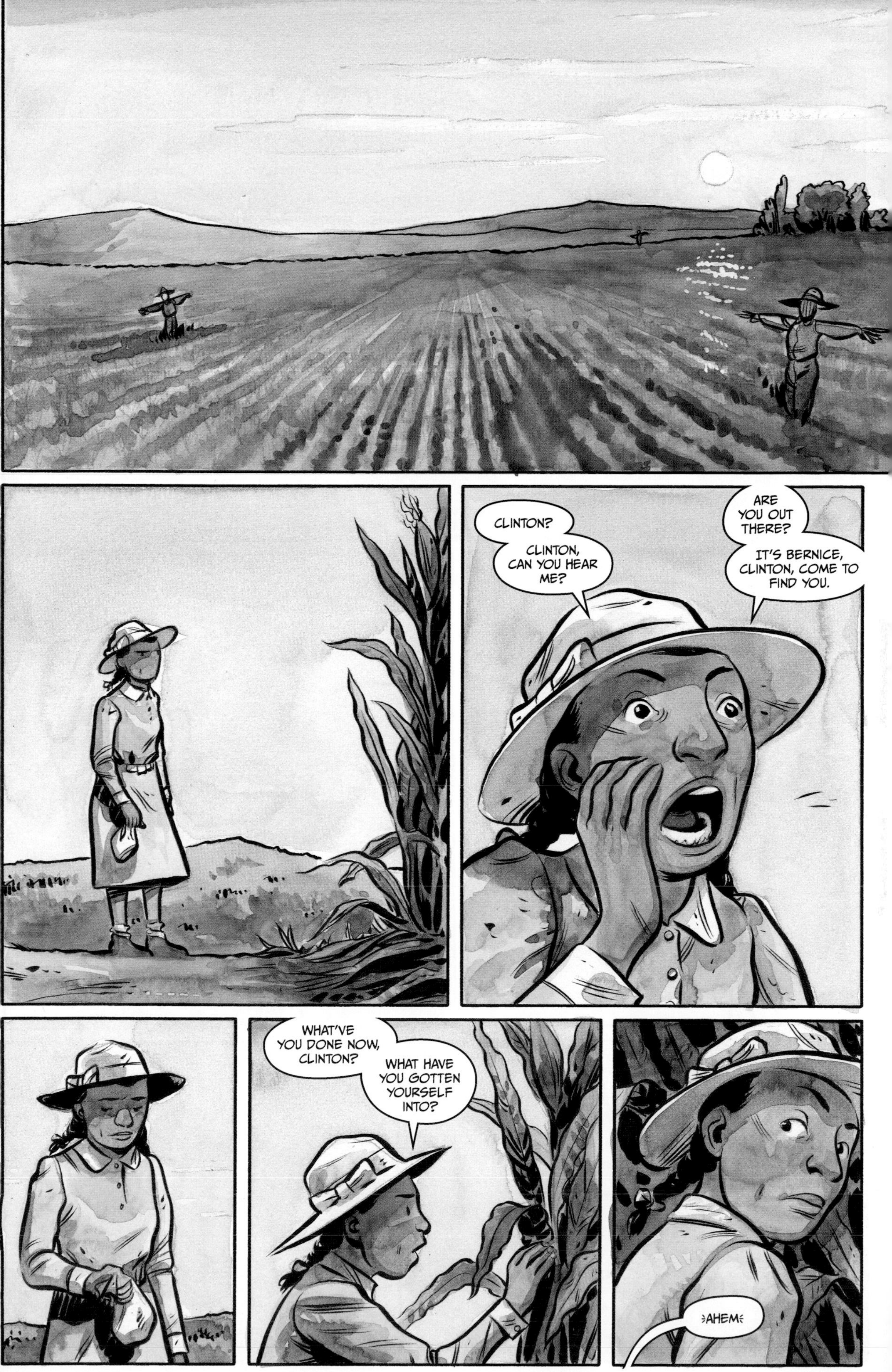
CLINTON?
CLINTON, CAN YOU HEAR ME?
ARE YOU OUT THERE?
IT'S BERNICE, CLINTON, COME TO FIND YOU.
WHAT'VE YOU DONE NOW, CLINTON?
WHAT HAVE YOU GOTTEN YOURSELF INTO?
AHEM

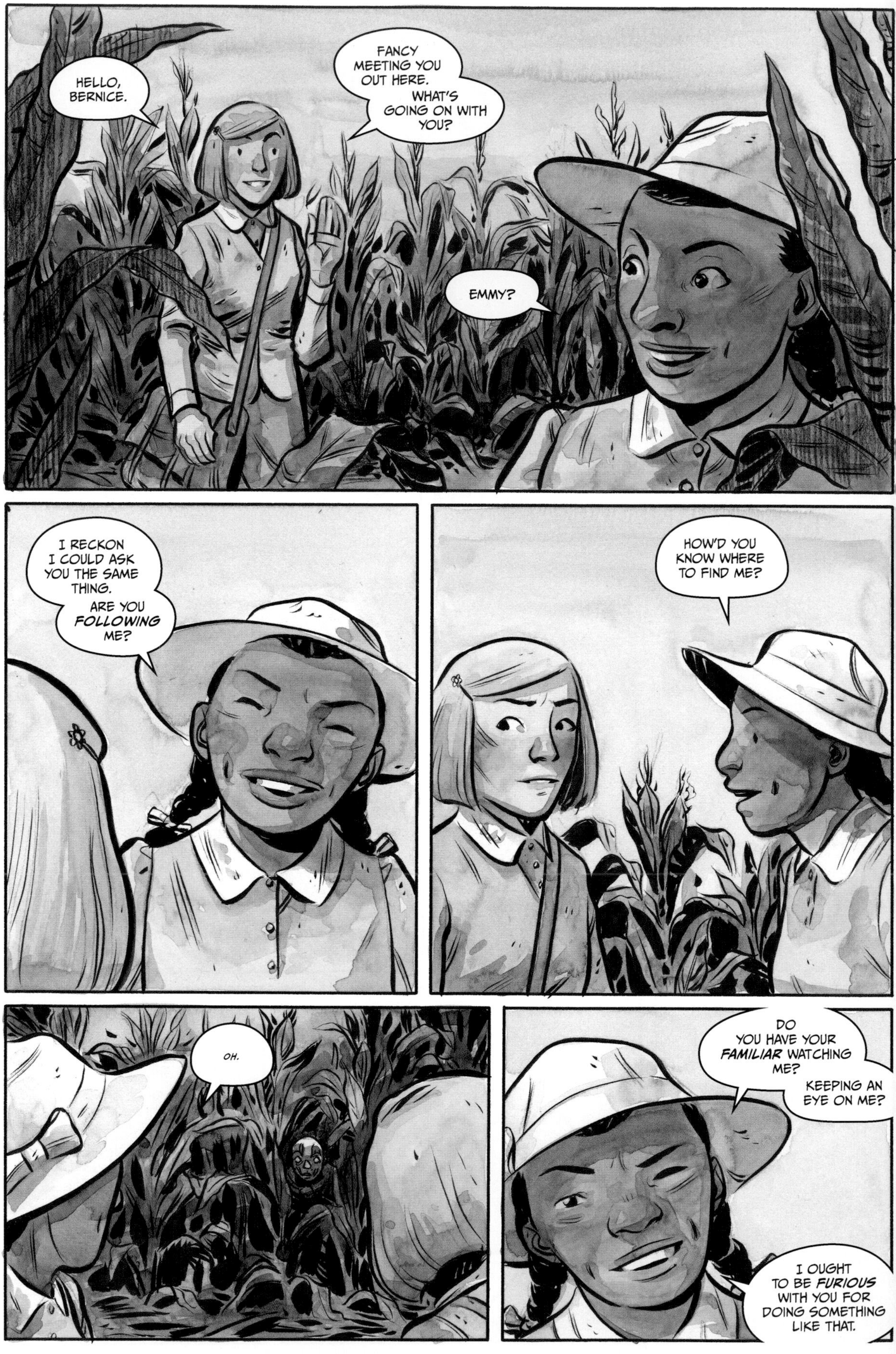
HELLO, BERNICE.
FANCY MEETING YOU OUT HERE.
WHAT'S GOING ON WITH YOU?
EMMY?
I RECKON I COULD ASK YOU THE SAME THING.
ARE YOU *FOLLOWING* ME?
HOW'D YOU KNOW WHERE TO FIND ME?
OH.
DO YOU HAVE YOUR *FAMILIAR* WATCHING ME?
KEEPING AN EYE ON ME?
I OUGHT TO BE *FURIOUS* WITH YOU FOR DOING SOMETHING LIKE THAT.

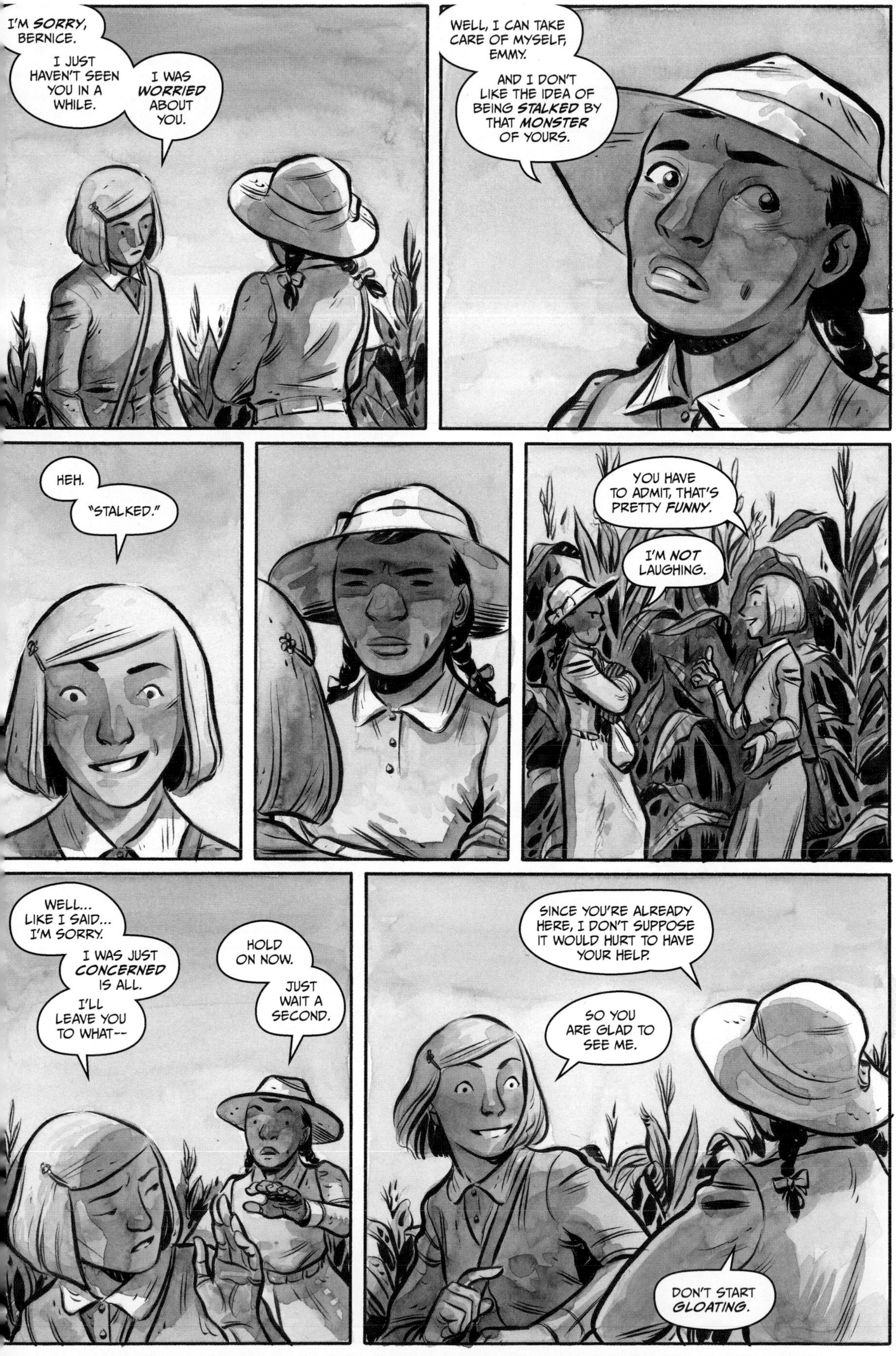
I'M SORRY, BERNICE.
I JUST HAVEN'T SEEN YOU IN A WHILE.
I WAS WORRIED ABOUT YOU.
WELL, I CAN TAKE CARE OF MYSELF, EMMY.
AND I DON'T LIKE THE IDEA OF BEING STALKED BY THAT MONSTER OF YOURS.
HEH.
"STALKED."
YOU HAVE TO ADMIT, THAT'S PRETTY FUNNY.
I'M NOT LAUGHING.
WELL... LIKE I SAID... I'M SORRY.
I WAS JUST CONCERNED IS ALL.
I'LL LEAVE YOU TO WHAT--
HOLD ON NOW.
JUST WAIT A SECOND.
SINCE YOU'RE ALREADY HERE, I DON'T SUPPOSE IT WOULD HURT TO HAVE YOUR HELP.
SO YOU ARE GLAD TO SEE ME.
DON'T START GLOATING.

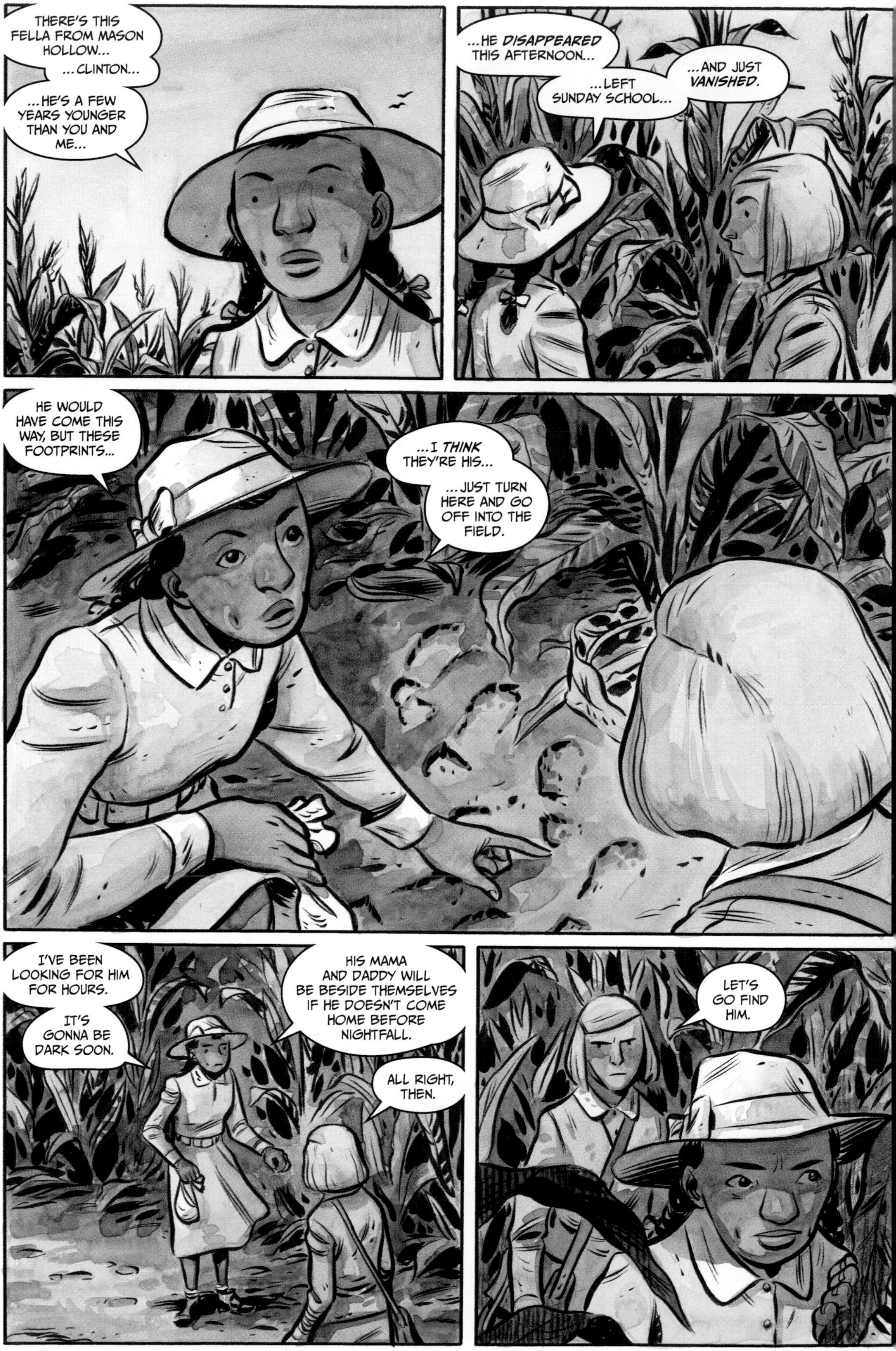

THERE'S THIS FELLA FROM MASON HOLLOW...
...CLINTON...
...HE'S A FEW YEARS YOUNGER THAN YOU AND ME...
...HE *DISAPPEARED* THIS AFTERNOON...
...LEFT SUNDAY SCHOOL...
...AND JUST *VANISHED.*
HE WOULD HAVE COME THIS WAY, BUT THESE FOOTPRINTS...
...I *THINK* THEY'RE HIS...
...JUST TURN HERE AND GO OFF INTO THE FIELD.
I'VE BEEN LOOKING FOR HIM FOR HOURS.
IT'S GONNA BE DARK SOON.
HIS MAMA AND DADDY WILL BE BESIDE THEMSELVES IF HE DOESN'T COME HOME BEFORE NIGHTFALL.
ALL RIGHT, THEN.
LET'S GO FIND HIM.

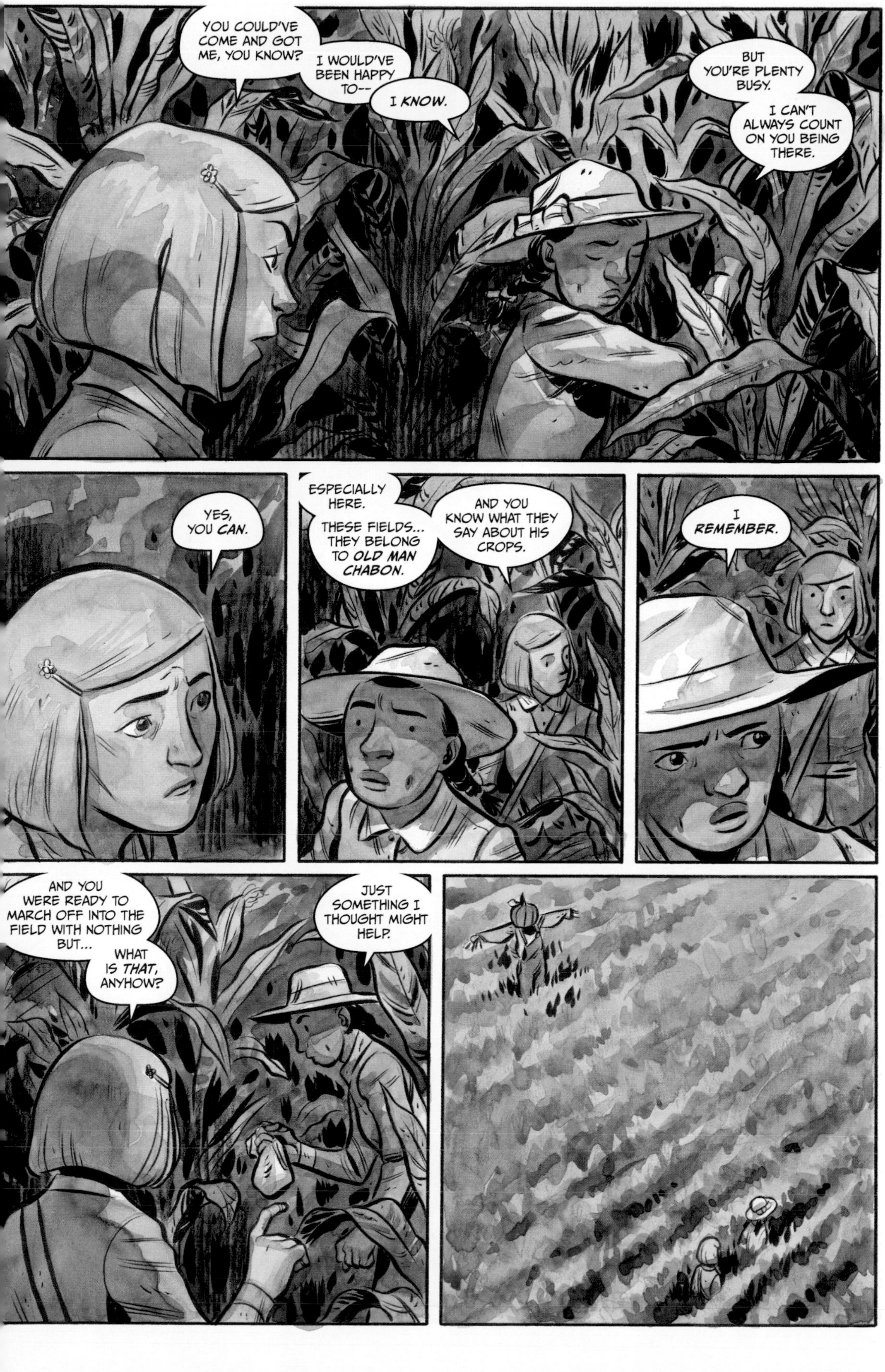
YOU COULD'VE COME AND GOT ME, YOU KNOW?
I WOULD'VE BEEN HAPPY TO--
I KNOW.
BUT YOU'RE PLENTY BUSY.
I CAN'T ALWAYS COUNT ON YOU BEING THERE.
YES, YOU CAN.
ESPECIALLY HERE.
THESE FIELDS... THEY BELONG TO OLD MAN CHABON.
AND YOU KNOW WHAT THEY SAY ABOUT HIS CROPS.
I REMEMBER.
AND YOU WERE READY TO MARCH OFF INTO THE FIELD WITH NOTHING BUT...
WHAT IS THAT, ANYHOW?
JUST SOMETHING I THOUGHT MIGHT HELP.

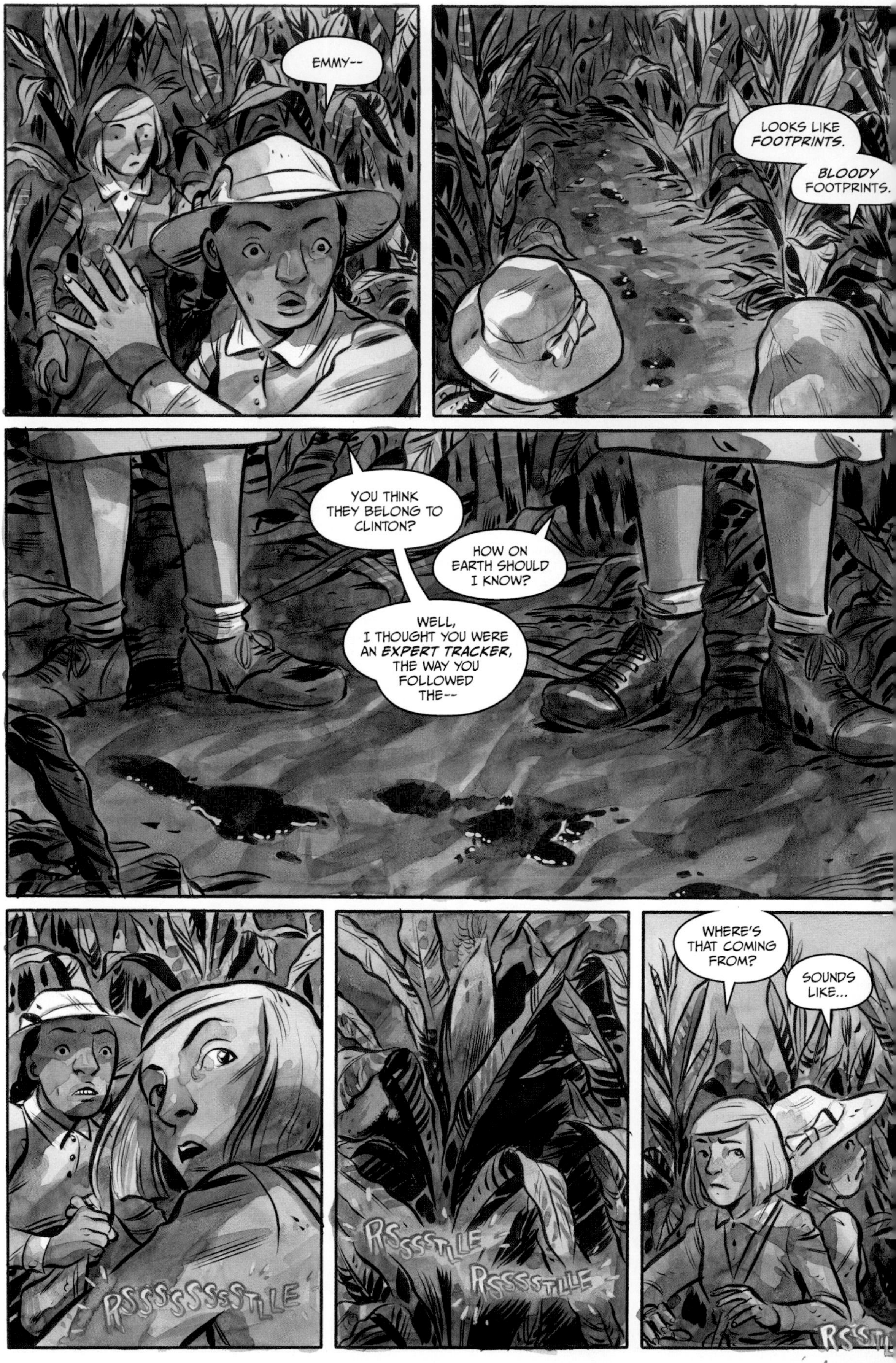
EMMY--
LOOKS LIKE FOOTPRINTS.
BLOODY FOOTPRINTS.
YOU THINK THEY BELONG TO CLINTON?
HOW ON EARTH SHOULD I KNOW?
WELL, I THOUGHT YOU WERE AN EXPERT TRACKER, THE WAY YOU FOLLOWED THE--
RSSSSSSSSTLLE
RSSSSTLLE
RSSSSTLLE
WHERE'S THAT COMING FROM?
SOUNDS LIKE...

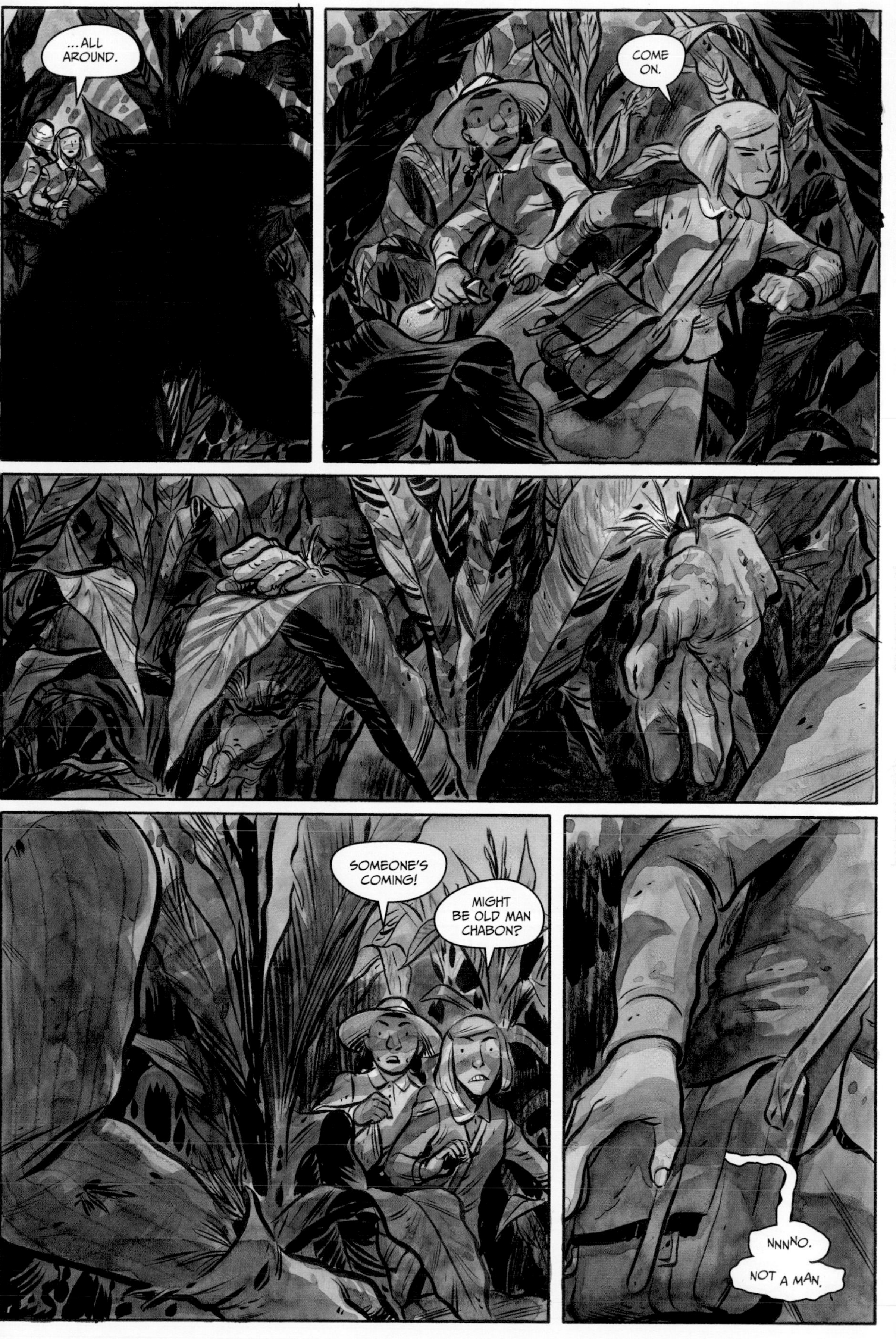
...ALL AROUND.
COME ON.
SOMEONE'S COMING!
MIGHT BE OLD MAN CHABON?
NNNNO.
NOT A MAN.

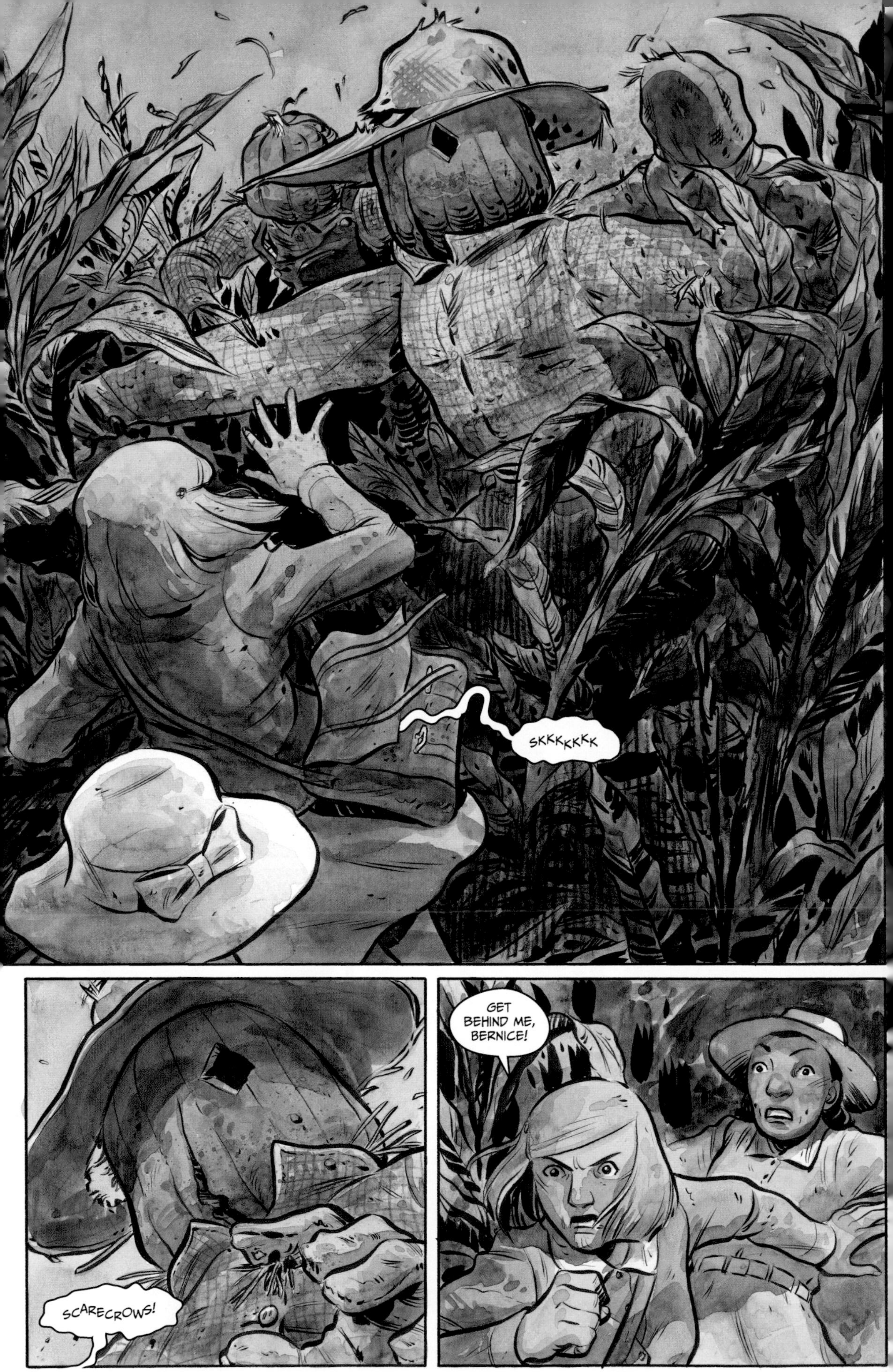
SKKKKKKK
SCARECROWS!
GET BEHIND ME, BERNICE!

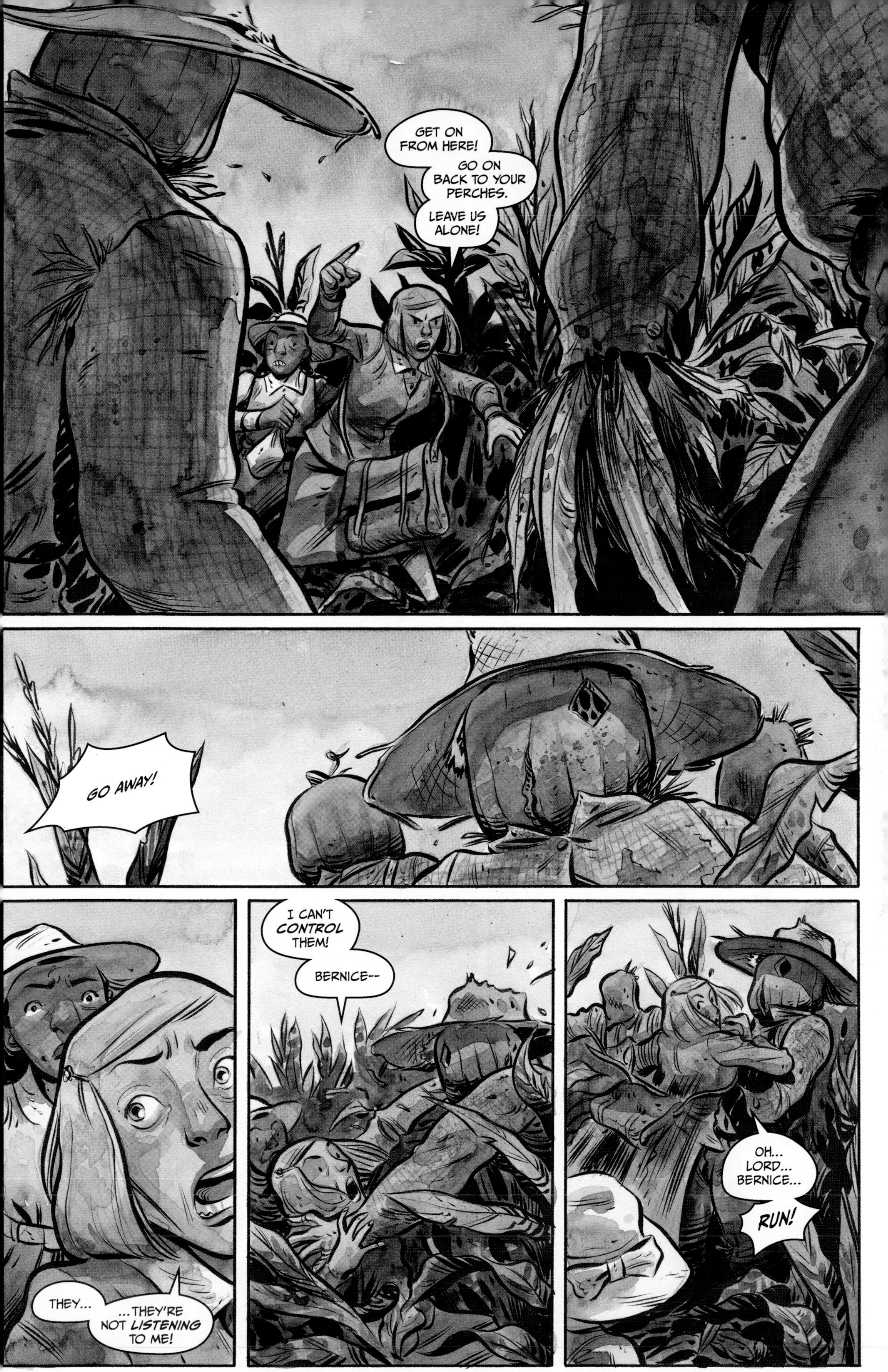
GET ON FROM HERE!
GO ON BACK TO YOUR PERCHES.
LEAVE US ALONE!
GO AWAY!
THEY...
...THEY'RE NOT LISTENING TO ME!
I CAN'T CONTROL THEM!
BERNICE--
OH... LORD... BERNICE...
RUN!

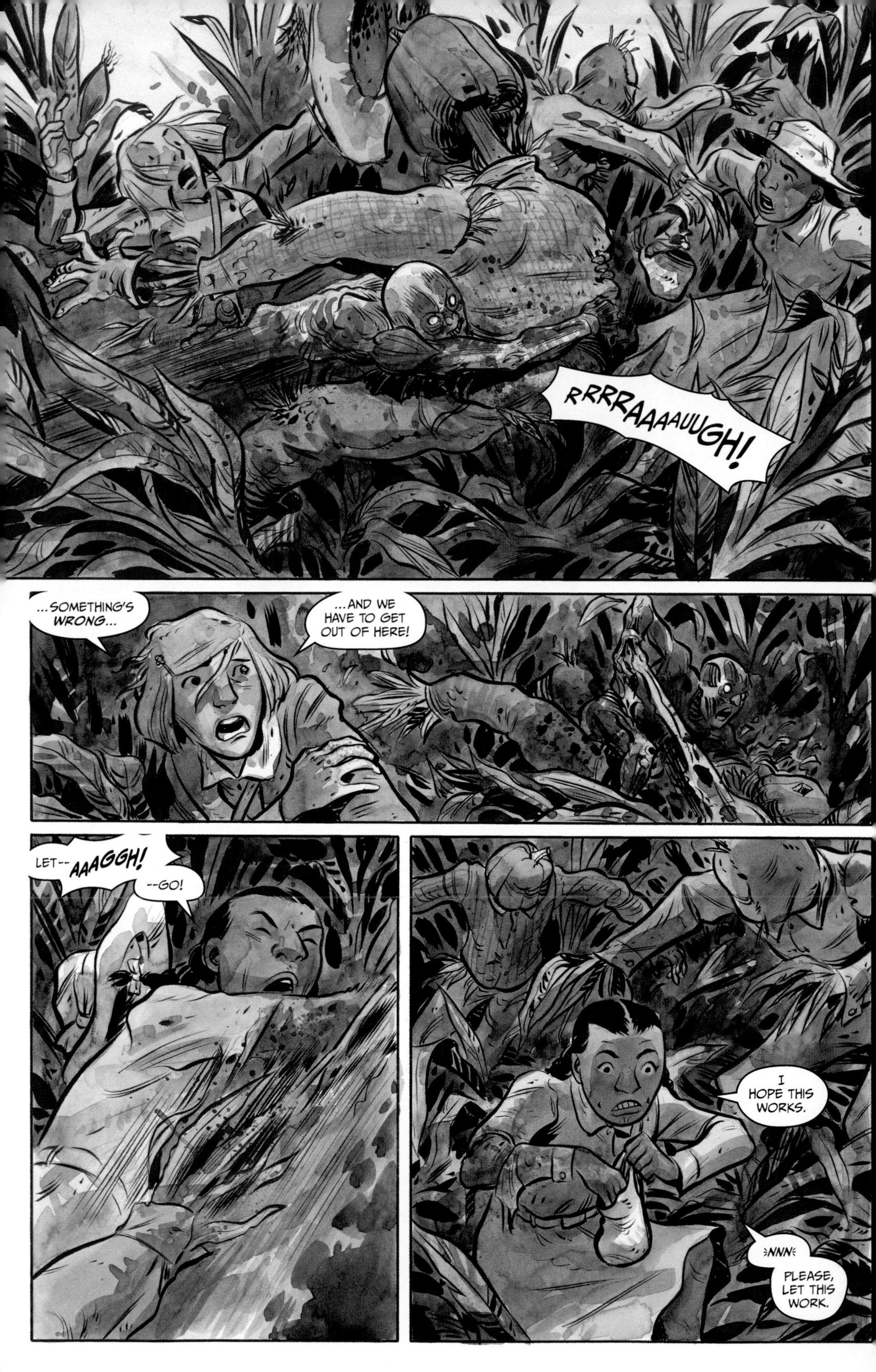
RRRRAAAAUUGH!
...SOMETHING'S WRONG...
...AND WE HAVE TO GET OUT OF HERE!
LET-- AAAGGH! --GO!
I HOPE THIS WORKS.
NNN
PLEASE, LET THIS WORK.

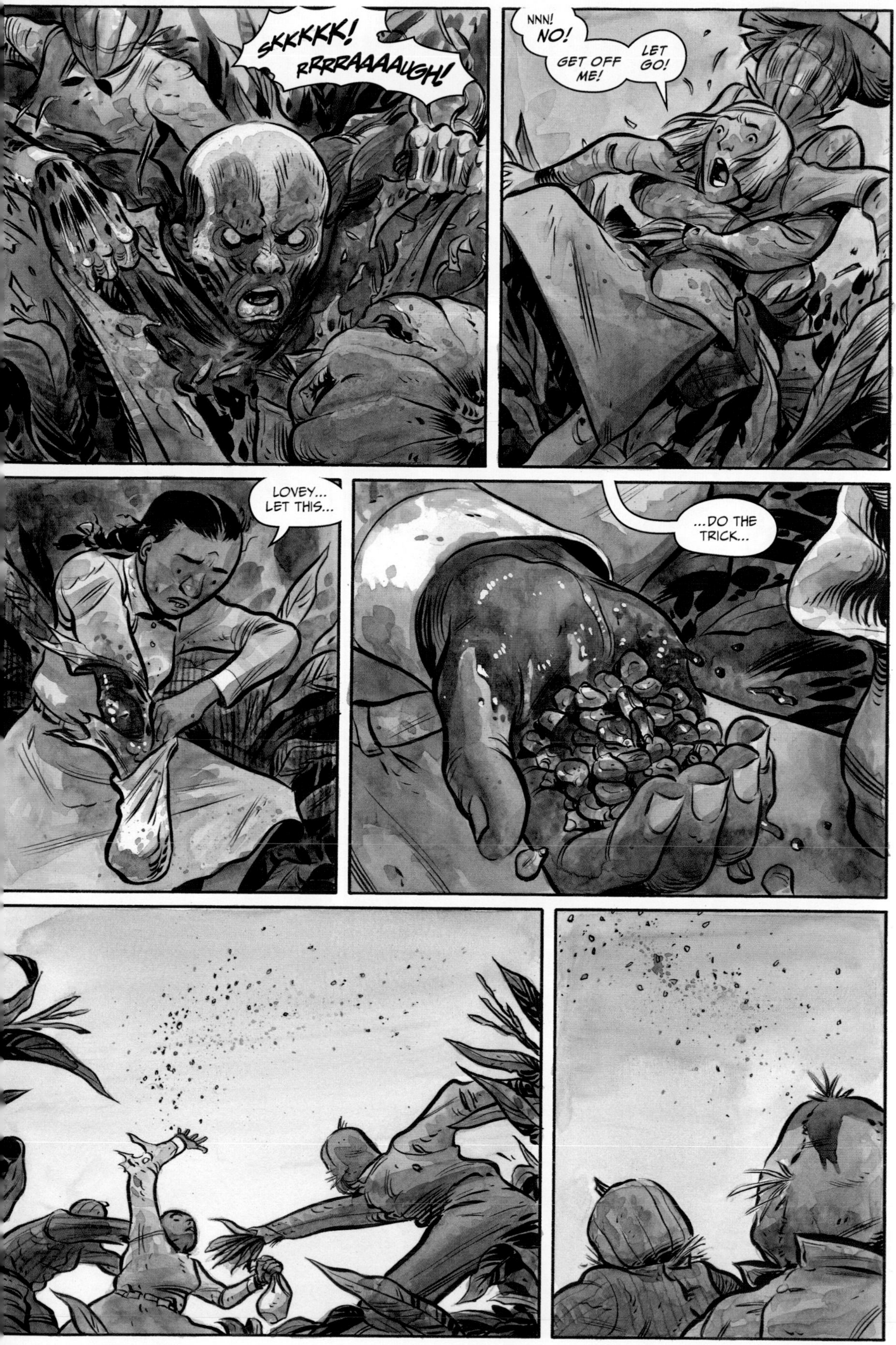
SKKKKK!
RRRRAAAAAUGH!
NNN!
NO!
GET OFF ME!
LET GO!
LOVEY... LET THIS...
...DO THE TRICK...

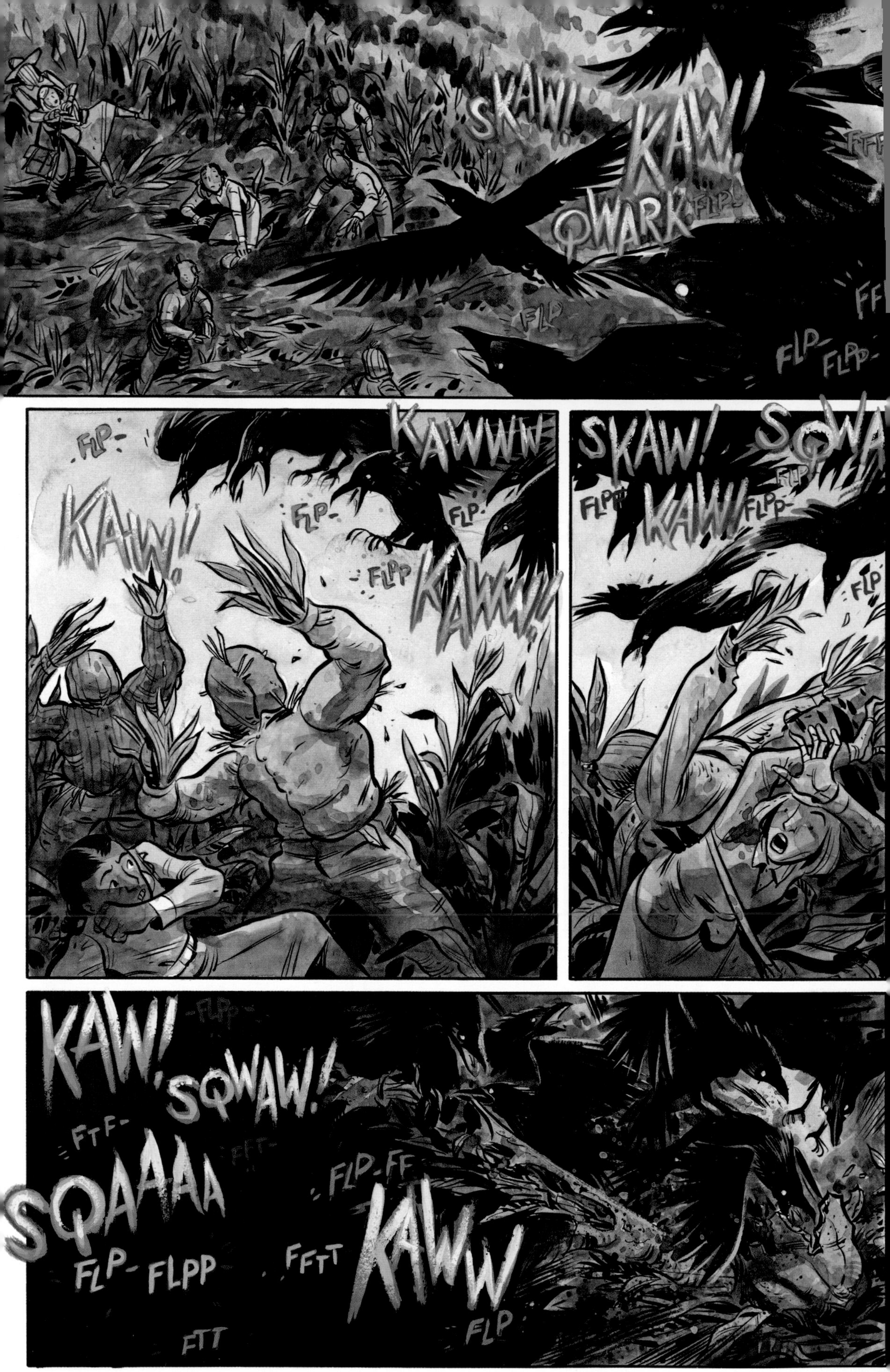
SKAW!
KAW!
QWARK
FLP-
FLP
FLP-
FLPP-
FLP-
KAWWW
KAW!
FLP-
FLP-
FLPP
KAWW!
SKAW!
SQWA
FLPP
KAW!
FLPP-
FLP
KAW!
-FLPP
SQWAW!
FTF-
SQAAAA
FLP-FLPP
FLP-FF
FFTT
KAWW
FLP
FTT

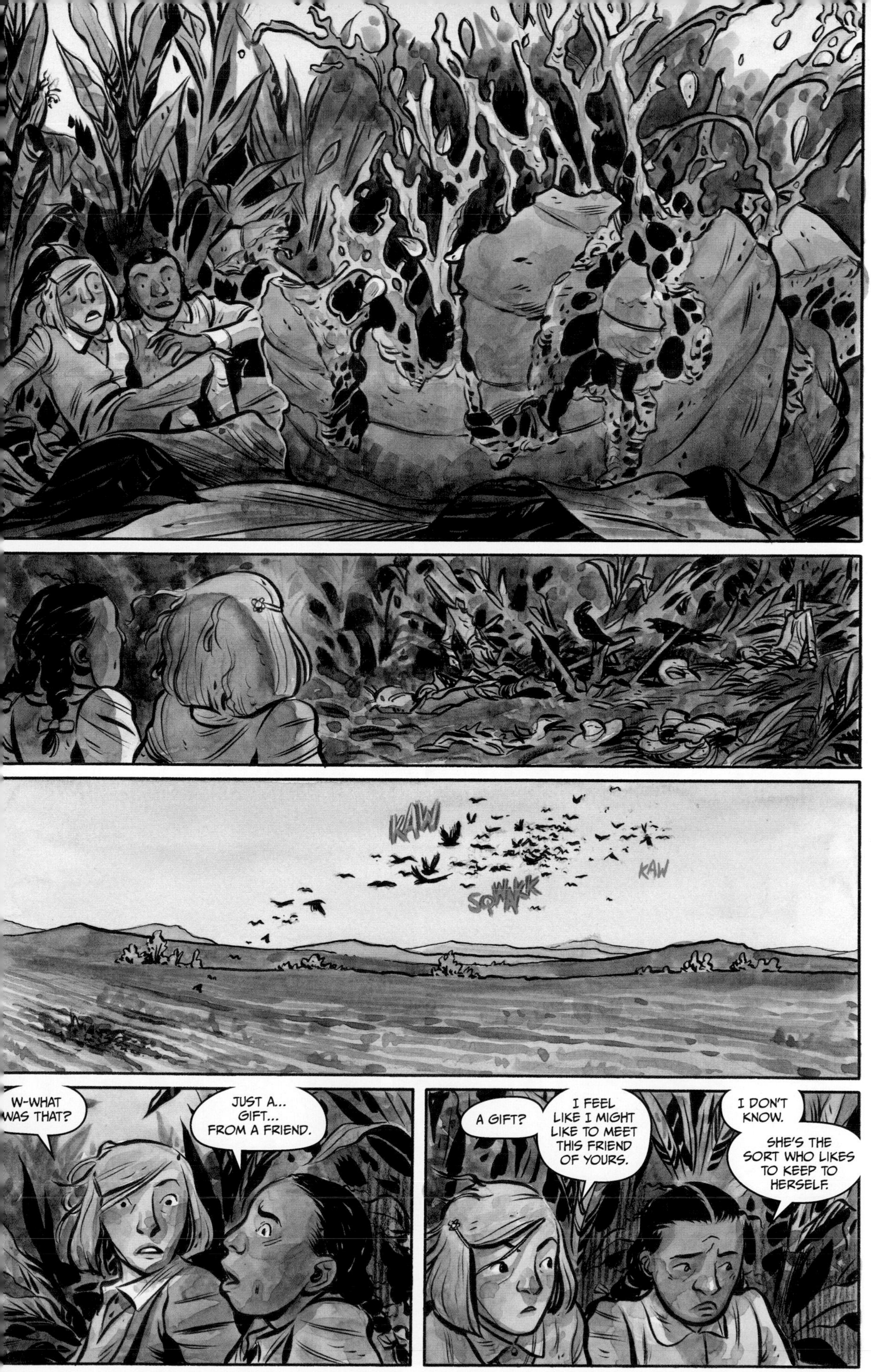
KAW
KAW
SQWAKK
W-WHAT WAS THAT?
JUST A... GIFT... FROM A FRIEND.
A GIFT?
I FEEL LIKE I MIGHT LIKE TO MEET THIS FRIEND OF YOURS.
I DON'T KNOW.
SHE'S THE SORT WHO LIKES TO KEEP TO HERSELF.

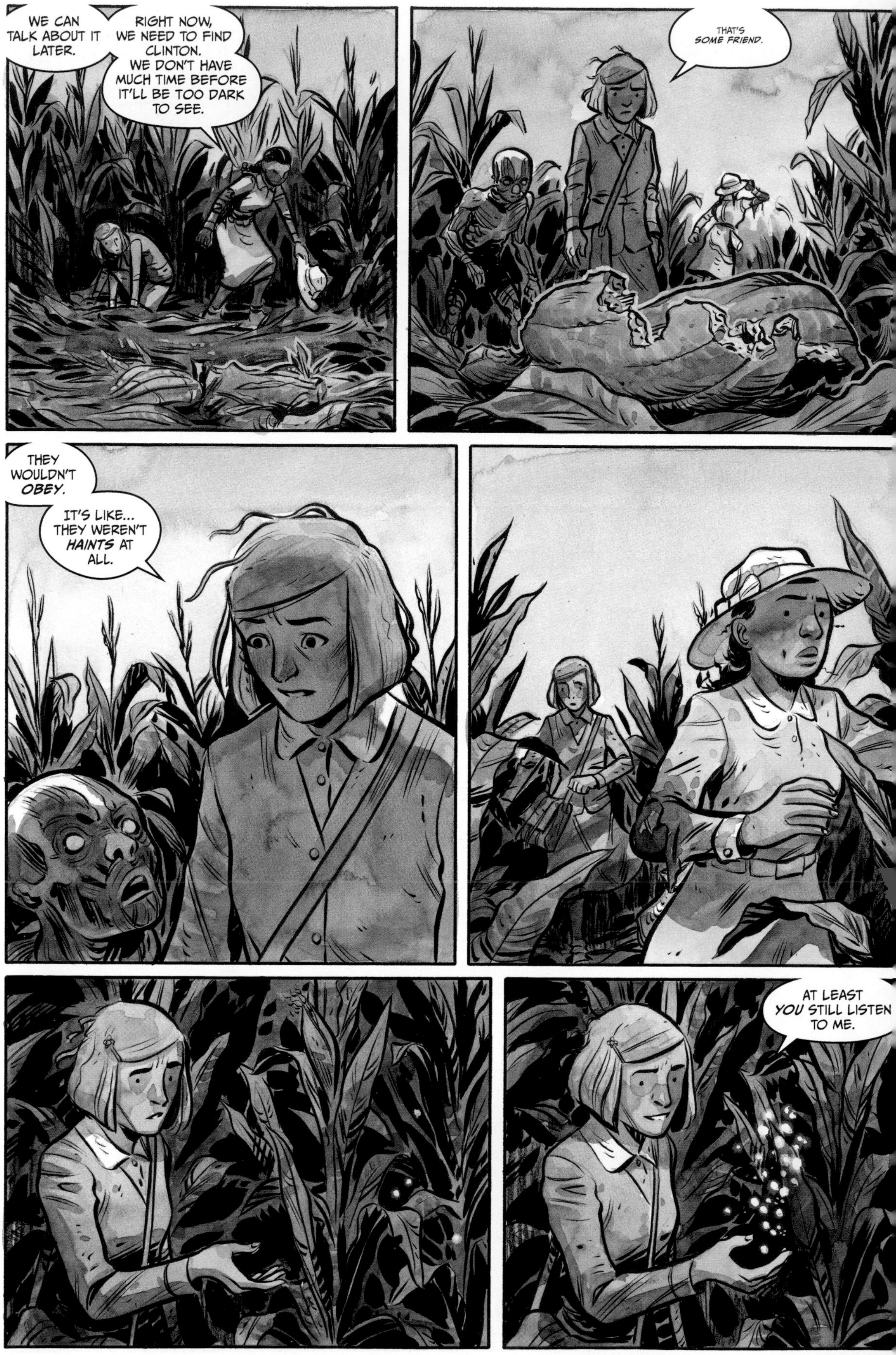

WE CAN TALK ABOUT IT LATER.
RIGHT NOW, WE NEED TO FIND CLINTON. WE DON'T HAVE MUCH TIME BEFORE IT'LL BE TOO DARK TO SEE.
THAT'S SOME FRIEND.
THEY WOULDN'T OBEY.
IT'S LIKE... THEY WEREN'T HAINTS AT ALL.
AT LEAST YOU STILL LISTEN TO ME.

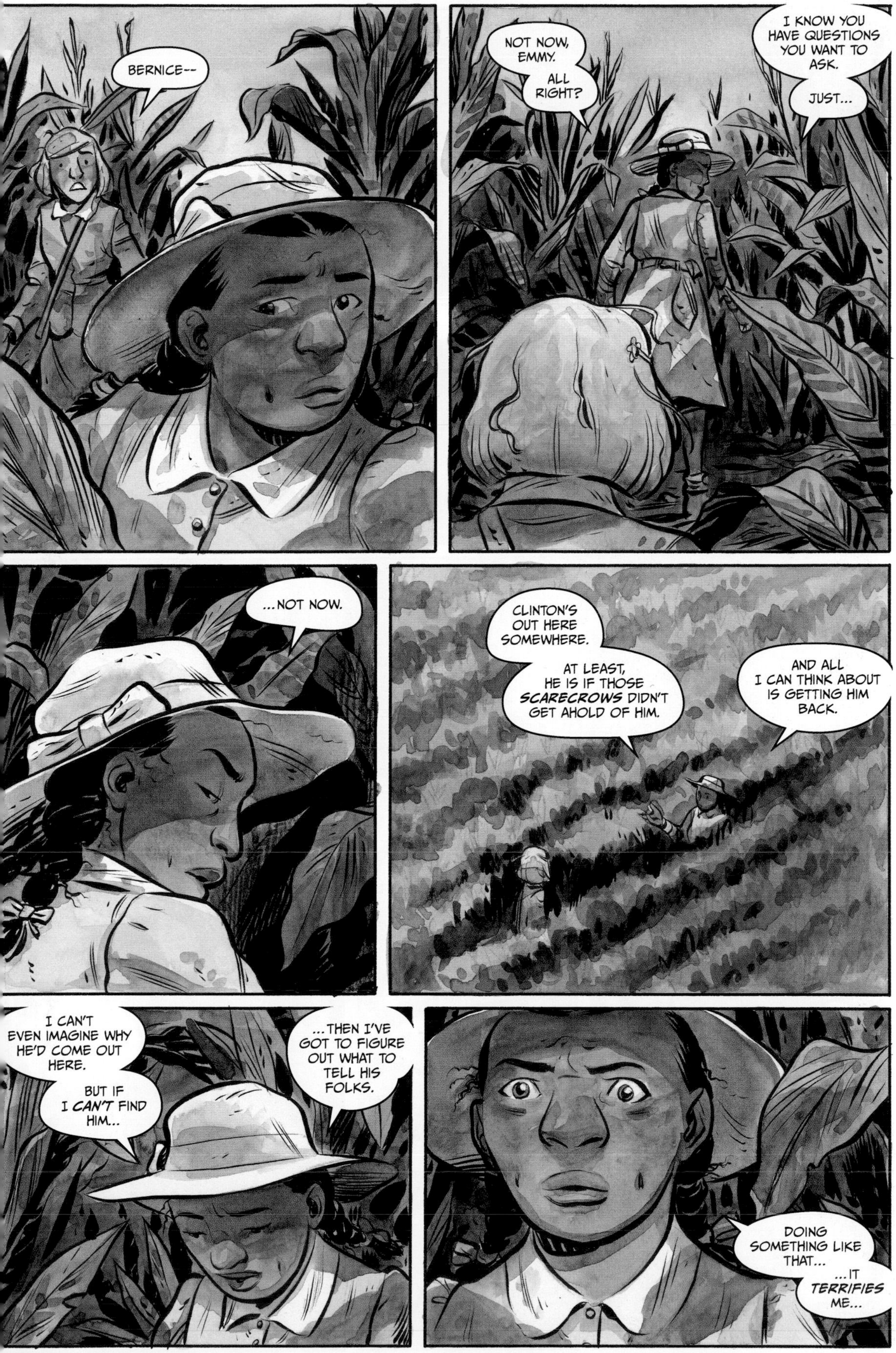
BERNICE--
NOT NOW, EMMY.
ALL RIGHT?
I KNOW YOU HAVE QUESTIONS YOU WANT TO ASK.
JUST...
...NOT NOW.
CLINTON'S OUT HERE SOMEWHERE.
AT LEAST, HE IS IF THOSE SCARECROWS DIDN'T GET AHOLD OF HIM.
AND ALL I CAN THINK ABOUT IS GETTING HIM BACK.
I CAN'T EVEN IMAGINE WHY HE'D COME OUT HERE.
BUT IF I CAN'T FIND HIM...
...THEN I'VE GOT TO FIGURE OUT WHAT TO TELL HIS FOLKS.
DOING SOMETHING LIKE THAT...
...IT TERRIFIES ME...

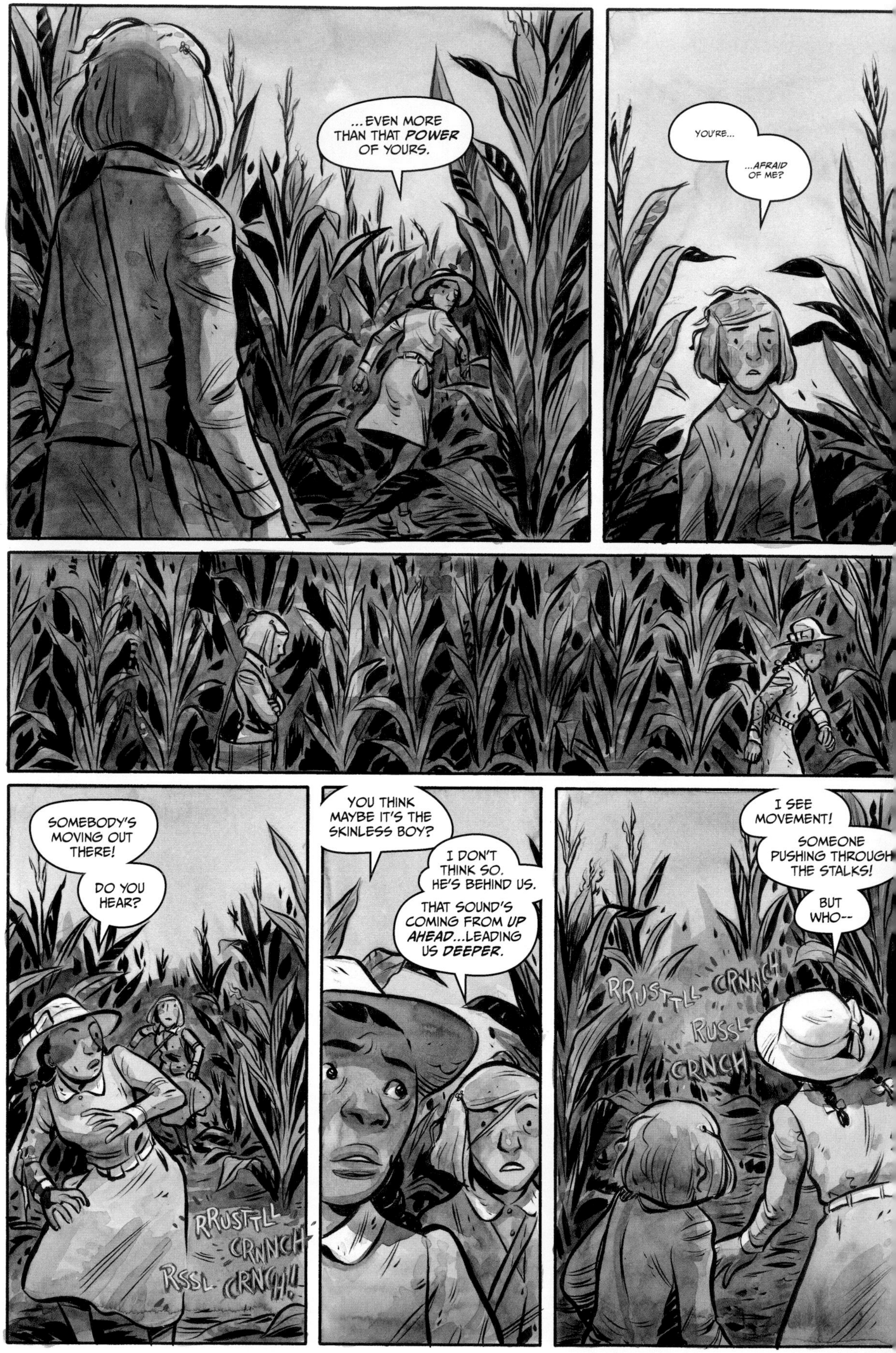
...EVEN MORE THAN THAT *POWER* OF YOURS.
YOU'RE...
...*AFRAID* OF ME?
SOMEBODY'S MOVING OUT THERE!
DO YOU HEAR?
RRUSTTLL CRNNCH
RSSL CRNCH!!
YOU THINK MAYBE IT'S THE SKINLESS BOY?
I DON'T THINK SO. HE'S BEHIND US.
THAT SOUND'S COMING FROM *UP AHEAD*...LEADING US *DEEPER*.
I SEE MOVEMENT!
SOMEONE PUSHING THROUGH THE STALKS!
BUT WHO--
RRUSTTLL CRNNCH
RUSSL
CRNCH

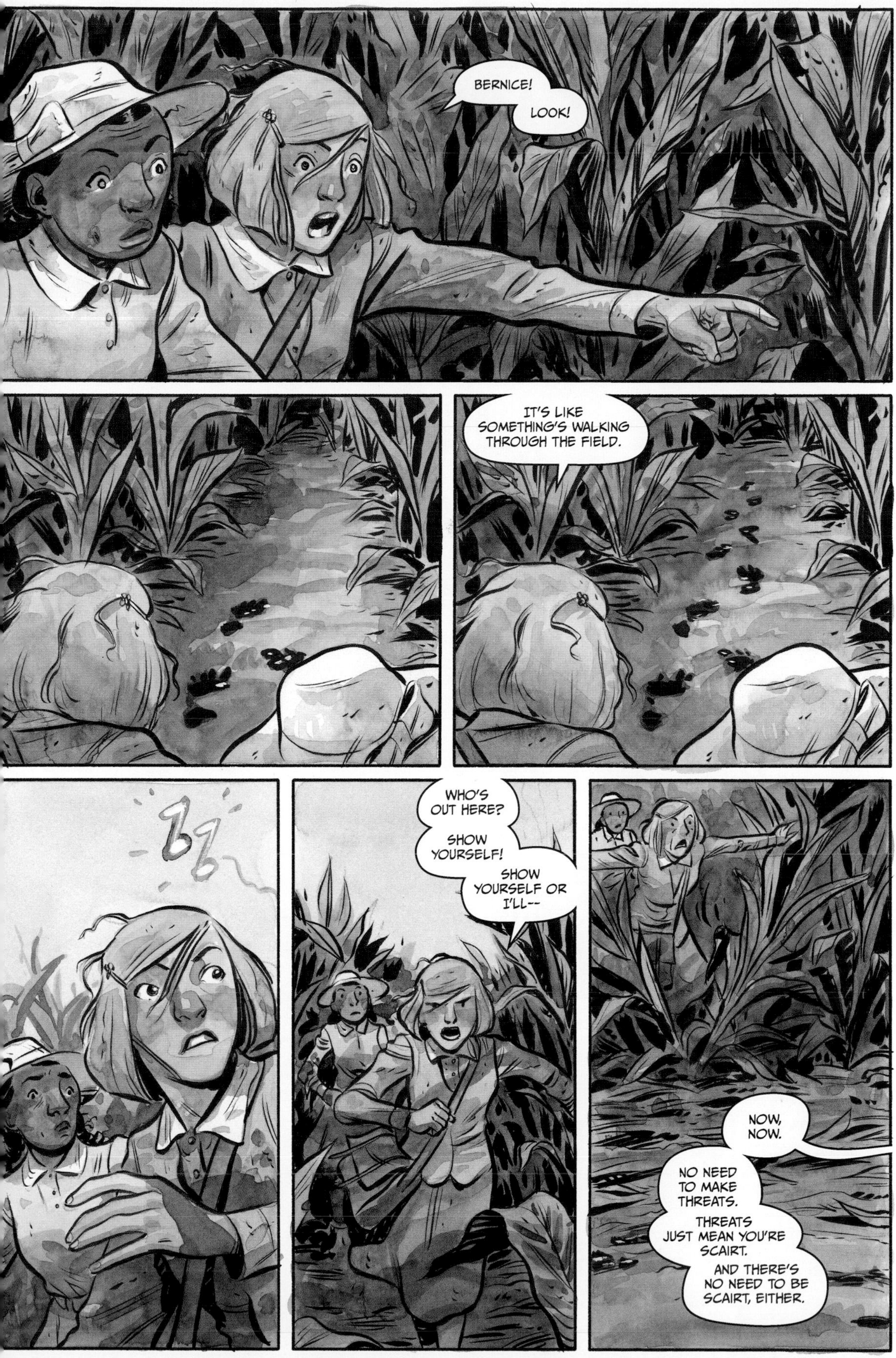
BERNICE!
LOOK!
IT'S LIKE SOMETHING'S WALKING THROUGH THE FIELD.
WHO'S OUT HERE?
SHOW YOURSELF!
SHOW YOURSELF OR I'LL--
NOW, NOW.
NO NEED TO MAKE THREATS.
THREATS JUST MEAN YOU'RE SCAIRT.
AND THERE'S NO NEED TO BE SCAIRT, EITHER.

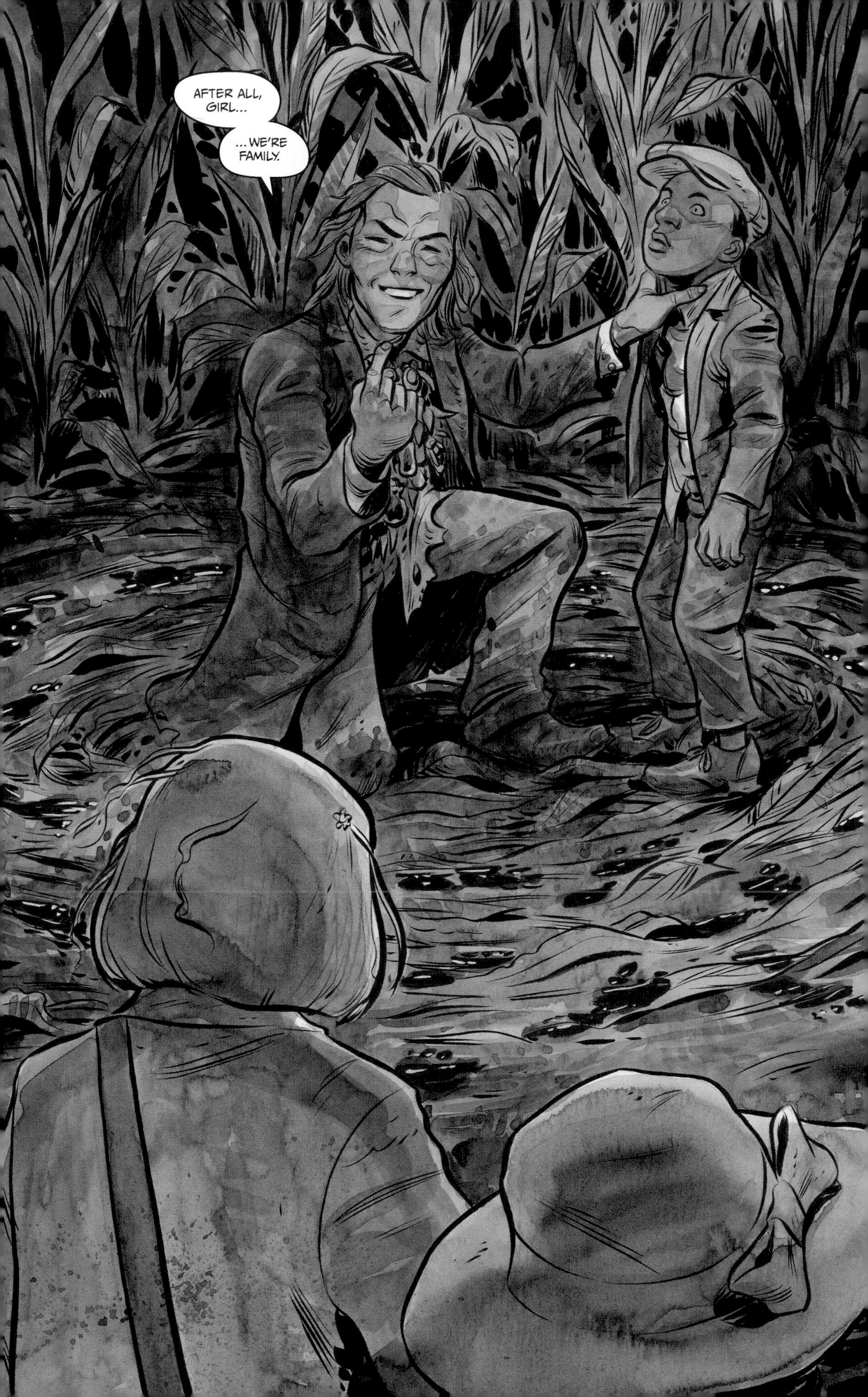
AFTER ALL, GIRL...
...WE'RE FAMILY.

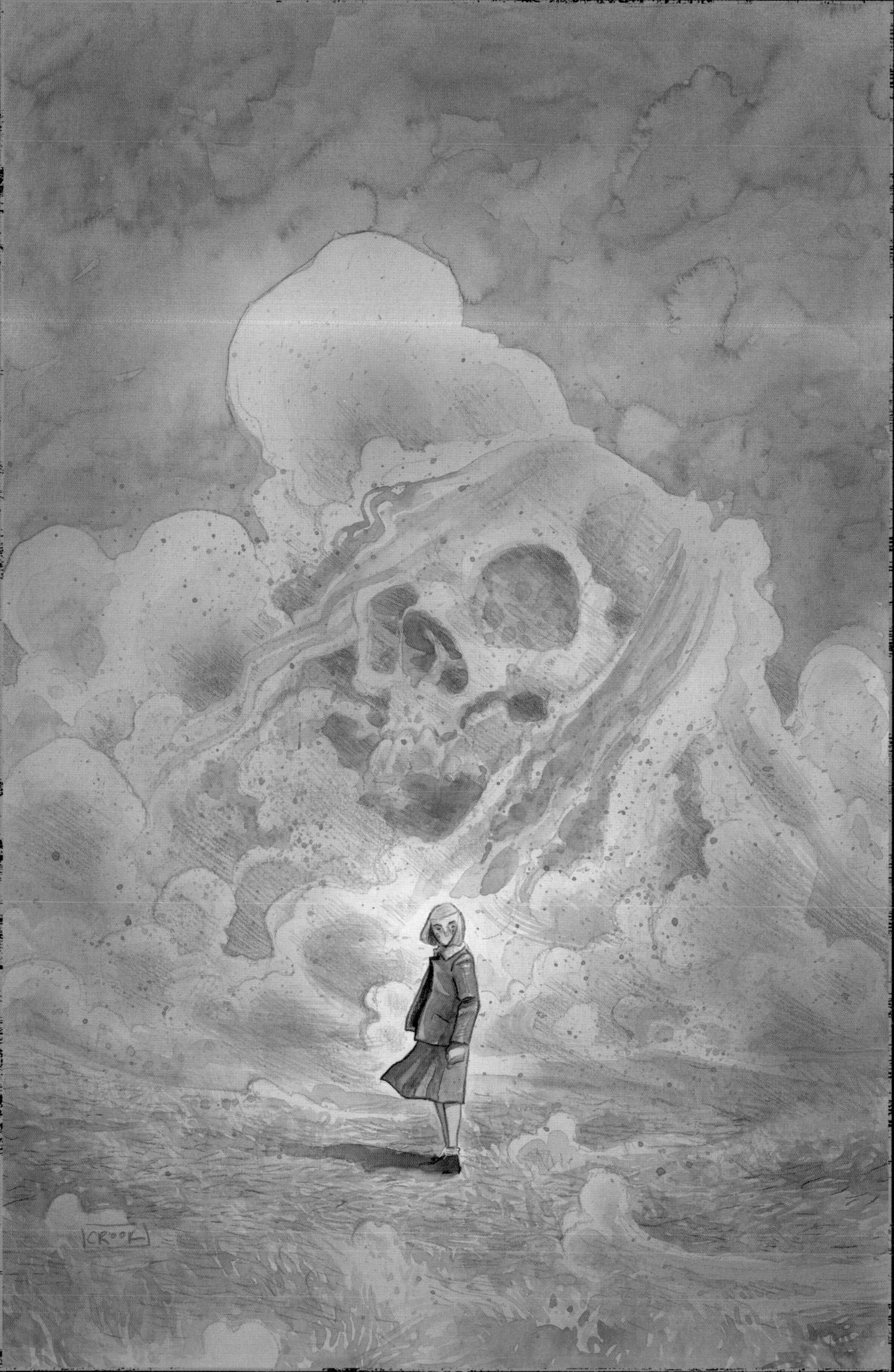
CROOK

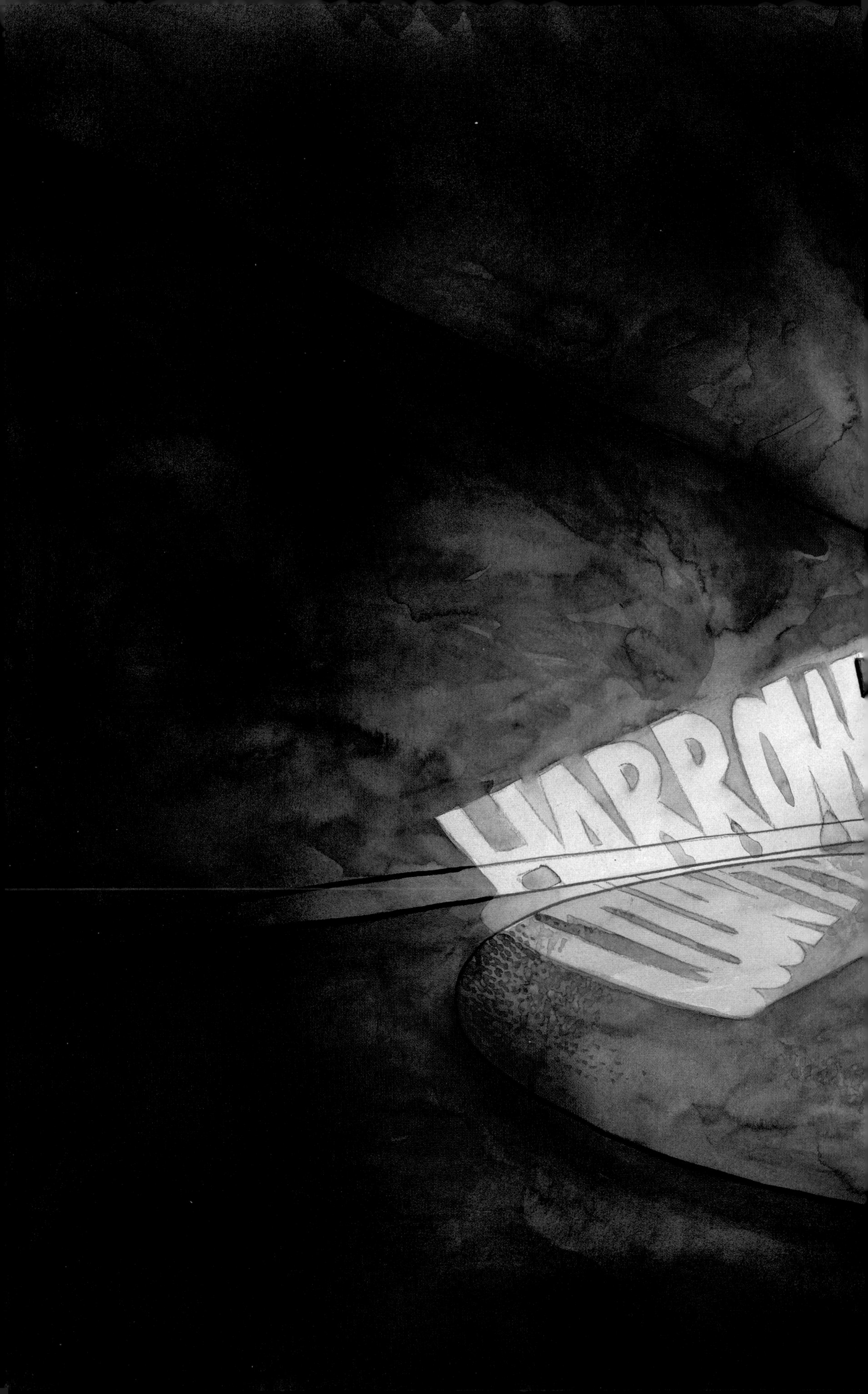
HARROW

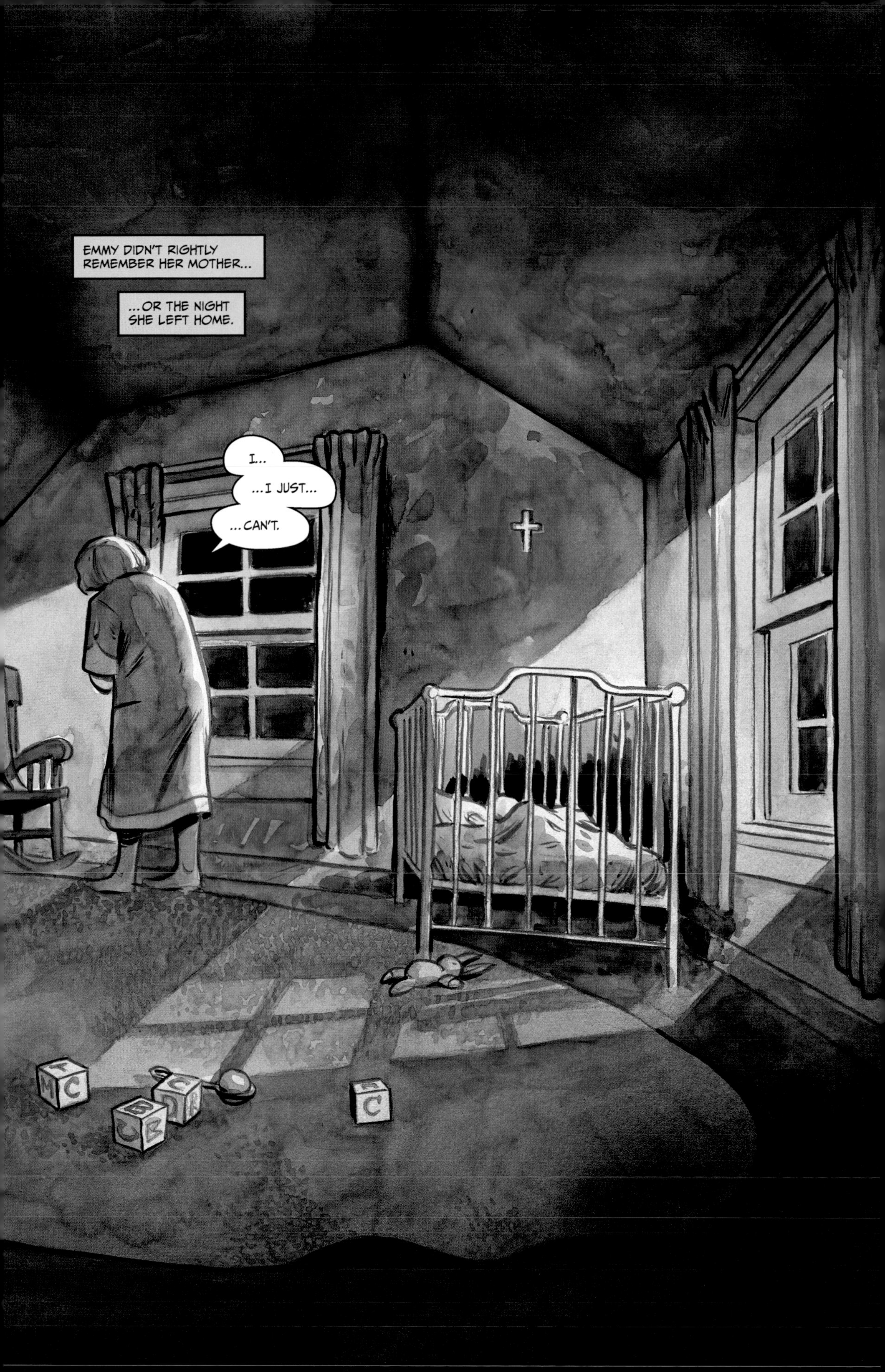
EMMY DIDN'T RIGHTLY REMEMBER HER MOTHER...
...OR THE NIGHT SHE LEFT HOME.
I...
...I JUST...
...CAN'T.

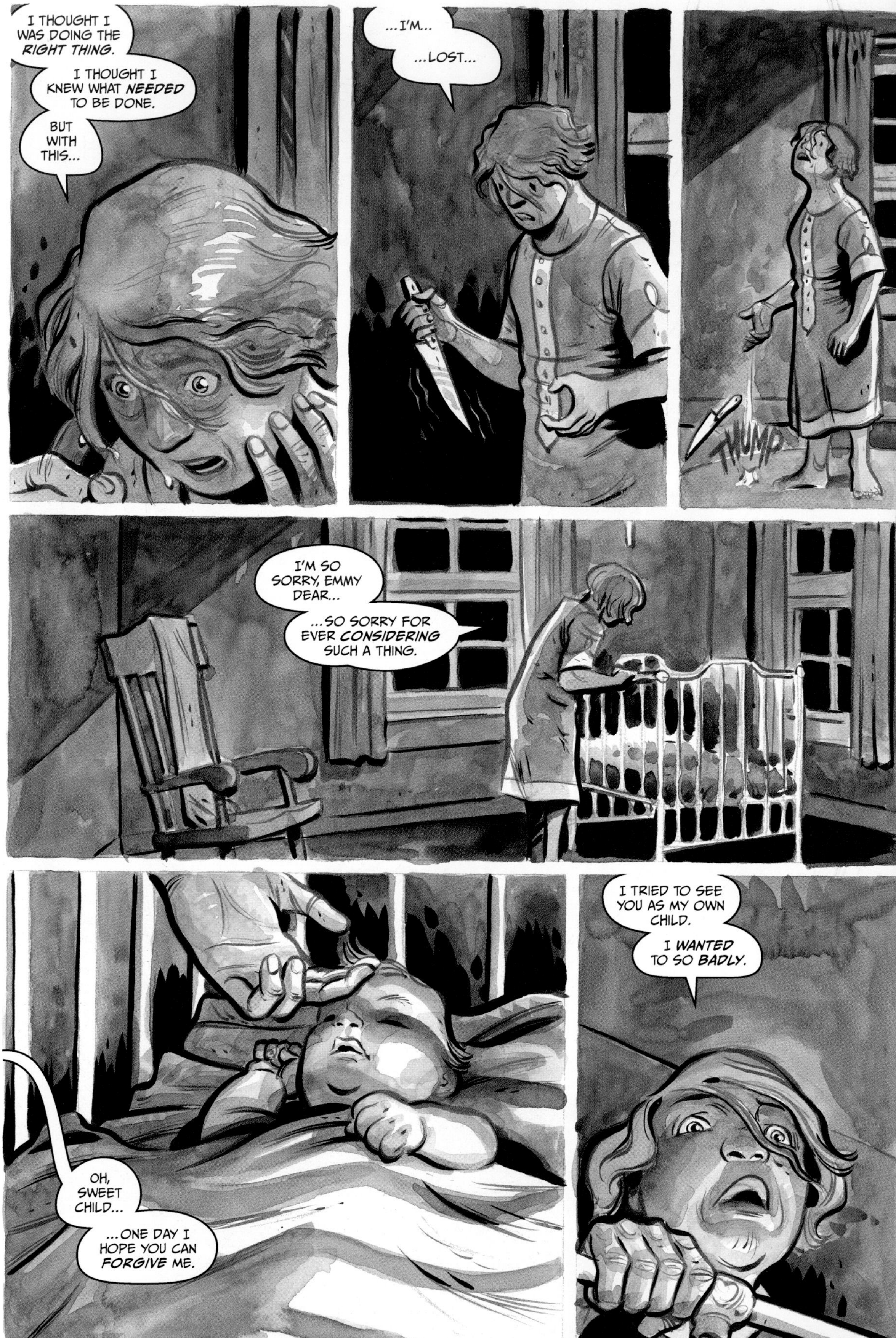
I THOUGHT I WAS DOING THE *RIGHT THING.*
I THOUGHT I KNEW WHAT *NEEDED* TO BE DONE.
BUT WITH THIS...
...I'M...
...LOST...
THUMP
I'M SO SORRY, EMMY DEAR...
...SO SORRY FOR EVER *CONSIDERING* SUCH A THING.
OH, SWEET CHILD...
...ONE DAY I HOPE YOU CAN *FORGIVE* ME.
I TRIED TO SEE YOU AS MY OWN CHILD.
I *WANTED* TO SO *BADLY.*

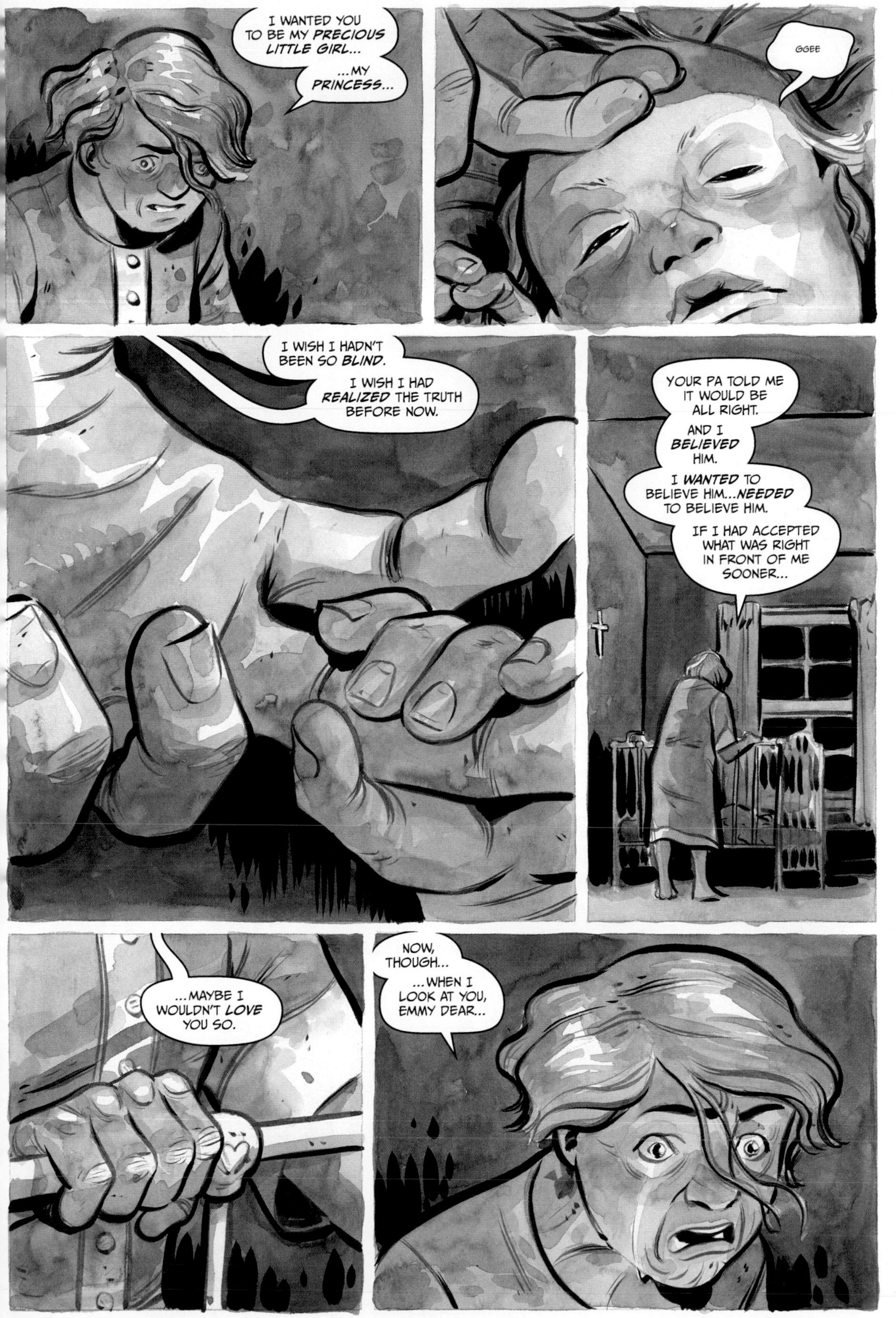

I WANTED YOU TO BE MY PRECIOUS LITTLE GIRL...
...MY PRINCESS...
GGEE
I WISH I HADN'T BEEN SO BLIND.
I WISH I HAD REALIZED THE TRUTH BEFORE NOW.
YOUR PA TOLD ME IT WOULD BE ALL RIGHT.
AND I BELIEVED HIM.
I WANTED TO BELIEVE HIM...NEEDED TO BELIEVE HIM.
IF I HAD ACCEPTED WHAT WAS RIGHT IN FRONT OF ME SOONER...
...MAYBE I WOULDN'T LOVE YOU SO.
NOW, THOUGH...
...WHEN I LOOK AT YOU, EMMY DEAR...

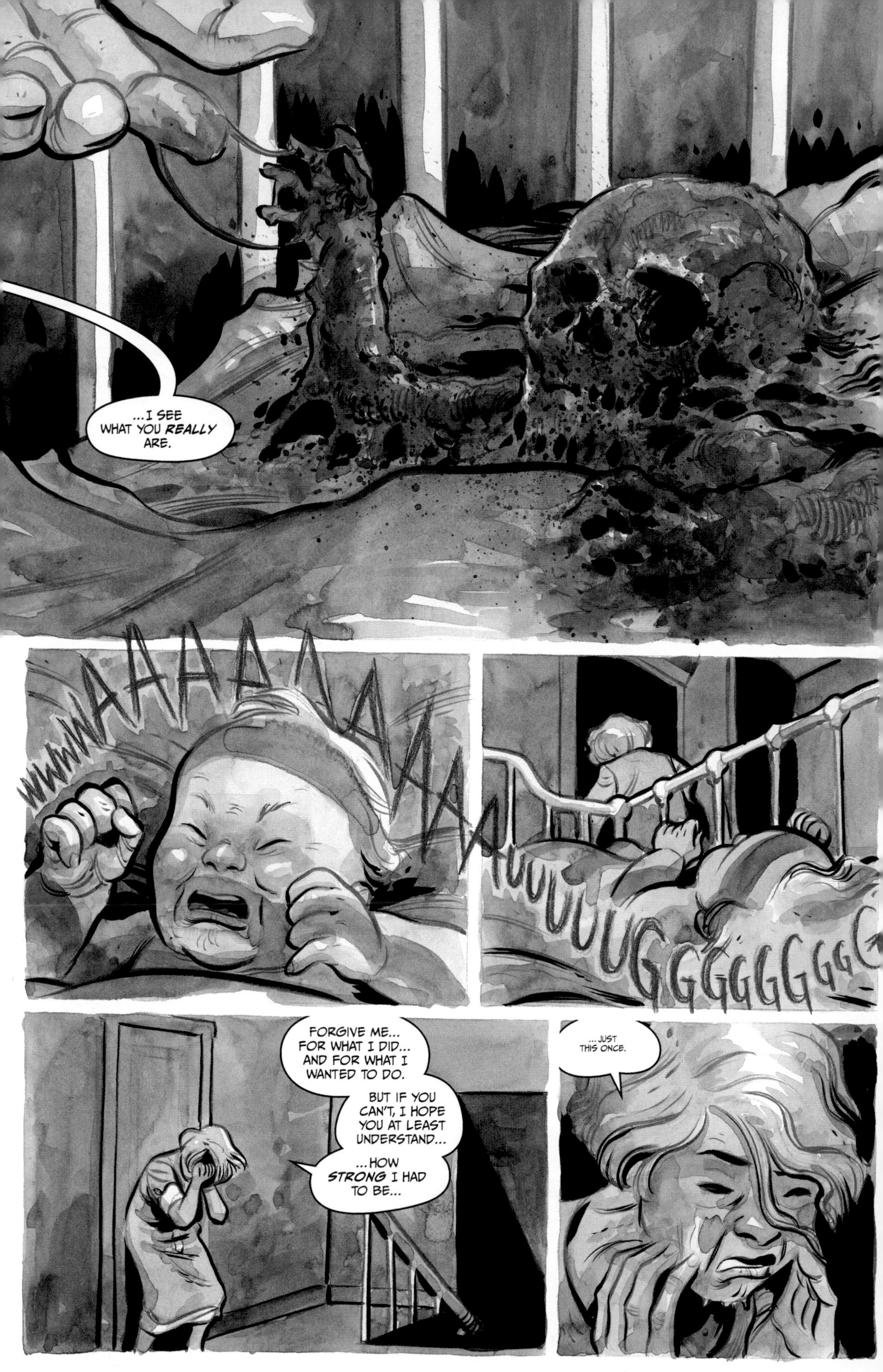
...I SEE WHAT YOU *REALLY* ARE.
WWWAAAAAAAAAAUUUUUUGGGGGGGGG
FORGIVE ME... FOR WHAT I DID... AND FOR WHAT I WANTED TO DO.
BUT IF YOU CAN'T, I HOPE YOU AT LEAST UNDERSTAND...
...HOW *STRONG* I HAD TO BE...
...JUST THIS ONCE.

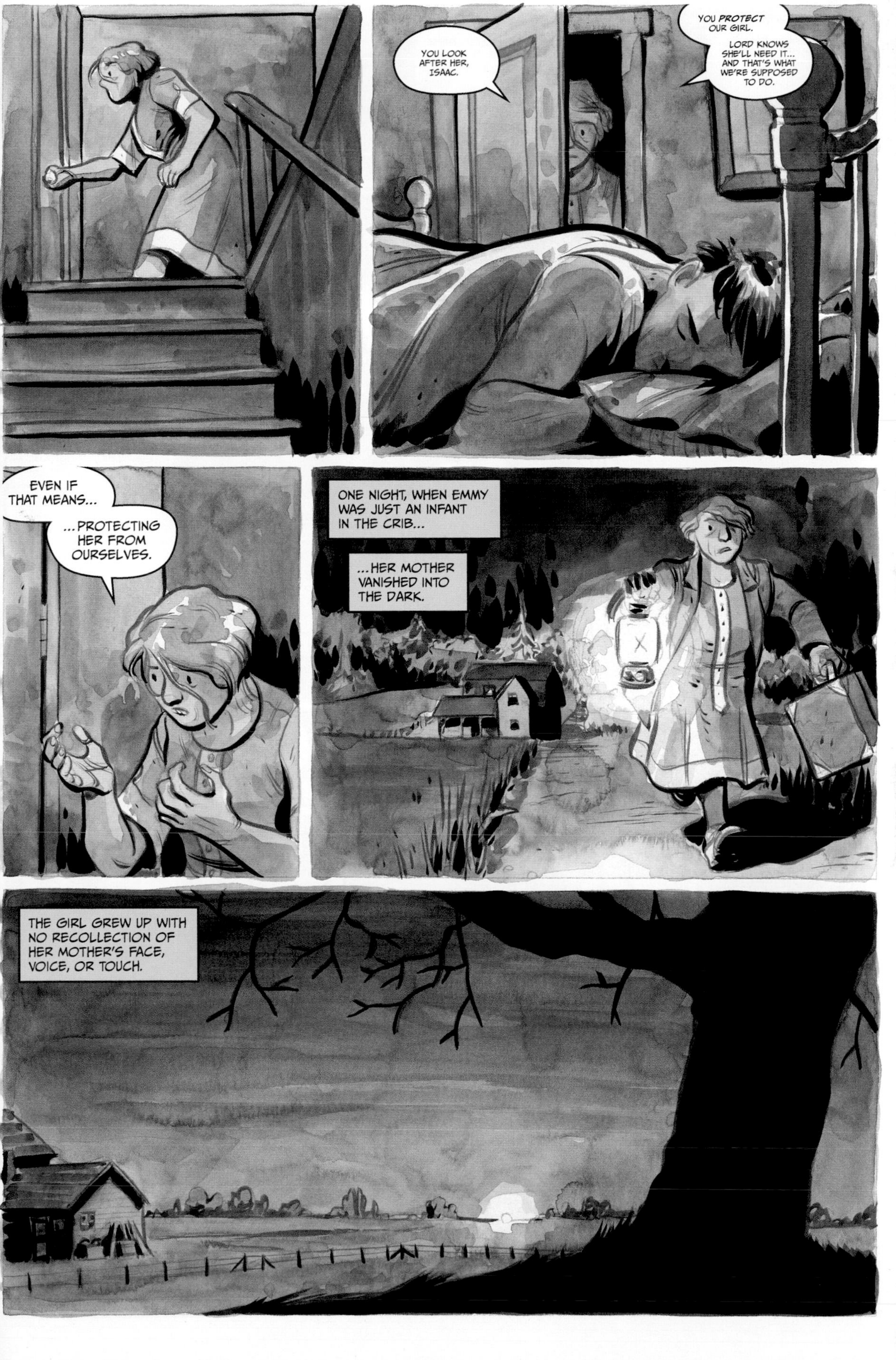
YOU LOOK AFTER HER, ISAAC.
YOU PROTECT OUR GIRL.
LORD KNOWS SHE'LL NEED IT... AND THAT'S WHAT WE'RE SUPPOSED TO DO.
EVEN IF THAT MEANS...
...PROTECTING HER FROM OURSELVES.
ONE NIGHT, WHEN EMMY WAS JUST AN INFANT IN THE CRIB...
...HER MOTHER VANISHED INTO THE DARK.
THE GIRL GREW UP WITH NO RECOLLECTION OF HER MOTHER'S FACE, VOICE, OR TOUCH.

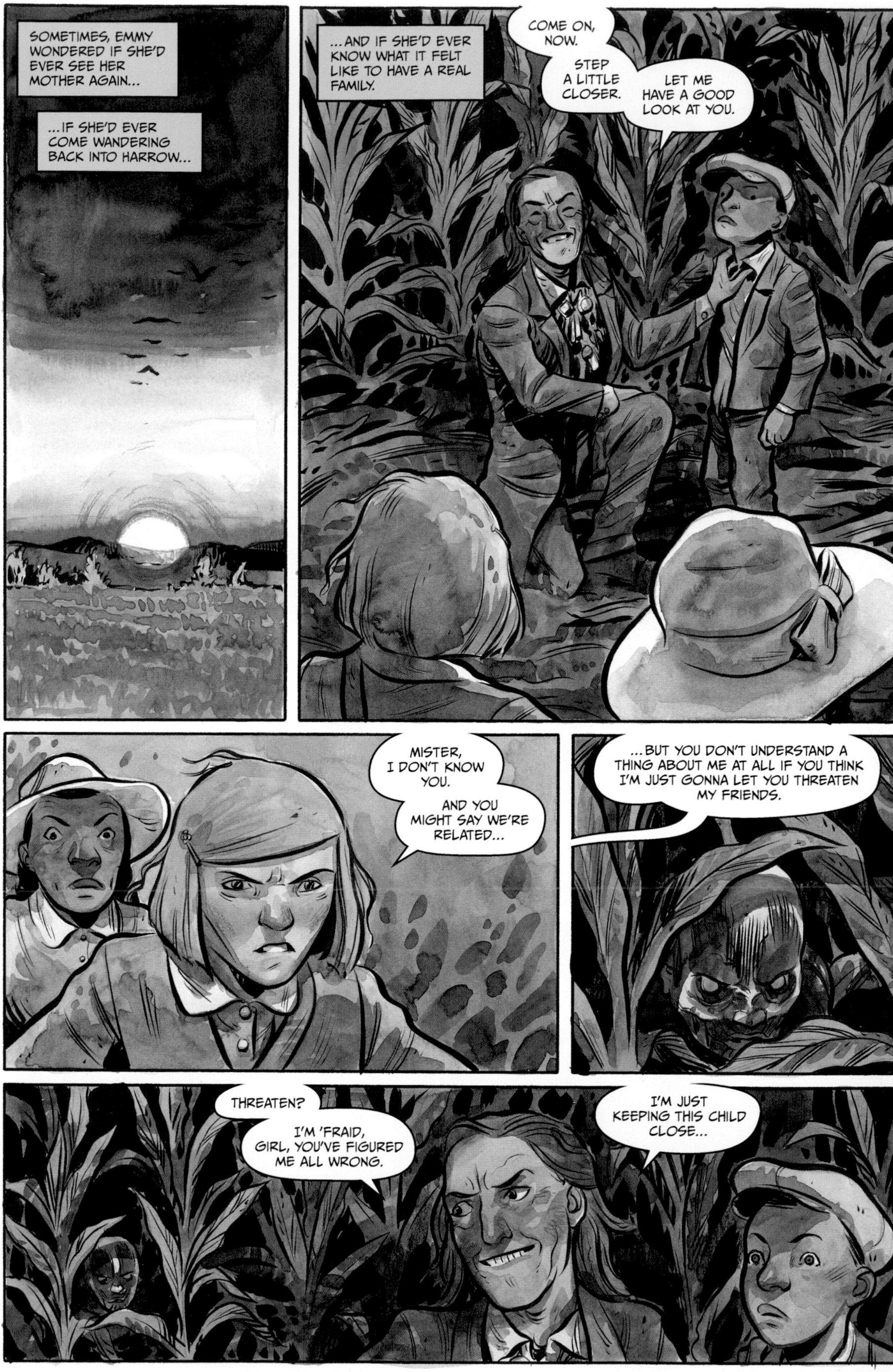
SOMETIMES, EMMY WONDERED IF SHE'D EVER SEE HER MOTHER AGAIN...
...IF SHE'D EVER COME WANDERING BACK INTO HARROW...
...AND IF SHE'D EVER KNOW WHAT IT FELT LIKE TO HAVE A REAL FAMILY.
COME ON, NOW.
STEP A LITTLE CLOSER.
LET ME HAVE A GOOD LOOK AT YOU.
MISTER, I DON'T KNOW YOU.
AND YOU MIGHT SAY WE'RE RELATED...
...BUT YOU DON'T UNDERSTAND A THING ABOUT ME AT ALL IF YOU THINK I'M JUST GONNA LET YOU THREATEN MY FRIENDS.
THREATEN?
I'M 'FRAID, GIRL, YOU'VE FIGURED ME ALL WRONG.
I'M JUST KEEPING THIS CHILD CLOSE...

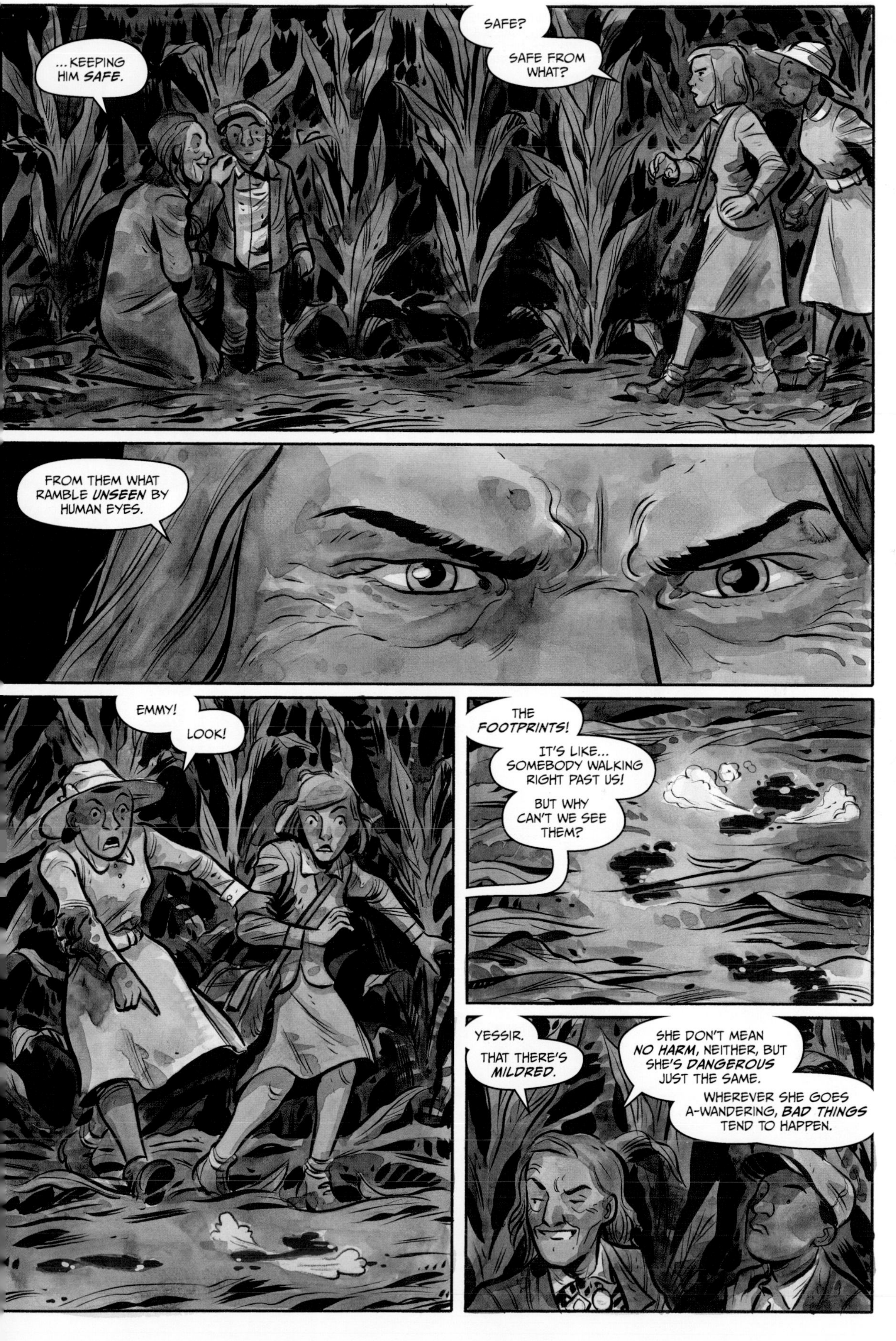
...KEEPING HIM SAFE.
SAFE?
SAFE FROM WHAT?
FROM THEM WHAT RAMBLE UNSEEN BY HUMAN EYES.
EMMY!
LOOK!
THE FOOTPRINTS!
IT'S LIKE... SOMEBODY WALKING RIGHT PAST US!
BUT WHY CAN'T WE SEE THEM?
YESSIR.
THAT THERE'S MILDRED.
SHE DON'T MEAN NO HARM, NEITHER, BUT SHE'S DANGEROUS JUST THE SAME.
WHEREVER SHE GOES A-WANDERING, BAD THINGS TEND TO HAPPEN.

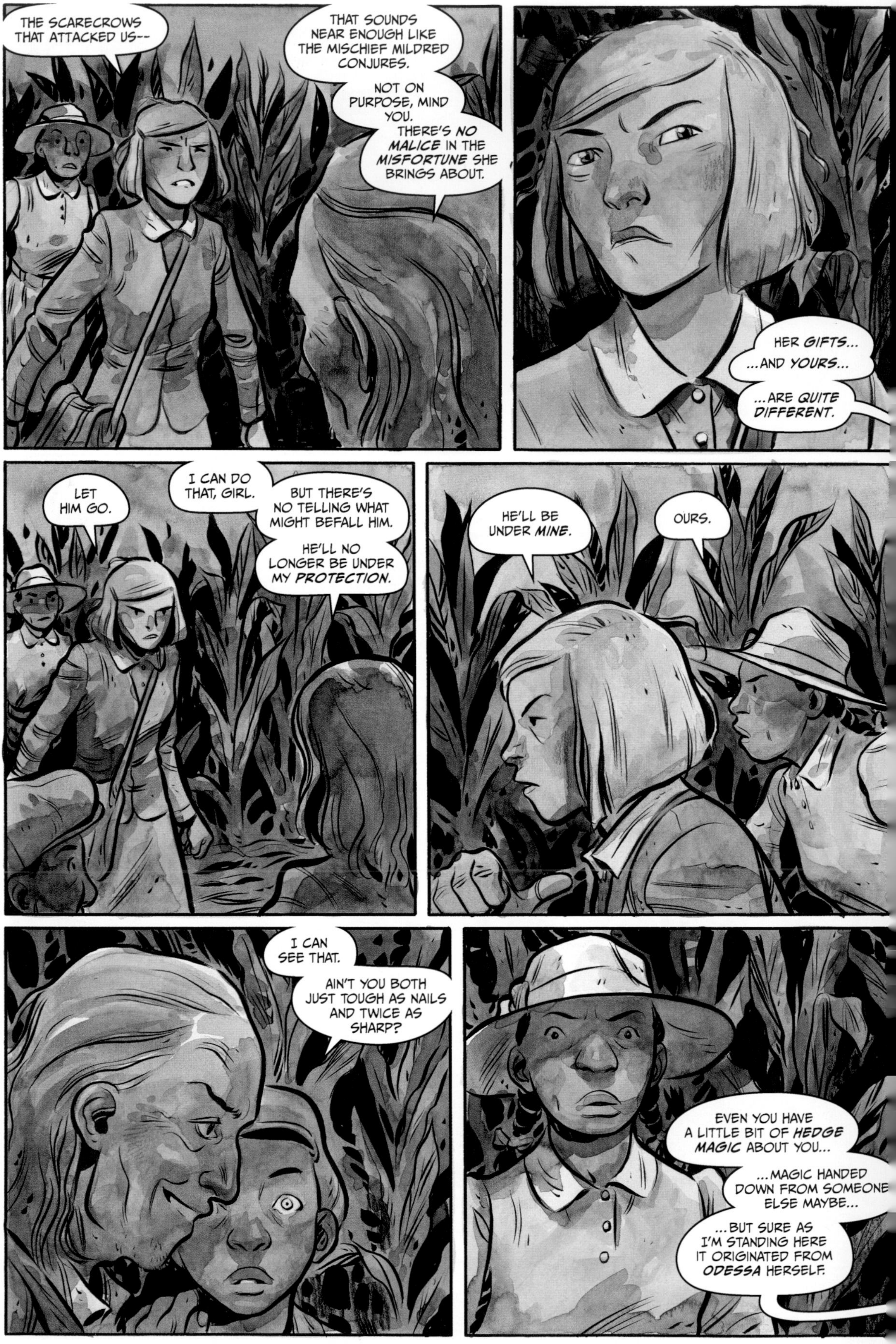
THE SCARECROWS THAT ATTACKED US--
THAT SOUNDS NEAR ENOUGH LIKE THE MISCHIEF MILDRED CONJURES.
NOT ON PURPOSE, MIND YOU.
THERE'S NO MALICE IN THE MISFORTUNE SHE BRINGS ABOUT.
HER GIFTS...
...AND YOURS...
...ARE QUITE DIFFERENT.
LET HIM GO.
I CAN DO THAT, GIRL.
BUT THERE'S NO TELLING WHAT MIGHT BEFALL HIM.
HE'LL NO LONGER BE UNDER MY PROTECTION.
HE'LL BE UNDER MINE.
OURS.
I CAN SEE THAT.
AIN'T YOU BOTH JUST TOUGH AS NAILS AND TWICE AS SHARP?
EVEN YOU HAVE A LITTLE BIT OF HEDGE MAGIC ABOUT YOU...
...MAGIC HANDED DOWN FROM SOMEONE ELSE MAYBE...
...BUT SURE AS I'M STANDING HERE IT ORIGINATED FROM ODESSA HERSELF.

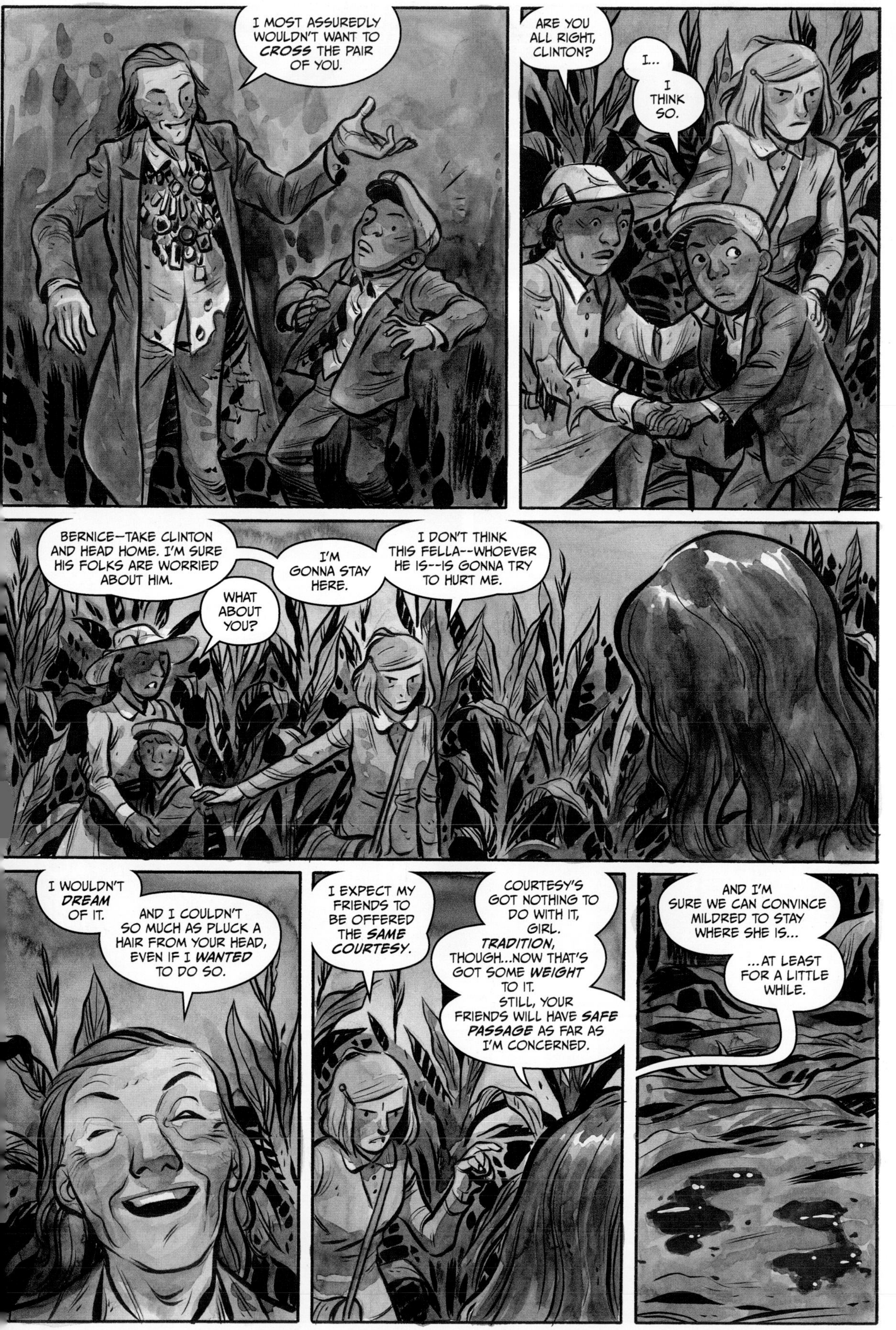
I MOST ASSUREDLY WOULDN'T WANT TO CROSS THE PAIR OF YOU.
ARE YOU ALL RIGHT, CLINTON?
I...
I THINK SO.
BERNICE—TAKE CLINTON AND HEAD HOME. I'M SURE HIS FOLKS ARE WORRIED ABOUT HIM.
WHAT ABOUT YOU?
I'M GONNA STAY HERE.
I DON'T THINK THIS FELLA--WHOEVER HE IS--IS GONNA TRY TO HURT ME.
I WOULDN'T DREAM OF IT.
AND I COULDN'T SO MUCH AS PLUCK A HAIR FROM YOUR HEAD, EVEN IF I WANTED TO DO SO.
I EXPECT MY FRIENDS TO BE OFFERED THE SAME COURTESY.
COURTESY'S GOT NOTHING TO DO WITH IT, GIRL. TRADITION, THOUGH...NOW THAT'S GOT SOME WEIGHT TO IT.
STILL, YOUR FRIENDS WILL HAVE SAFE PASSAGE AS FAR AS I'M CONCERNED.
AND I'M SURE WE CAN CONVINCE MILDRED TO STAY WHERE SHE IS...
...AT LEAST FOR A LITTLE WHILE.

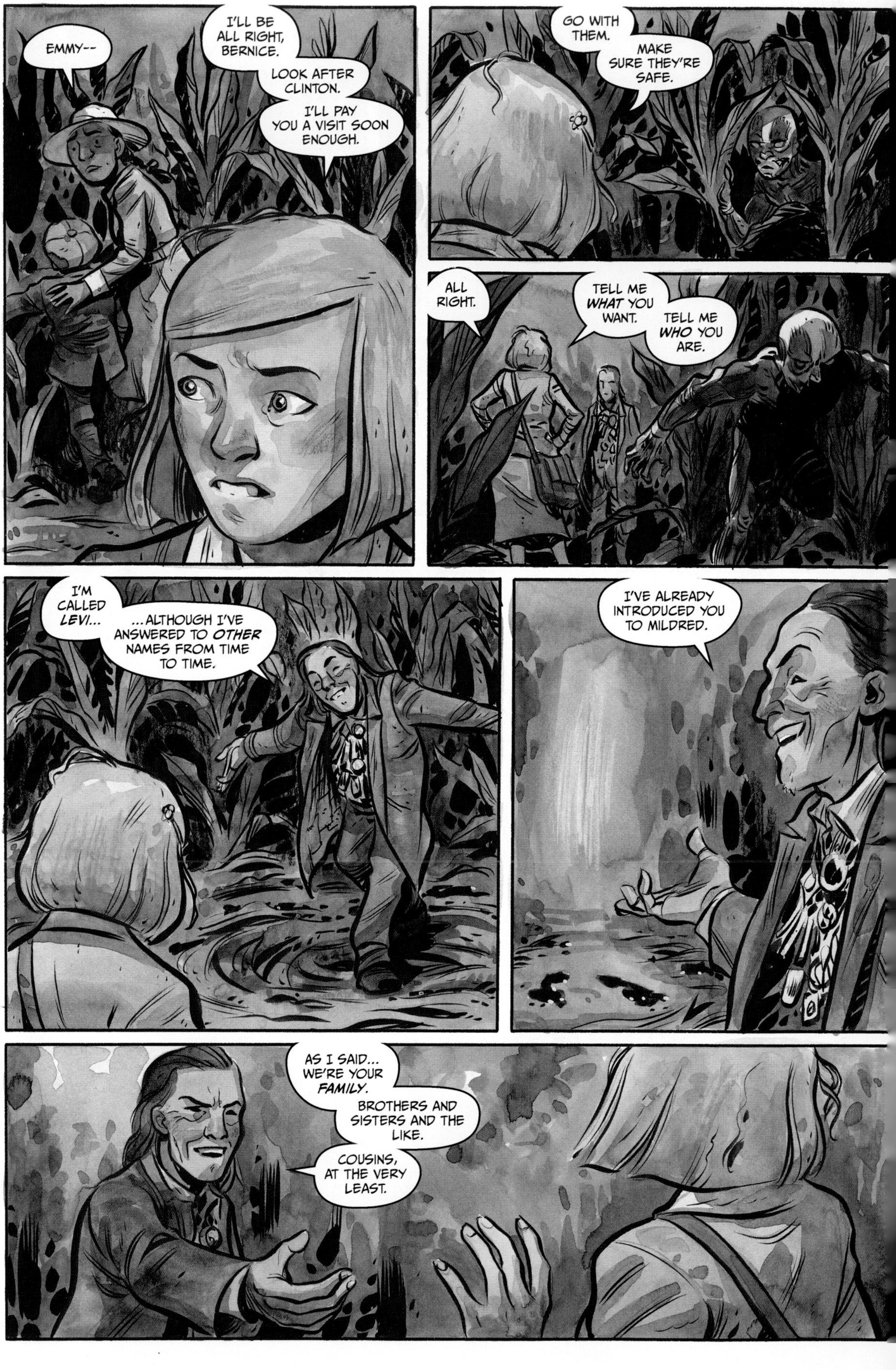
EMMY--
I'LL BE ALL RIGHT, BERNICE.
LOOK AFTER CLINTON.
I'LL PAY YOU A VISIT SOON ENOUGH.
GO WITH THEM.
MAKE SURE THEY'RE SAFE.
ALL RIGHT.
TELL ME *WHAT* YOU WANT.
TELL ME *WHO* YOU ARE.
I'M CALLED *LEVI*...
...ALTHOUGH I'VE ANSWERED TO *OTHER* NAMES FROM TIME TO TIME.
I'VE ALREADY INTRODUCED YOU TO MILDRED.
AS I SAID... WE'RE YOUR *FAMILY*.
BROTHERS AND SISTERS AND THE LIKE.
COUSINS, AT THE VERY LEAST.

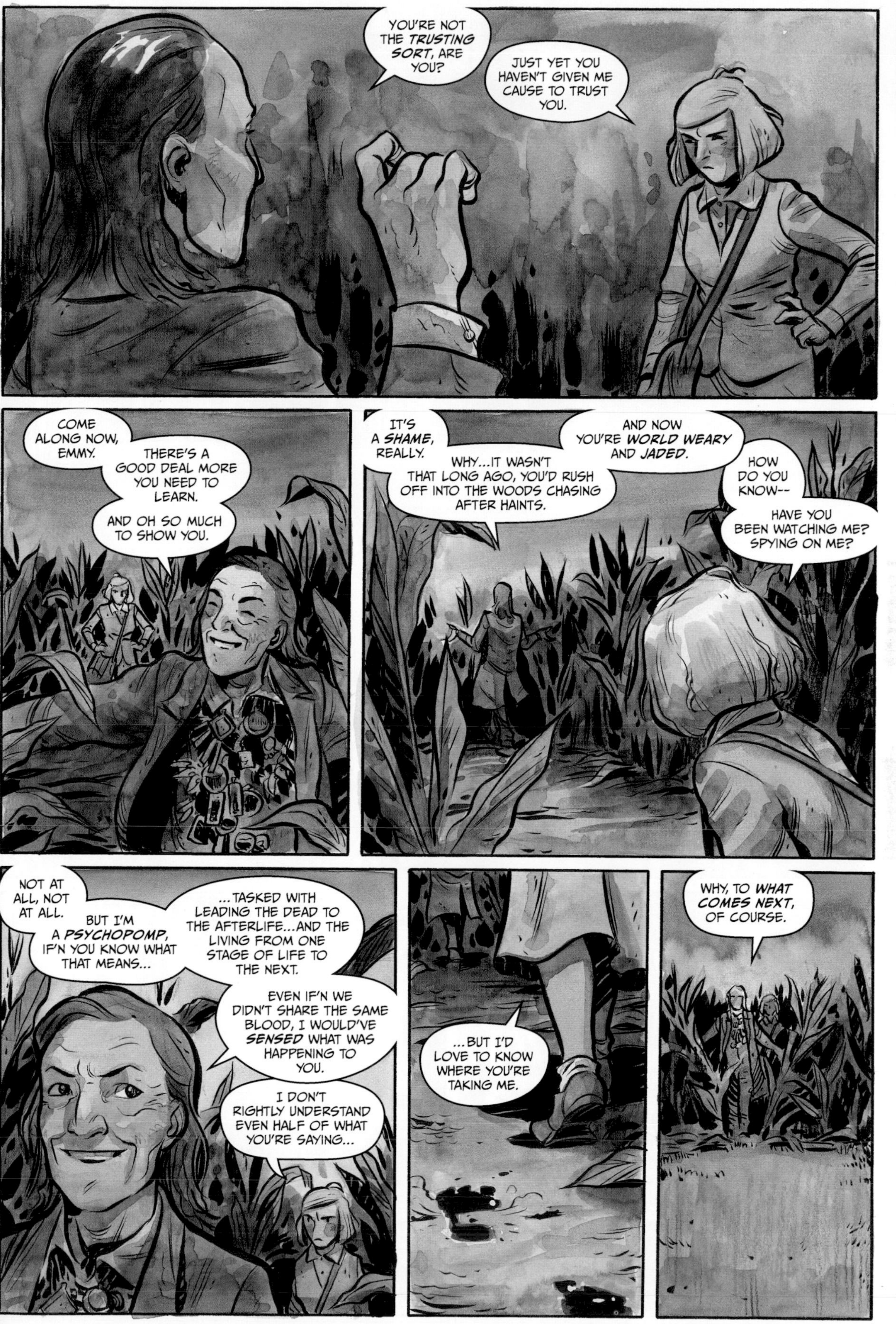

YOU'RE NOT THE TRUSTING SORT, ARE YOU?
JUST YET YOU HAVEN'T GIVEN ME CAUSE TO TRUST YOU.
COME ALONG NOW, EMMY.
THERE'S A GOOD DEAL MORE YOU NEED TO LEARN.
AND OH SO MUCH TO SHOW YOU.
IT'S A SHAME, REALLY.
WHY...IT WASN'T THAT LONG AGO, YOU'D RUSH OFF INTO THE WOODS CHASING AFTER HAINTS.
AND NOW YOU'RE WORLD WEARY AND JADED.
HOW DO YOU KNOW--
HAVE YOU BEEN WATCHING ME? SPYING ON ME?
NOT AT ALL, NOT AT ALL.
BUT I'M A PSYCHOPOMP, IF'N YOU KNOW WHAT THAT MEANS...
...TASKED WITH LEADING THE DEAD TO THE AFTERLIFE...AND THE LIVING FROM ONE STAGE OF LIFE TO THE NEXT.
EVEN IF'N WE DIDN'T SHARE THE SAME BLOOD, I WOULD'VE SENSED WHAT WAS HAPPENING TO YOU.
I DON'T RIGHTLY UNDERSTAND EVEN HALF OF WHAT YOU'RE SAYING...
...BUT I'D LOVE TO KNOW WHERE YOU'RE TAKING ME.
WHY, TO WHAT COMES NEXT, OF COURSE.

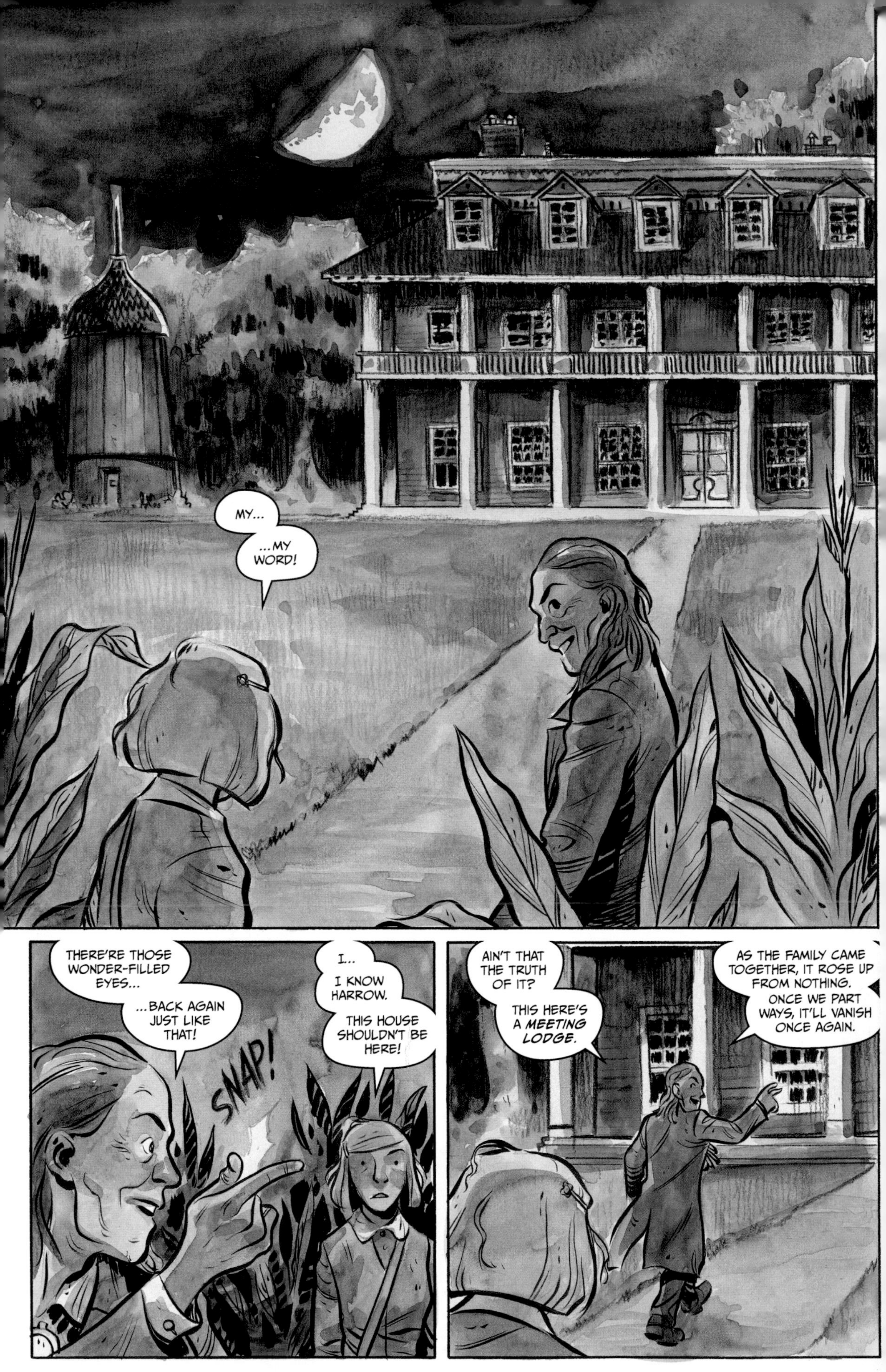
MY...
...MY WORD!
THERE'RE THOSE WONDER-FILLED EYES...
...BACK AGAIN JUST LIKE THAT!
SNAP!
I...
I KNOW HARROW.
THIS HOUSE SHOULDN'T BE HERE!
AIN'T THAT THE TRUTH OF IT?
THIS HERE'S A *MEETING LODGE.*
AS THE FAMILY CAME TOGETHER, IT ROSE UP FROM NOTHING.
ONCE WE PART WAYS, IT'LL VANISH ONCE AGAIN.

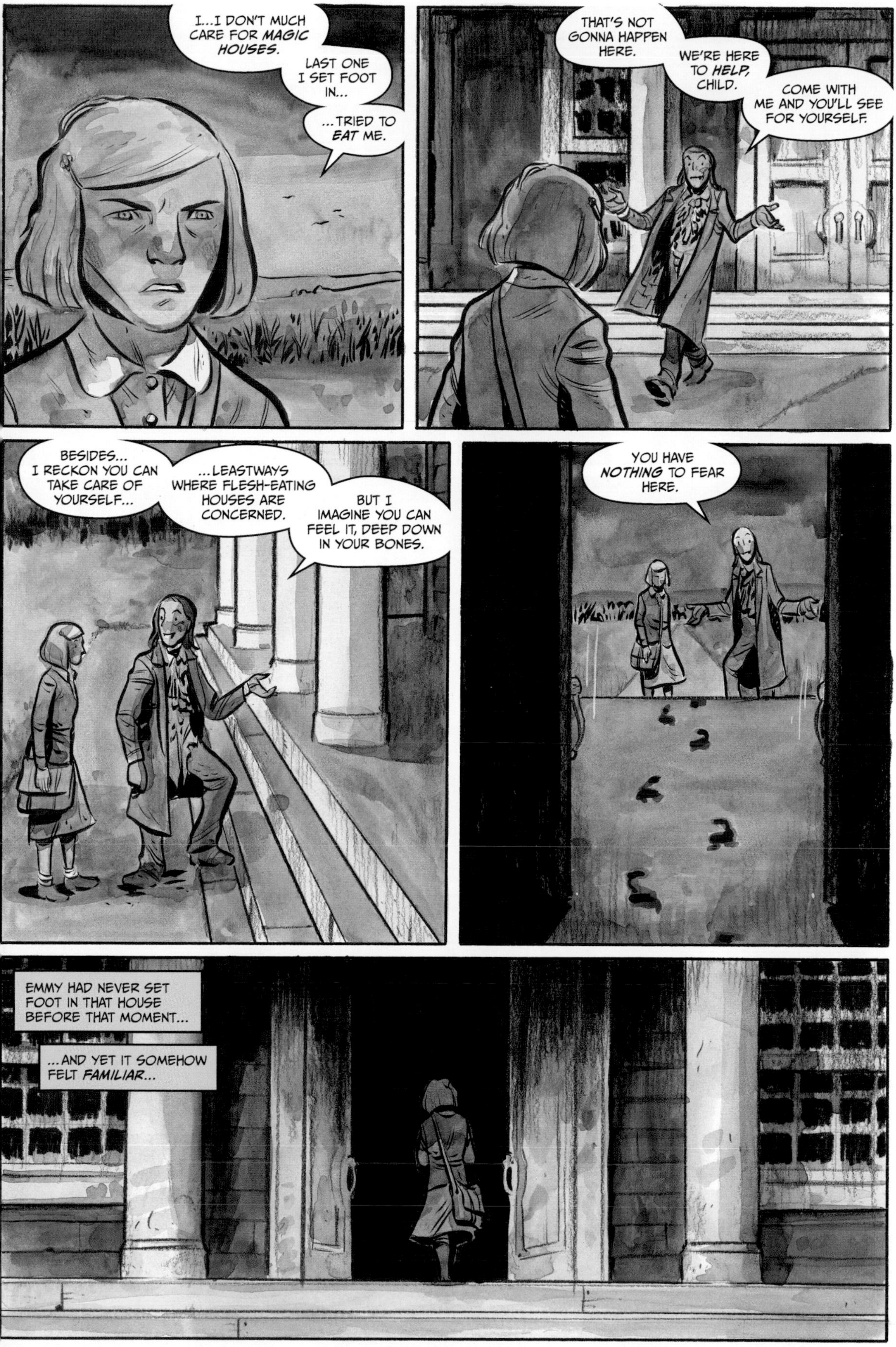
I...I DON'T MUCH CARE FOR MAGIC HOUSES.
LAST ONE I SET FOOT IN...
...TRIED TO EAT ME.
THAT'S NOT GONNA HAPPEN HERE.
WE'RE HERE TO HELP, CHILD.
COME WITH ME AND YOU'LL SEE FOR YOURSELF.
BESIDES... I RECKON YOU CAN TAKE CARE OF YOURSELF...
...LEASTWAYS WHERE FLESH-EATING HOUSES ARE CONCERNED.
BUT I IMAGINE YOU CAN FEEL IT, DEEP DOWN IN YOUR BONES.
YOU HAVE NOTHING TO FEAR HERE.
EMMY HAD NEVER SET FOOT IN THAT HOUSE BEFORE THAT MOMENT...
...AND YET IT SOMEHOW FELT FAMILIAR...

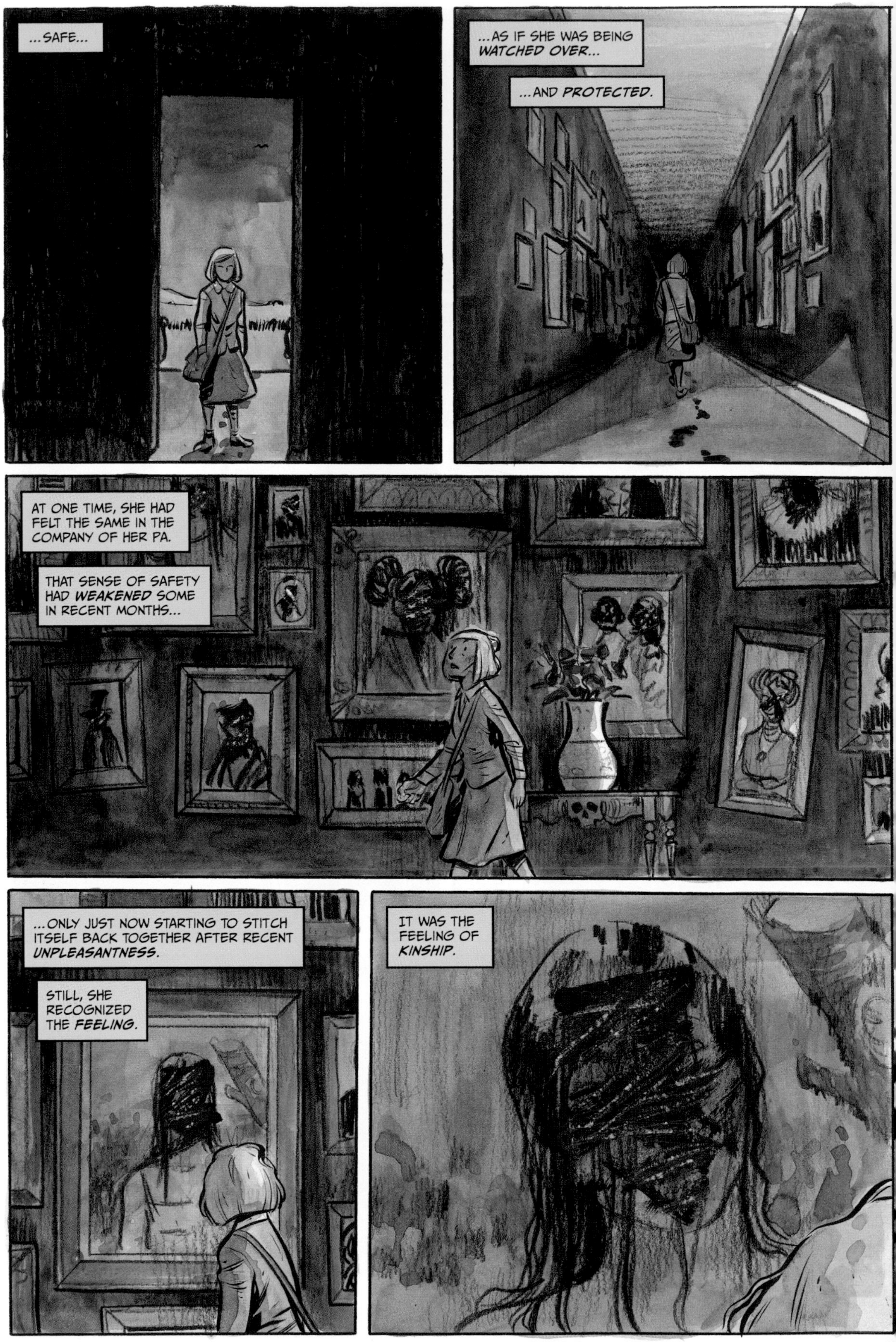
...SAFE...
...AS IF SHE WAS BEING *WATCHED OVER*...
...AND *PROTECTED*.
AT ONE TIME, SHE HAD FELT THE SAME IN THE COMPANY OF HER PA.
THAT SENSE OF SAFETY HAD *WEAKENED* SOME IN RECENT MONTHS...
...ONLY JUST NOW STARTING TO STITCH ITSELF BACK TOGETHER AFTER RECENT *UNPLEASANTNESS*.
STILL, SHE RECOGNIZED THE *FEELING*.
IT WAS THE FEELING OF *KINSHIP*.

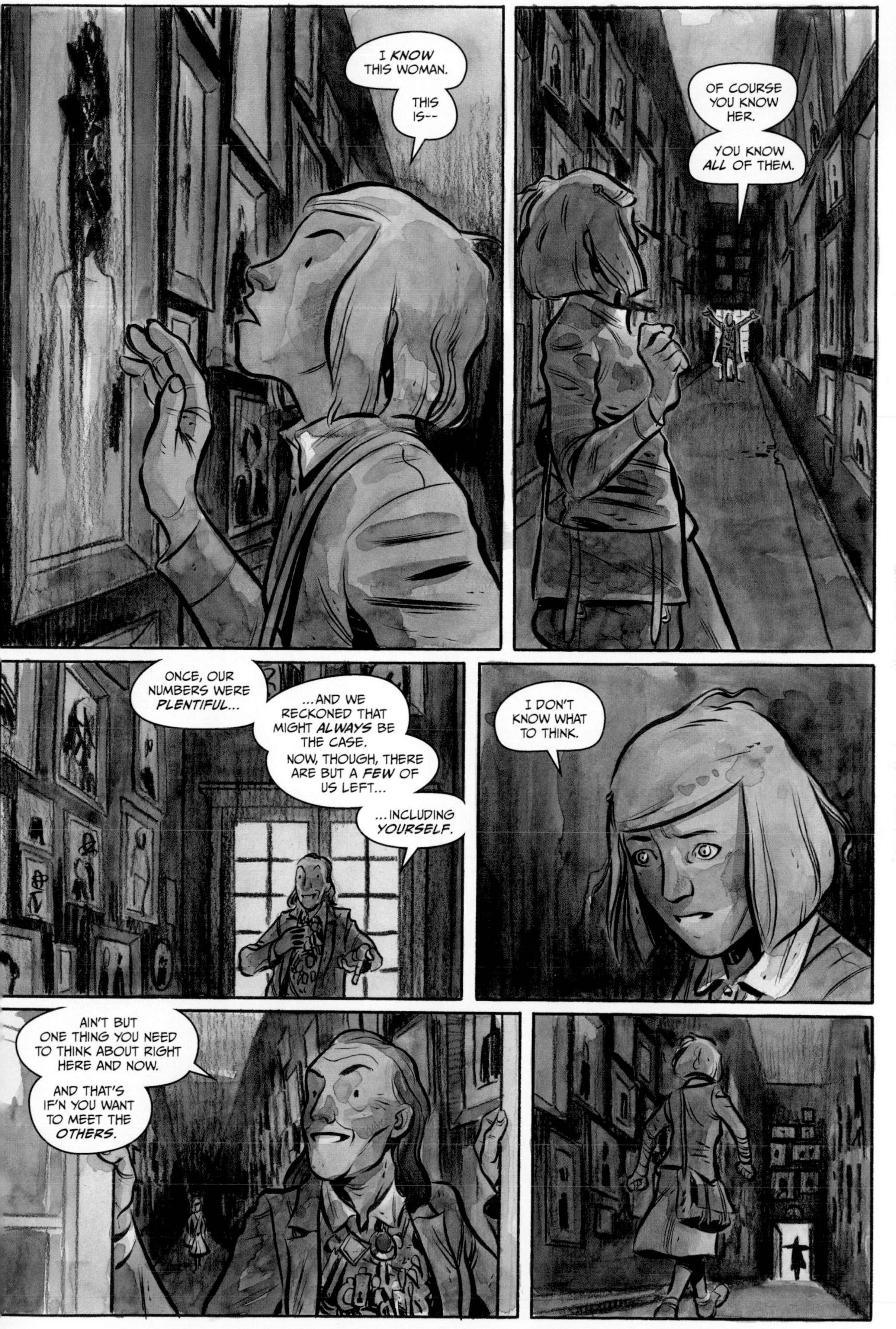
I *KNOW* THIS WOMAN.
THIS IS--
OF COURSE YOU KNOW HER.
YOU KNOW *ALL* OF THEM.
ONCE, OUR NUMBERS WERE *PLENTIFUL*...
...AND WE RECKONED THAT MIGHT *ALWAYS* BE THE CASE.
NOW, THOUGH, THERE ARE BUT A *FEW* OF US LEFT...
...INCLUDING *YOURSELF*.
I DON'T KNOW WHAT TO THINK.
AIN'T BUT ONE THING YOU NEED TO THINK ABOUT RIGHT HERE AND NOW.
AND THAT'S IF'N YOU WANT TO MEET THE *OTHERS*.

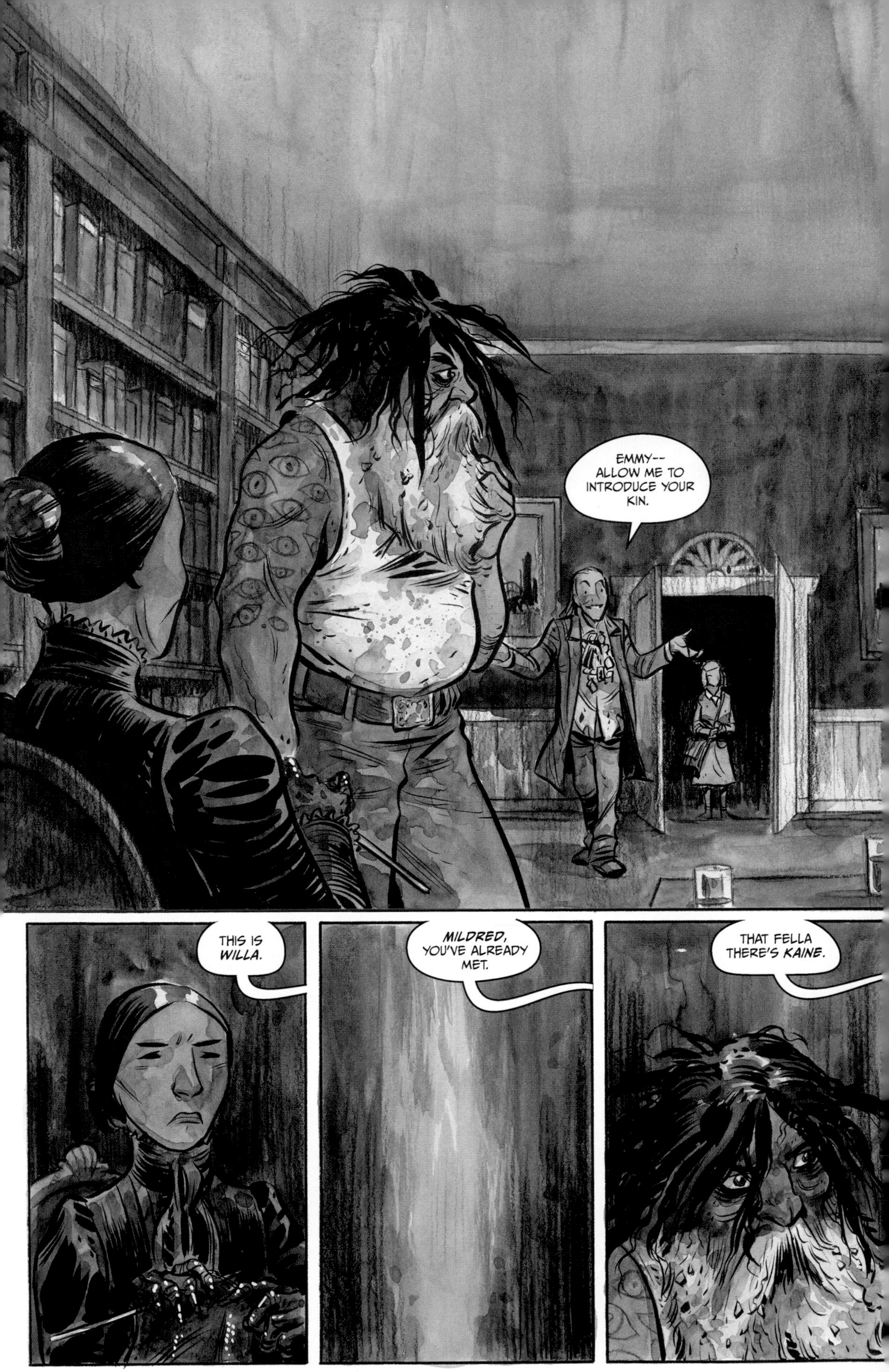
EMMY--
ALLOW ME TO INTRODUCE YOUR KIN.
THIS IS *WILLA*.
MILDRED, YOU'VE ALREADY MET.
THAT FELLA THERE'S *KAINE*.

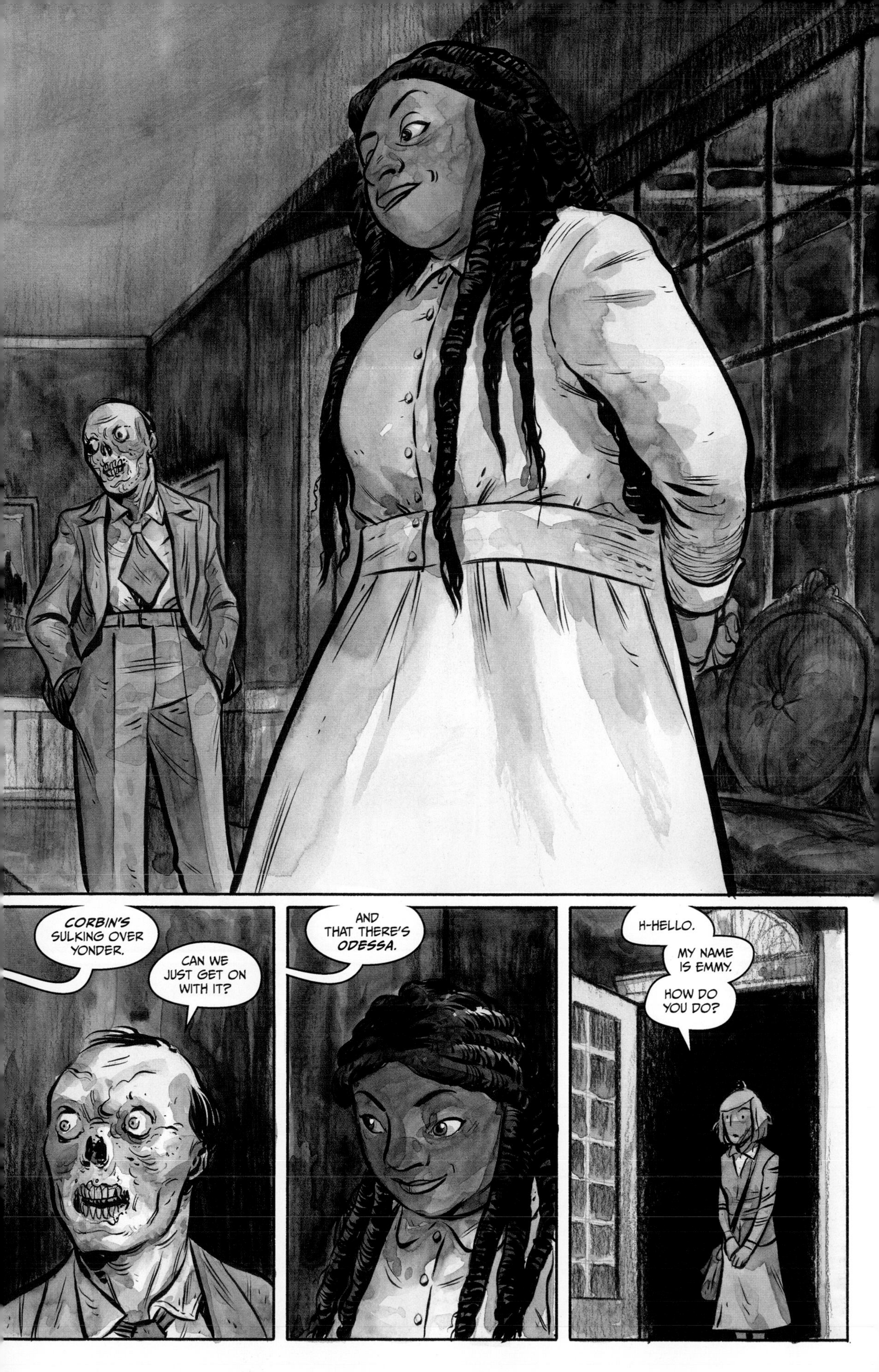
CORBIN'S SULKING OVER YONDER.
CAN WE JUST GET ON WITH IT?
AND THAT THERE'S ODESSA.
H-HELLO.
MY NAME IS EMMY.
HOW DO YOU DO?

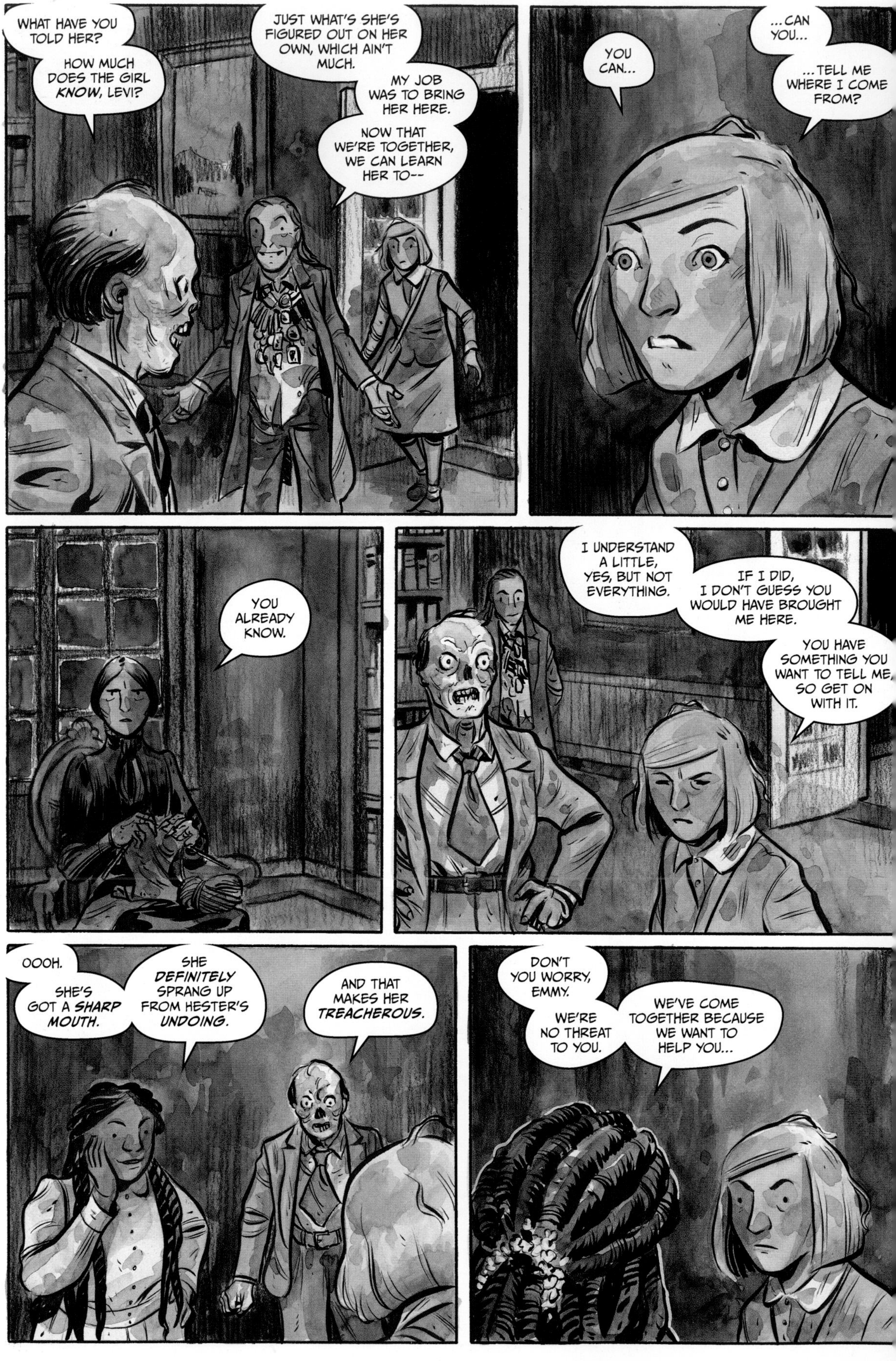
WHAT HAVE YOU TOLD HER?
HOW MUCH DOES THE GIRL *KNOW*, LEVI?
JUST WHAT'S SHE'S FIGURED OUT ON HER OWN, WHICH AIN'T MUCH.
MY JOB WAS TO BRING HER HERE.
NOW THAT WE'RE TOGETHER, WE CAN LEARN HER TO--
YOU CAN...
...CAN YOU...
...TELL ME WHERE I COME FROM?
YOU ALREADY KNOW.
I UNDERSTAND A LITTLE, YES, BUT NOT EVERYTHING.
IF I DID, I DON'T GUESS YOU WOULD HAVE BROUGHT ME HERE.
YOU HAVE SOMETHING YOU WANT TO TELL ME, SO GET ON WITH IT.
OOOH.
SHE'S GOT A *SHARP MOUTH.*
SHE *DEFINITELY* SPRANG UP FROM HESTER'S *UNDOING.*
AND THAT MAKES HER *TREACHEROUS.*
DON'T YOU WORRY, EMMY.
WE'RE NO THREAT TO YOU.
WE'VE COME TOGETHER BECAUSE WE WANT TO HELP YOU...

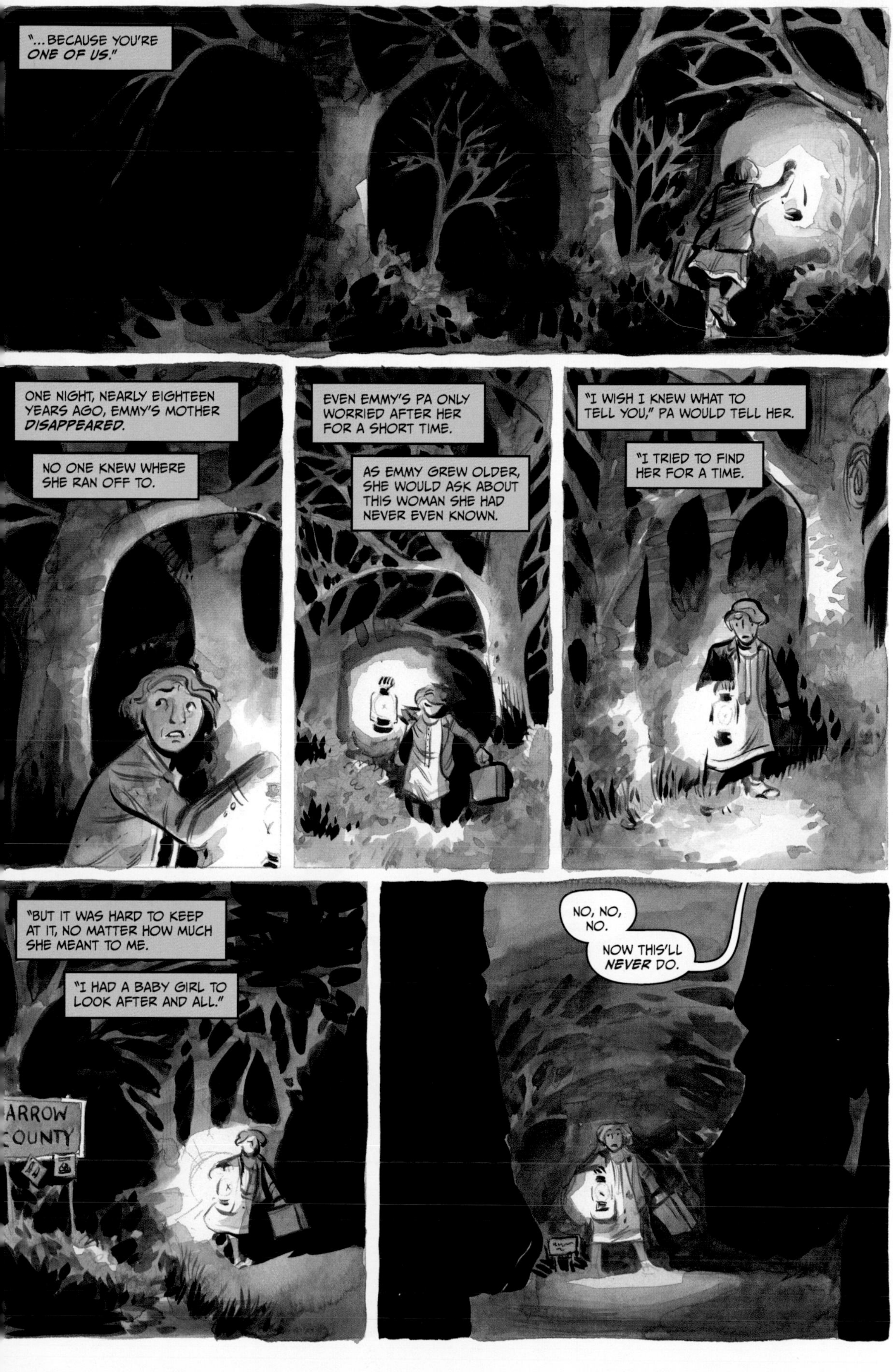
"...BECAUSE YOU'RE *ONE OF US.*"
ONE NIGHT, NEARLY EIGHTEEN YEARS AGO, EMMY'S MOTHER *DISAPPEARED.*
NO ONE KNEW WHERE SHE RAN OFF TO.
EVEN EMMY'S PA ONLY WORRIED AFTER HER FOR A SHORT TIME.
AS EMMY GREW OLDER, SHE WOULD ASK ABOUT THIS WOMAN SHE HAD NEVER EVEN KNOWN.
"I WISH I KNEW WHAT TO TELL YOU," PA WOULD TELL HER.
"I TRIED TO FIND HER FOR A TIME.
"BUT IT WAS HARD TO KEEP AT IT, NO MATTER HOW MUCH SHE MEANT TO ME.
"I HAD A BABY GIRL TO LOOK AFTER AND ALL."
ARROW
COUNTY
NO, NO, NO.
NOW THIS'LL *NEVER* DO.

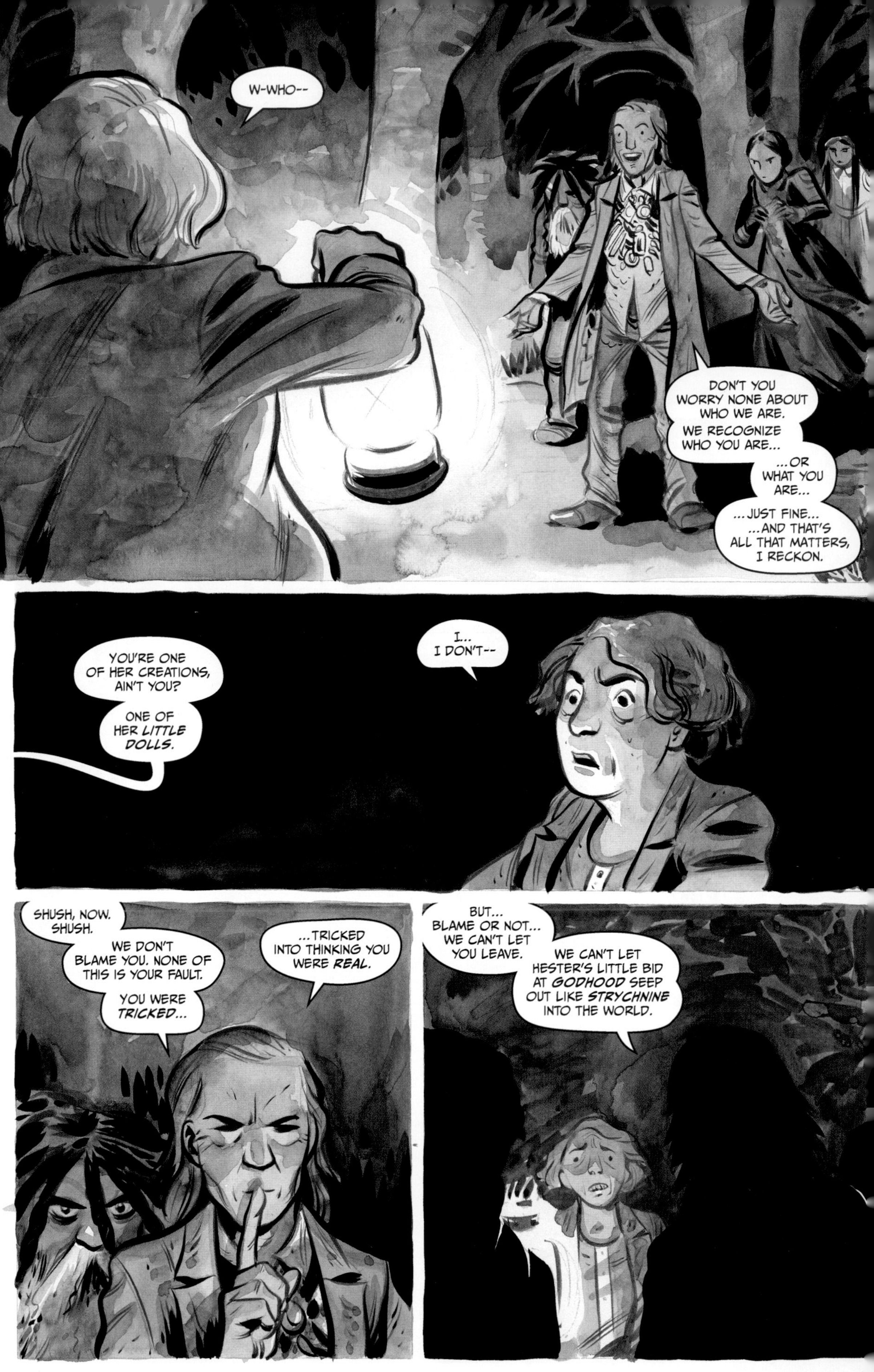
W-WHO--
DON'T YOU WORRY NONE ABOUT WHO WE ARE.
WE RECOGNIZE WHO YOU ARE...
...OR WHAT YOU ARE...
...JUST FINE... ...AND THAT'S ALL THAT MATTERS, I RECKON.
YOU'RE ONE OF HER CREATIONS, AIN'T YOU?
ONE OF HER *LITTLE DOLLS*.
I... I DON'T--
SHUSH, NOW. SHUSH.
WE DON'T BLAME YOU. NONE OF THIS IS YOUR FAULT.
YOU WERE *TRICKED*...
...TRICKED INTO THINKING YOU WERE *REAL*.
BUT... BLAME OR NOT... WE CAN'T LET YOU LEAVE.
WE CAN'T LET HESTER'S LITTLE BID AT *GODHOOD* SEEP OUT LIKE *STRYCHNINE* INTO THE WORLD.

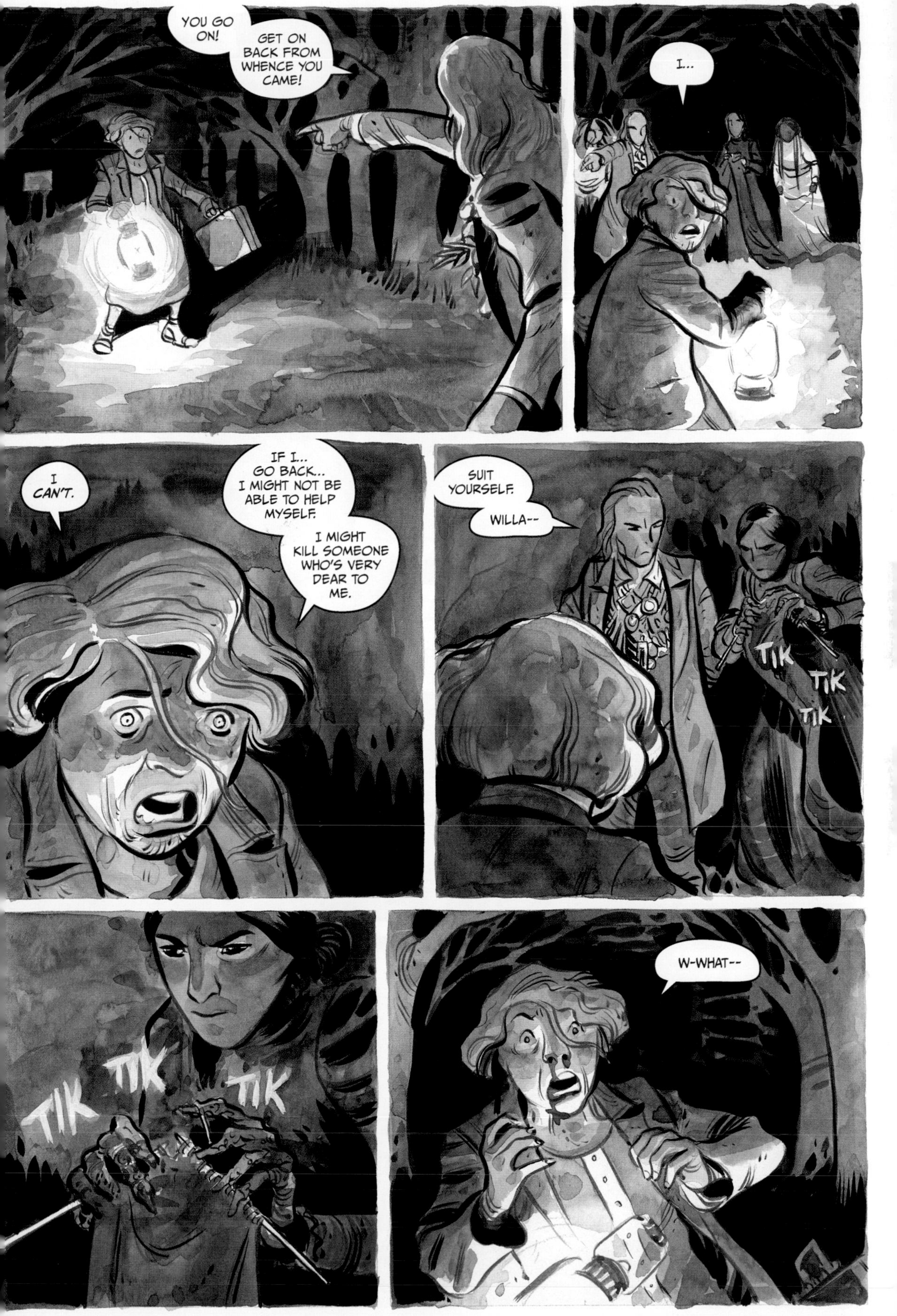
YOU GO ON!
GET ON BACK FROM WHENCE YOU CAME!
I...
I CAN'T.
IF I... GO BACK... I MIGHT NOT BE ABLE TO HELP MYSELF.
I MIGHT KILL SOMEONE WHO'S VERY DEAR TO ME.
SUIT YOURSELF.
WILLA--
TIK TIK TIK
TIK TIK TIK
W-WHAT--

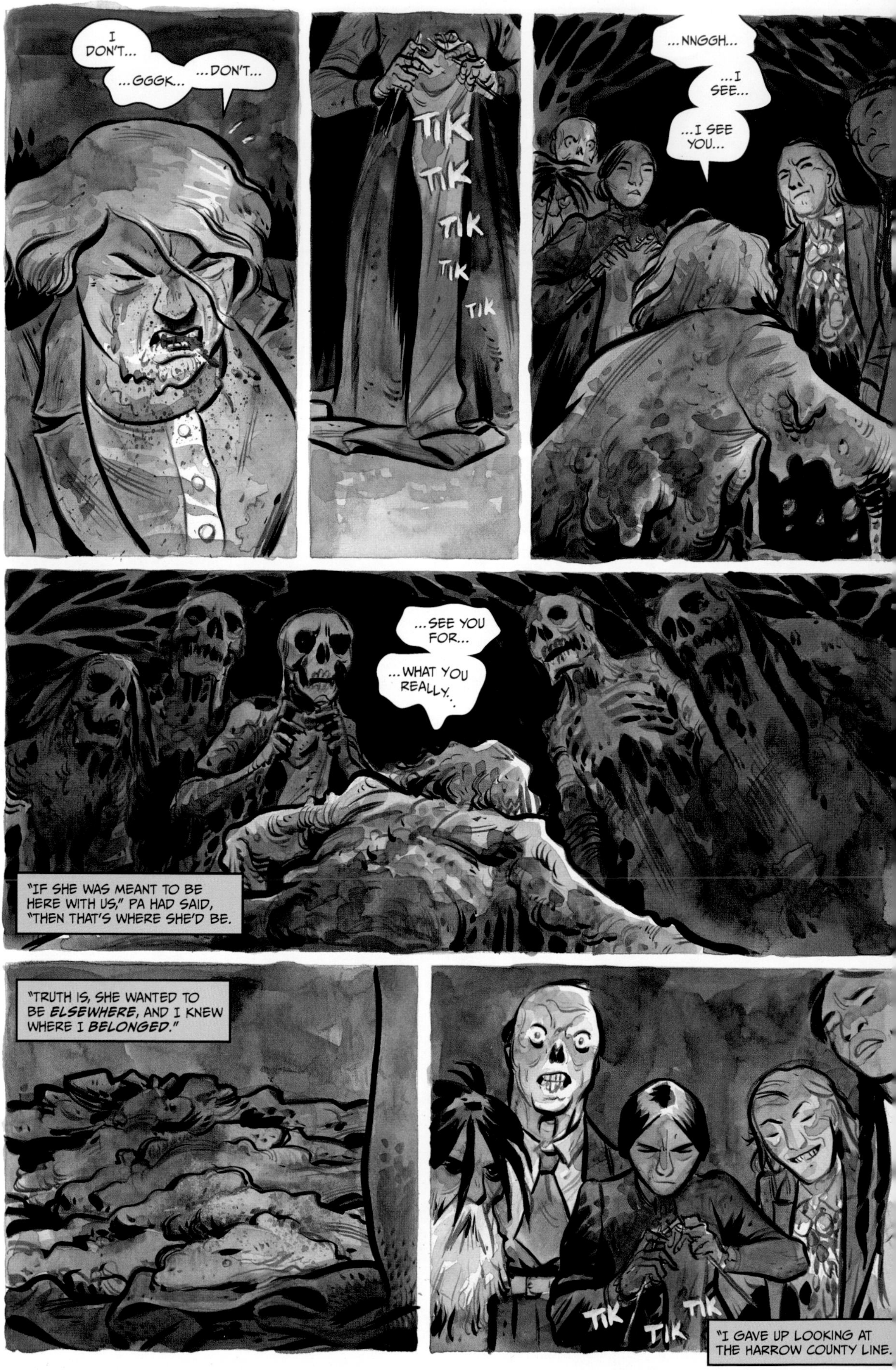
I DON'T... ...GGGK... ...DON'T...
TIK TIK TIK TIK TIK
...NNGGH...
...I SEE...
...I SEE YOU...
...SEE YOU FOR...
...WHAT YOU REALLY...
"IF SHE WAS MEANT TO BE HERE WITH US," PA HAD SAID, "THEN THAT'S WHERE SHE'D BE.
"TRUTH IS, SHE WANTED TO BE *ELSEWHERE*, AND I KNEW WHERE I *BELONGED*."
TIK TIK TIK
"I GAVE UP LOOKING AT THE HARROW COUNTY LINE.

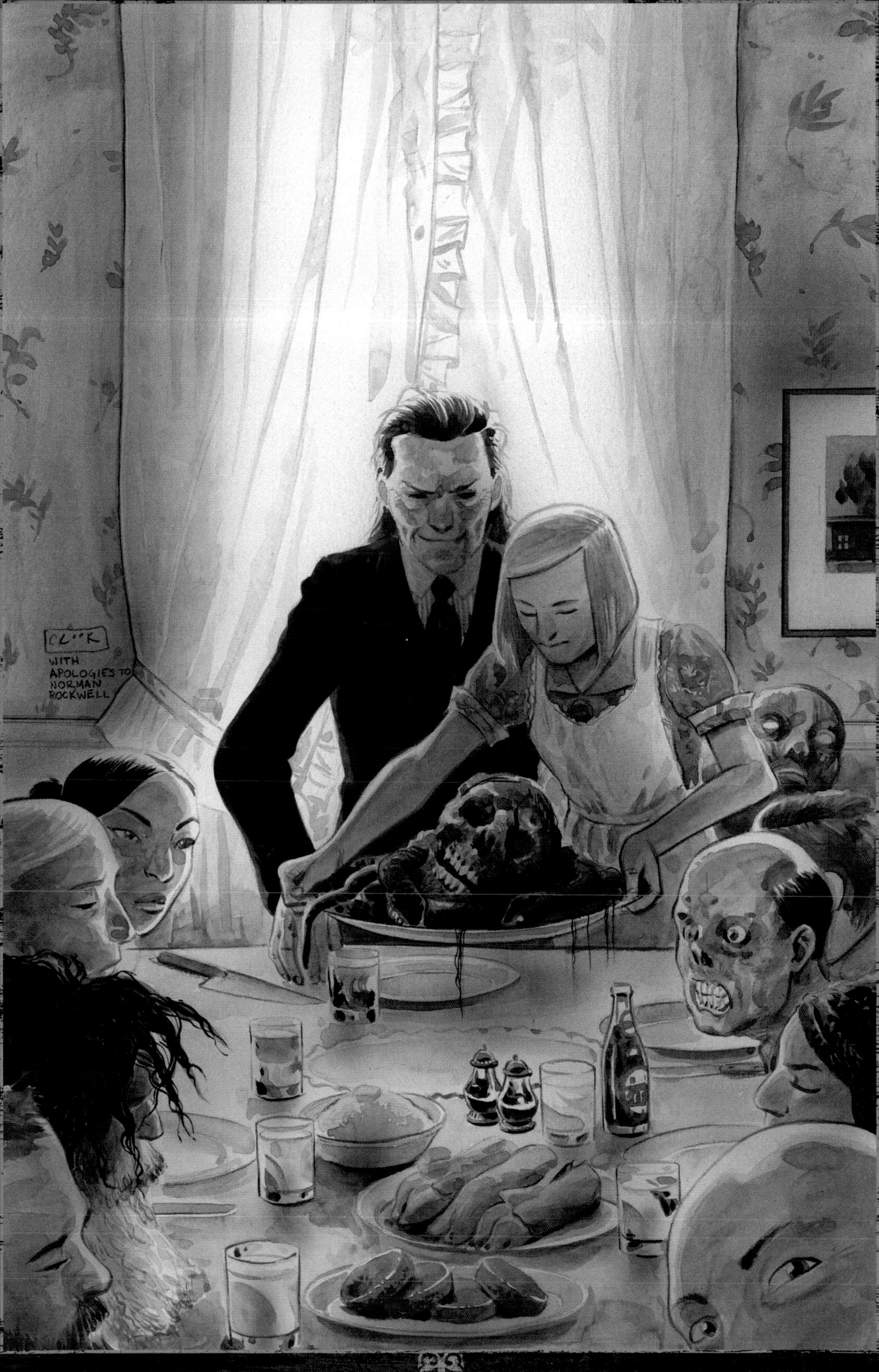
WITH APOLOGIES TO NORMAN ROCKWELL

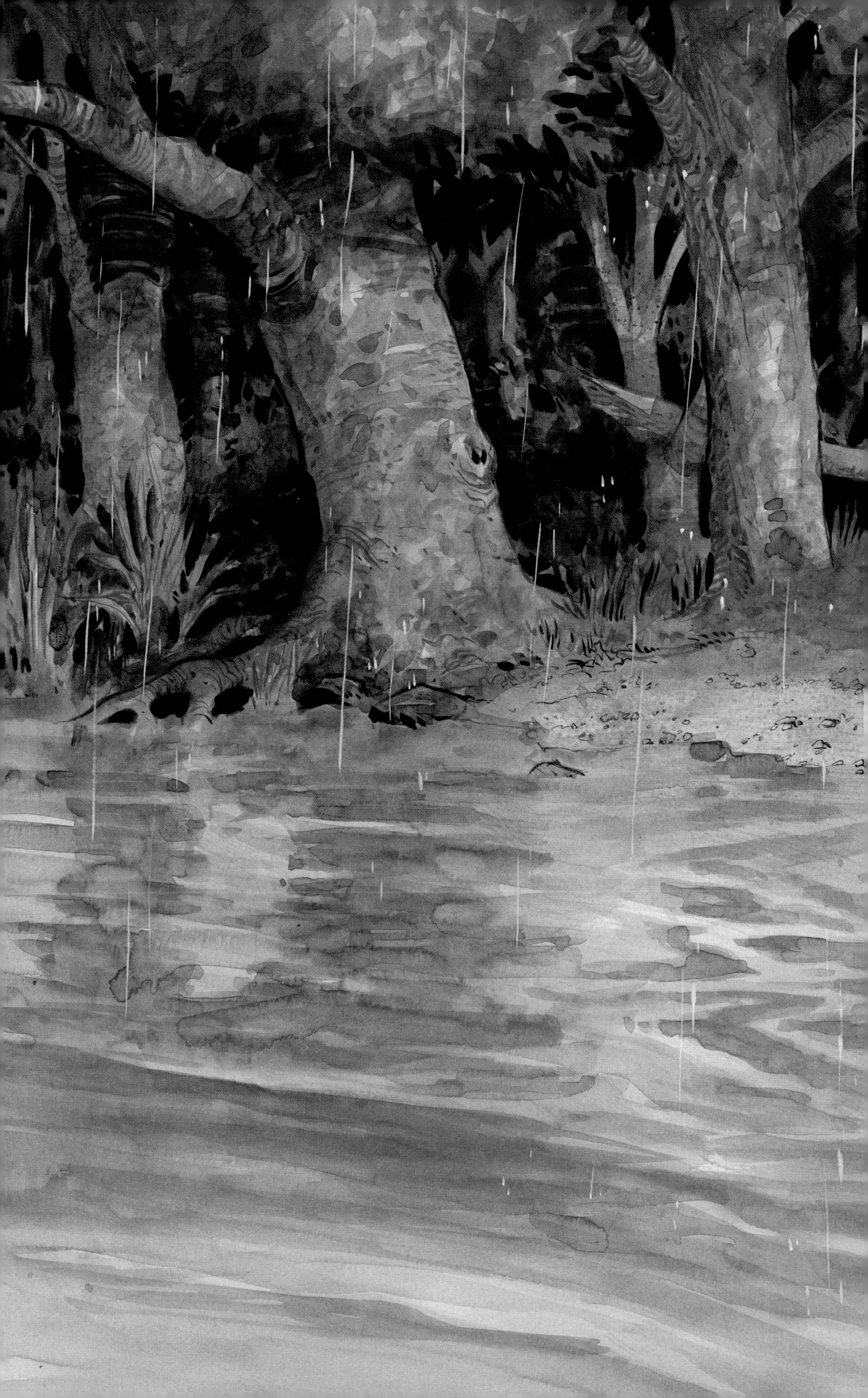

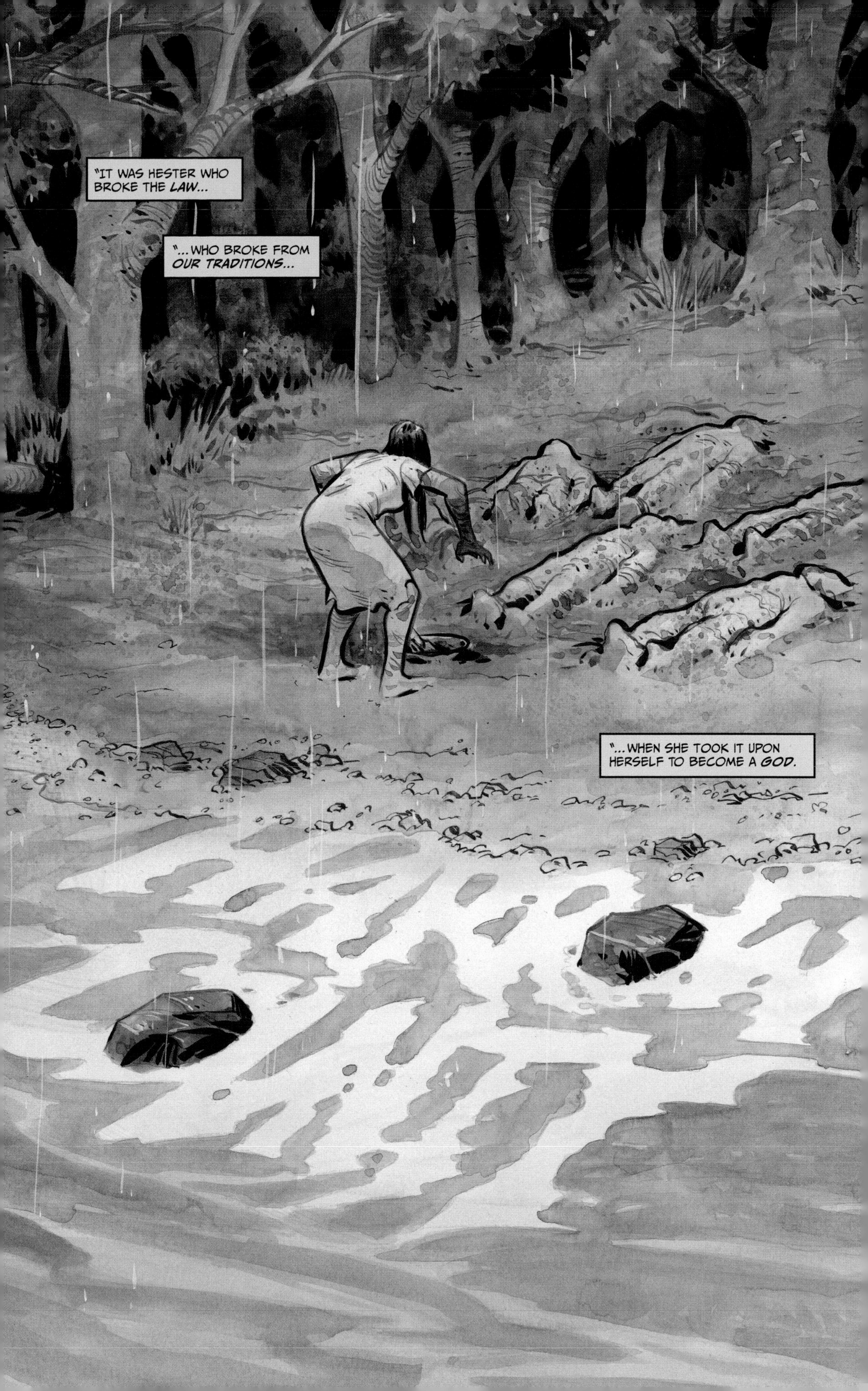
"IT WAS HESTER WHO BROKE THE *LAW*...
"...WHO BROKE FROM *OUR TRADITIONS*...
"...WHEN SHE TOOK IT UPON HERSELF TO BECOME A *GOD*.

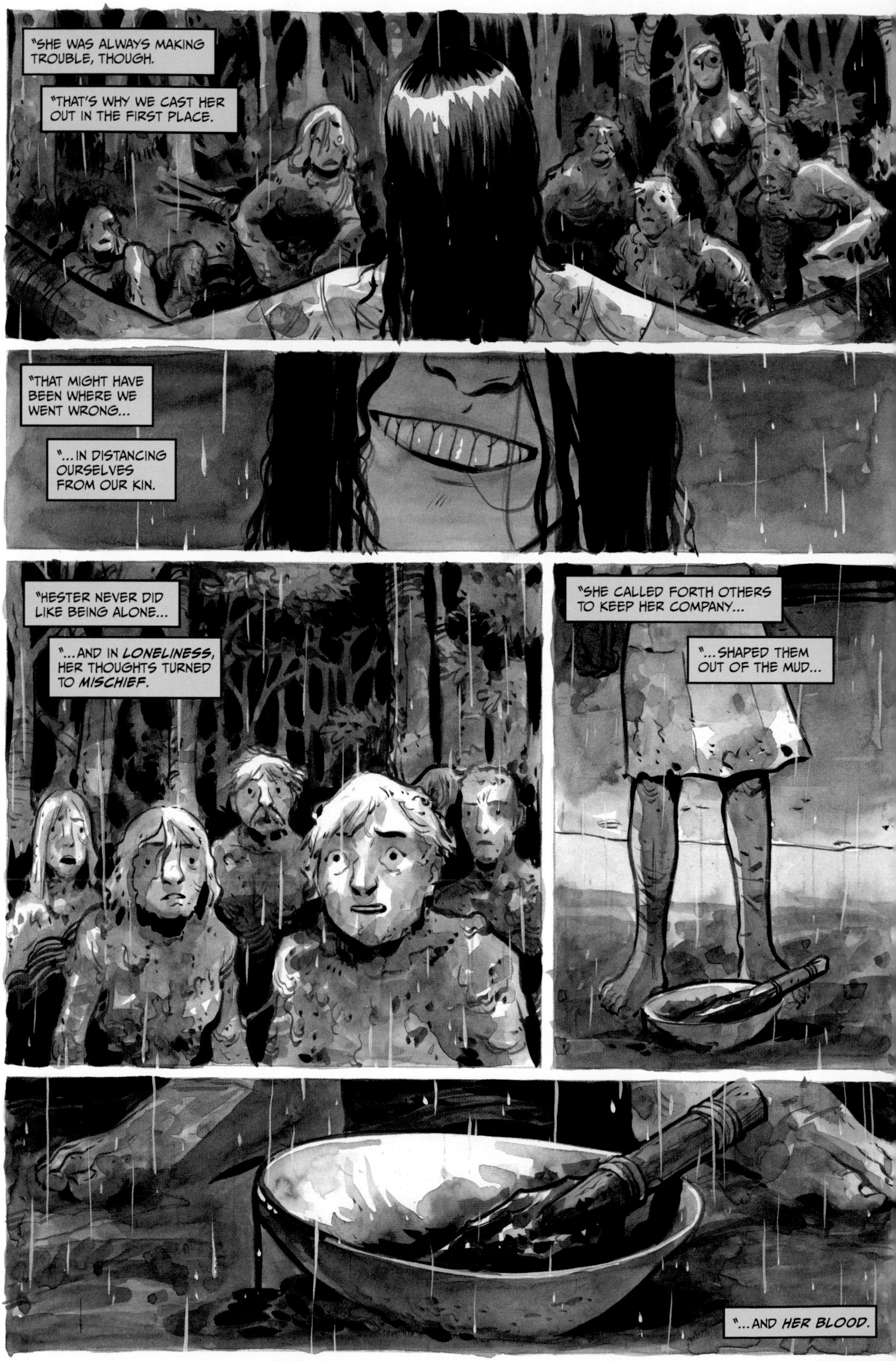
"SHE WAS ALWAYS MAKING TROUBLE, THOUGH.
"THAT'S WHY WE CAST HER OUT IN THE FIRST PLACE.
"THAT MIGHT HAVE BEEN WHERE WE WENT WRONG...
"...IN DISTANCING OURSELVES FROM OUR KIN.
"HESTER NEVER DID LIKE BEING ALONE...
"...AND IN *LONELINESS*, HER THOUGHTS TURNED TO *MISCHIEF*.
"SHE CALLED FORTH OTHERS TO KEEP HER COMPANY...
"...SHAPED THEM OUT OF THE MUD...
"...AND *HER BLOOD*.

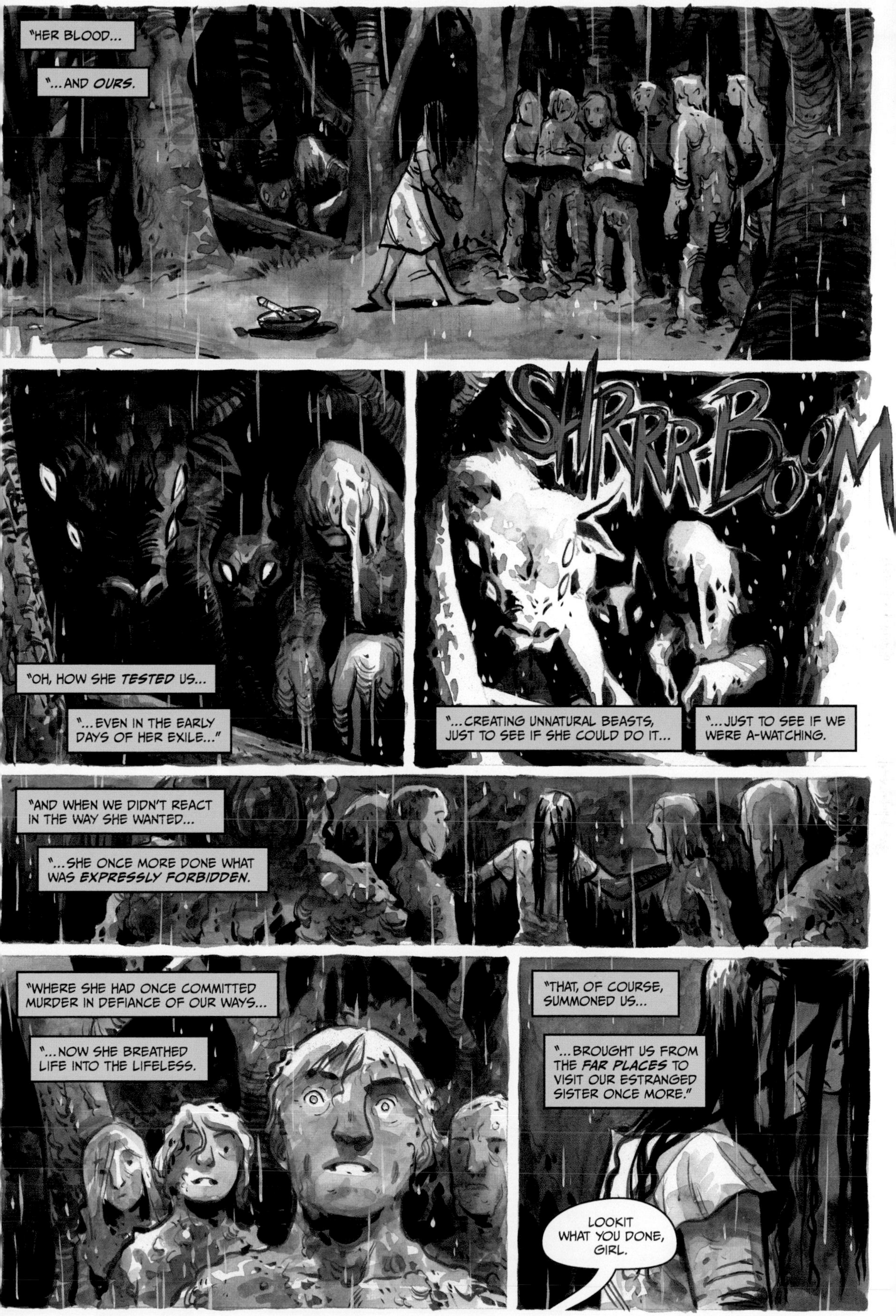
"HER BLOOD...
"...AND *OURS*.
"OH, HOW SHE *TESTED* US...
"...EVEN IN THE EARLY DAYS OF HER EXILE..."
SHRRRBOOM
"...CREATING UNNATURAL BEASTS, JUST TO SEE IF SHE COULD DO IT...
"...JUST TO SEE IF WE WERE A-WATCHING.
"AND WHEN WE DIDN'T REACT IN THE WAY SHE WANTED...
"...SHE ONCE MORE DONE WHAT WAS *EXPRESSLY FORBIDDEN*.
"WHERE SHE HAD ONCE COMMITTED MURDER IN DEFIANCE OF OUR WAYS...
"...NOW SHE BREATHED LIFE INTO THE LIFELESS.
"THAT, OF COURSE, SUMMONED US...
"...BROUGHT US FROM THE *FAR PLACES* TO VISIT OUR ESTRANGED SISTER ONCE MORE."
LOOKIT WHAT YOU DONE, GIRL.

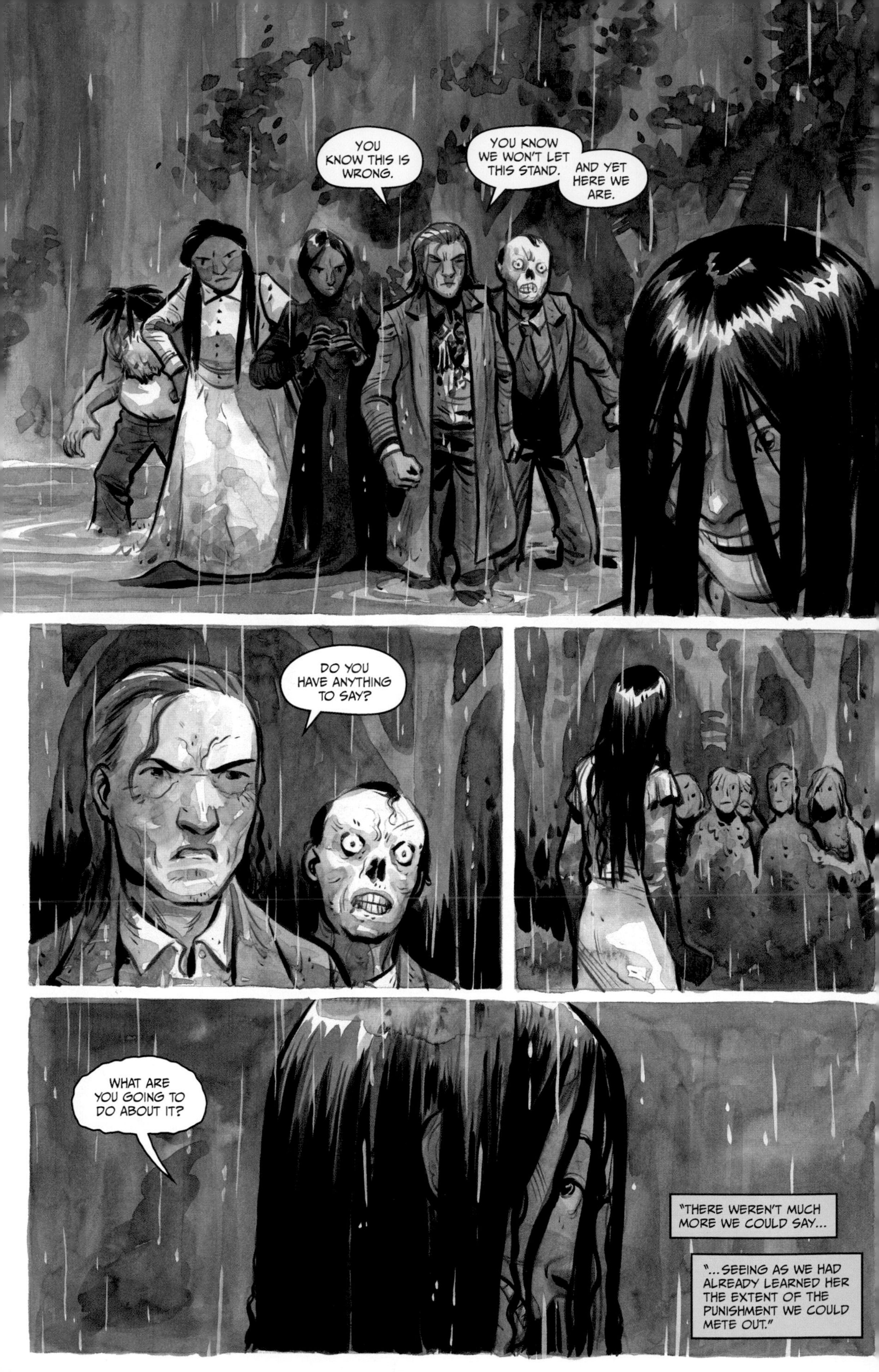
YOU KNOW THIS IS WRONG.
YOU KNOW WE WON'T LET THIS STAND.
AND YET HERE WE ARE.
DO YOU HAVE ANYTHING TO SAY?
WHAT ARE YOU GOING TO DO ABOUT IT?
"THERE WEREN'T MUCH MORE WE COULD SAY...
"...SEEING AS WE HAD ALREADY LEARNED HER THE EXTENT OF THE PUNISHMENT WE COULD METE OUT."

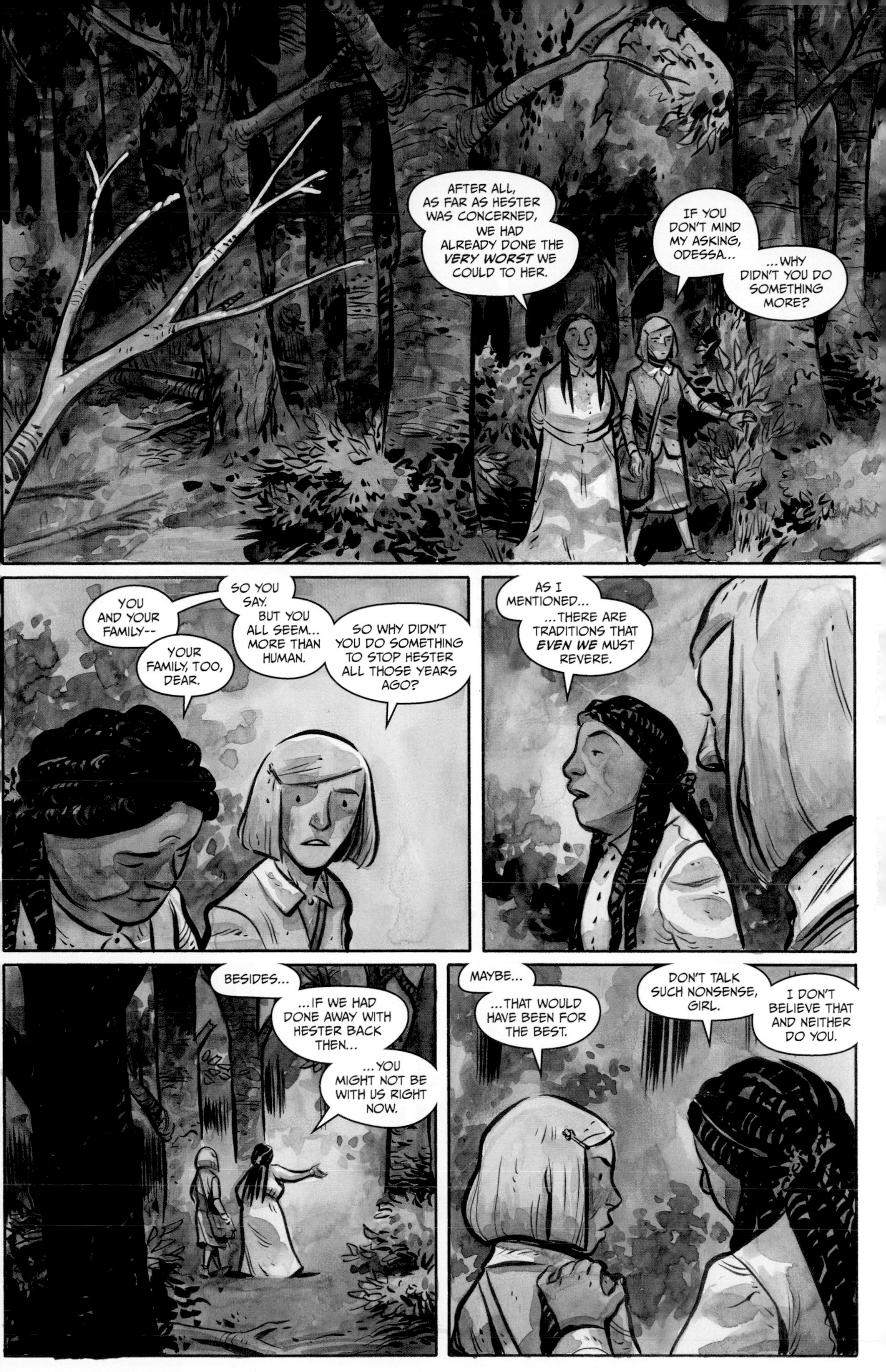
AFTER ALL, AS FAR AS HESTER WAS CONCERNED, WE HAD ALREADY DONE THE *VERY WORST* WE COULD TO HER.
IF YOU DON'T MIND MY ASKING, ODESSA...
...WHY DIDN'T YOU DO SOMETHING MORE?
YOU AND YOUR FAMILY--
YOUR FAMILY, TOO, DEAR.
SO YOU SAY.
BUT YOU ALL SEEM... MORE THAN HUMAN.
SO WHY DIDN'T YOU DO SOMETHING TO STOP HESTER ALL THOSE YEARS AGO?
AS I MENTIONED...
...THERE ARE TRADITIONS THAT *EVEN WE* MUST REVERE.
BESIDES...
...IF WE HAD DONE AWAY WITH HESTER BACK THEN...
...YOU MIGHT NOT BE WITH US RIGHT NOW.
MAYBE...
...THAT WOULD HAVE BEEN FOR THE BEST.
DON'T TALK SUCH NONSENSE, GIRL.
I DON'T BELIEVE THAT AND NEITHER DO YOU.

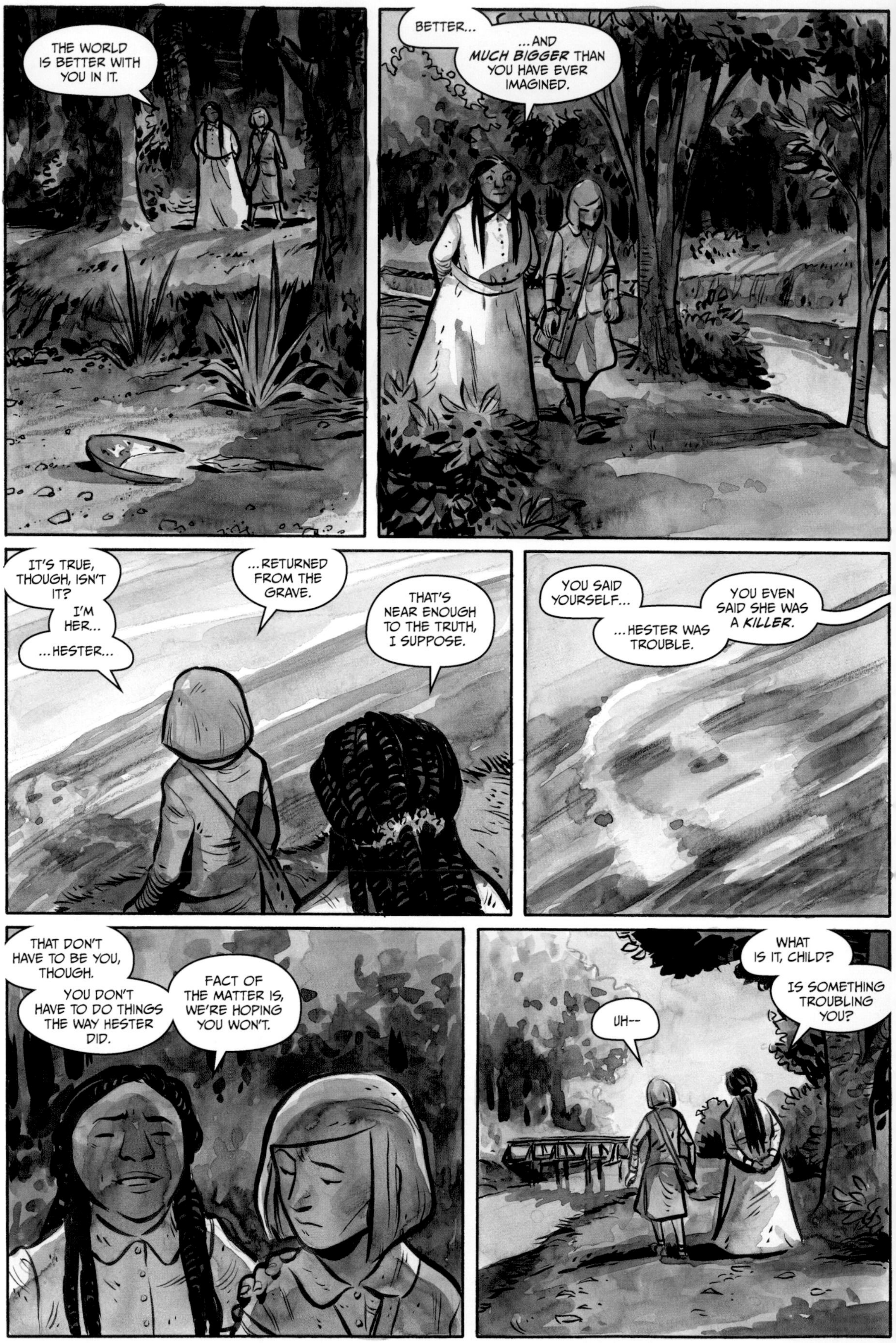
THE WORLD IS BETTER WITH YOU IN IT.
BETTER...
...AND *MUCH BIGGER* THAN YOU HAVE EVER IMAGINED.
IT'S TRUE, THOUGH, ISN'T IT?
I'M HER...
...HESTER...
...RETURNED FROM THE GRAVE.
THAT'S NEAR ENOUGH TO THE TRUTH, I SUPPOSE.
YOU SAID YOURSELF...
...HESTER WAS TROUBLE.
YOU EVEN SAID SHE WAS A *KILLER*.
THAT DON'T HAVE TO BE YOU, THOUGH.
YOU DON'T HAVE TO DO THINGS THE WAY HESTER DID.
FACT OF THE MATTER IS, WE'RE HOPING YOU WON'T.
WHAT IS IT, CHILD?
IS SOMETHING TROUBLING YOU?
UH--

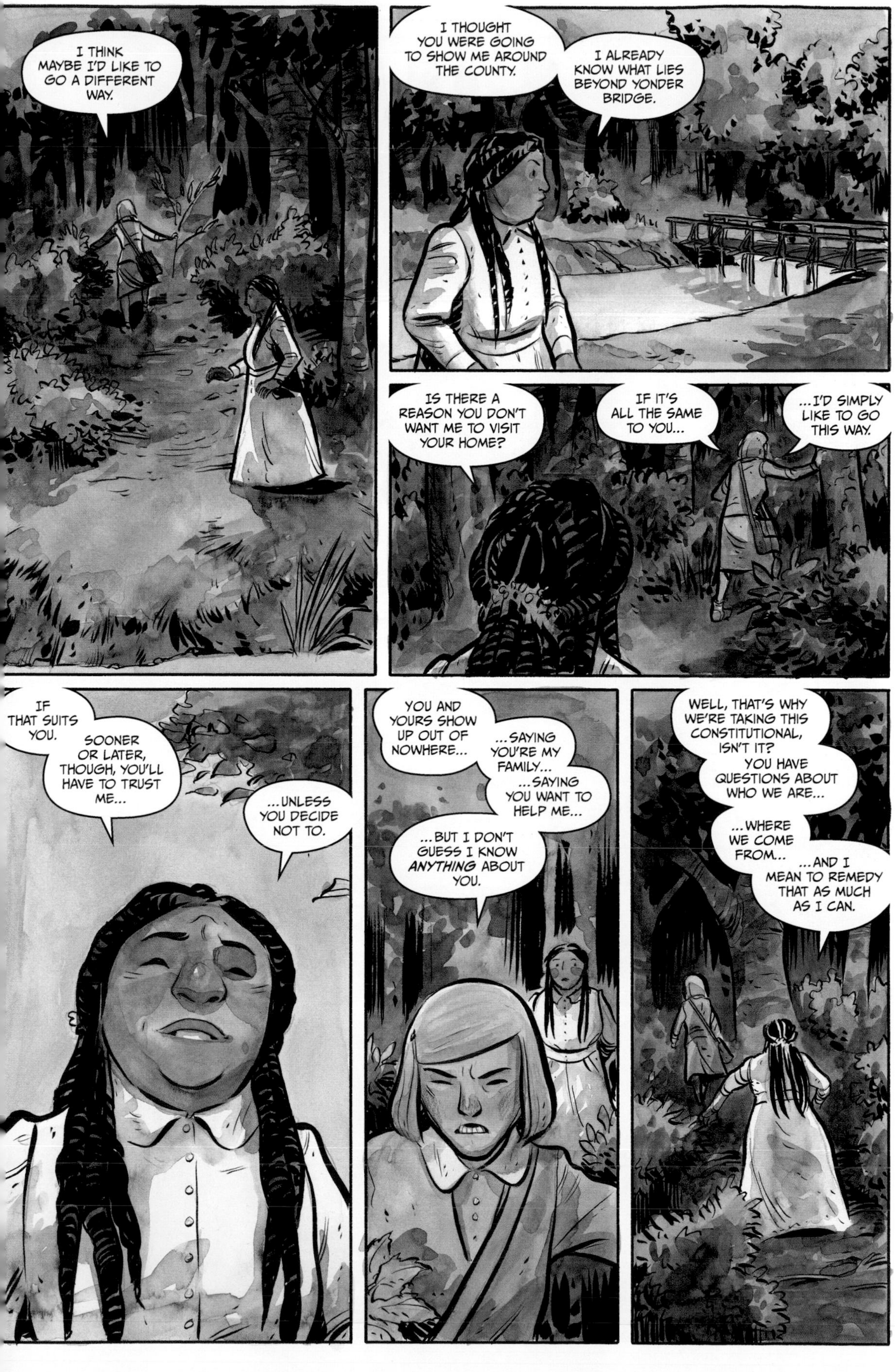
I THINK MAYBE I'D LIKE TO GO A DIFFERENT WAY.
I THOUGHT YOU WERE GOING TO SHOW ME AROUND THE COUNTY.
I ALREADY KNOW WHAT LIES BEYOND YONDER BRIDGE.
IS THERE A REASON YOU DON'T WANT ME TO VISIT YOUR HOME?
IF IT'S ALL THE SAME TO YOU...
...I'D SIMPLY LIKE TO GO THIS WAY.
IF THAT SUITS YOU.
SOONER OR LATER, THOUGH, YOU'LL HAVE TO TRUST ME...
...UNLESS YOU DECIDE NOT TO.
YOU AND YOURS SHOW UP OUT OF NOWHERE...
...SAYING YOU'RE MY FAMILY...
...SAYING YOU WANT TO HELP ME...
...BUT I DON'T GUESS I KNOW *ANYTHING* ABOUT YOU.
WELL, THAT'S WHY WE'RE TAKING THIS CONSTITUTIONAL, ISN'T IT?
YOU HAVE QUESTIONS ABOUT WHO WE ARE...
...WHERE WE COME FROM...
...AND I MEAN TO REMEDY THAT AS MUCH AS I CAN.

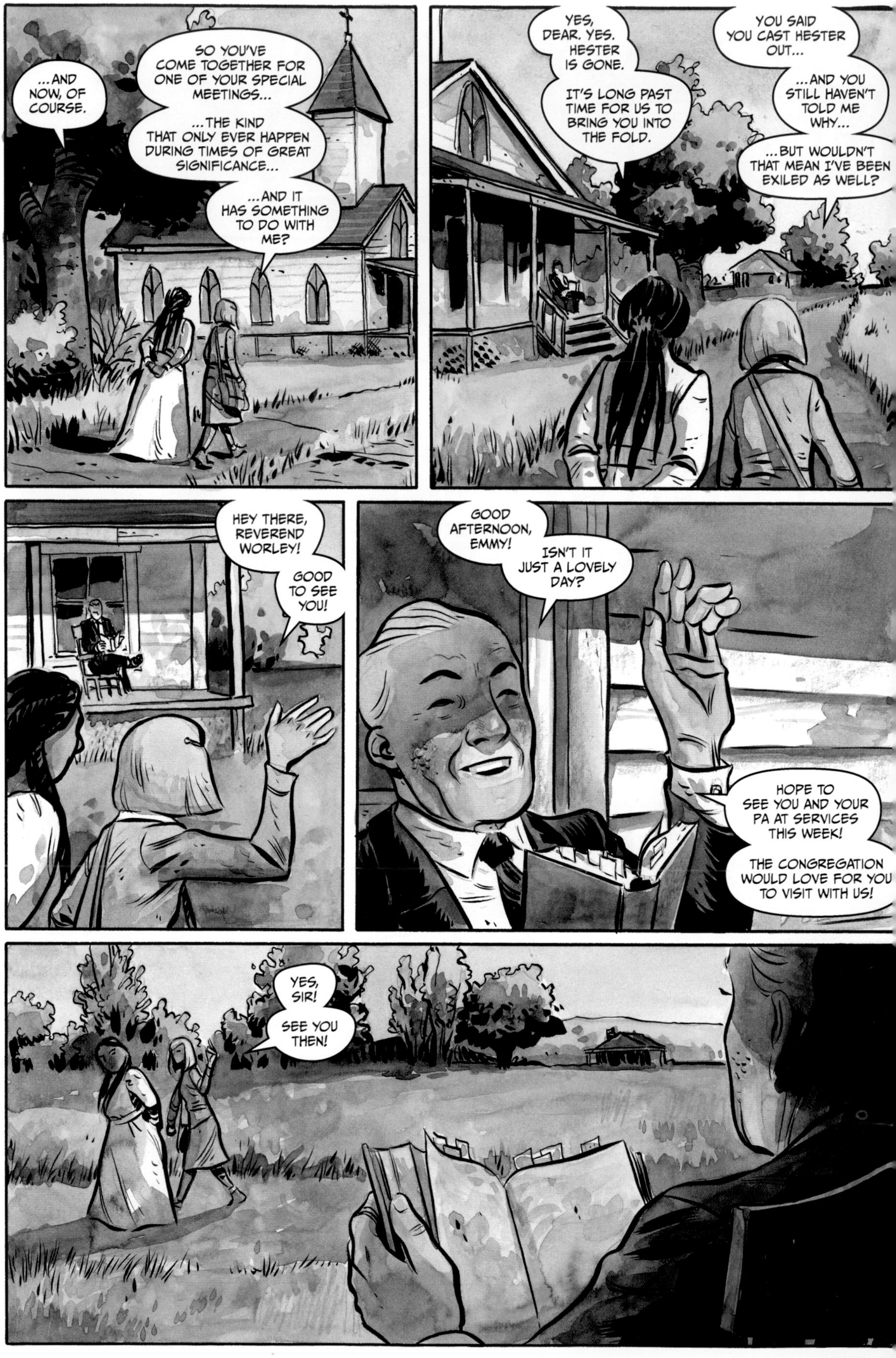
...AND NOW, OF COURSE.
SO YOU'VE COME TOGETHER FOR ONE OF YOUR SPECIAL MEETINGS...
...THE KIND THAT ONLY EVER HAPPEN DURING TIMES OF GREAT SIGNIFICANCE...
...AND IT HAS SOMETHING TO DO WITH ME?
YES, DEAR. YES. HESTER IS GONE.
IT'S LONG PAST TIME FOR US TO BRING YOU INTO THE FOLD.
YOU SAID YOU CAST HESTER OUT...
...AND YOU STILL HAVEN'T TOLD ME WHY...
...BUT WOULDN'T THAT MEAN I'VE BEEN EXILED AS WELL?
HEY THERE, REVEREND WORLEY!
GOOD TO SEE YOU!
GOOD AFTERNOON, EMMY!
ISN'T IT JUST A LOVELY DAY?
HOPE TO SEE YOU AND YOUR PA AT SERVICES THIS WEEK!
THE CONGREGATION WOULD LOVE FOR YOU TO VISIT WITH US!
YES, SIR!
SEE YOU THEN!

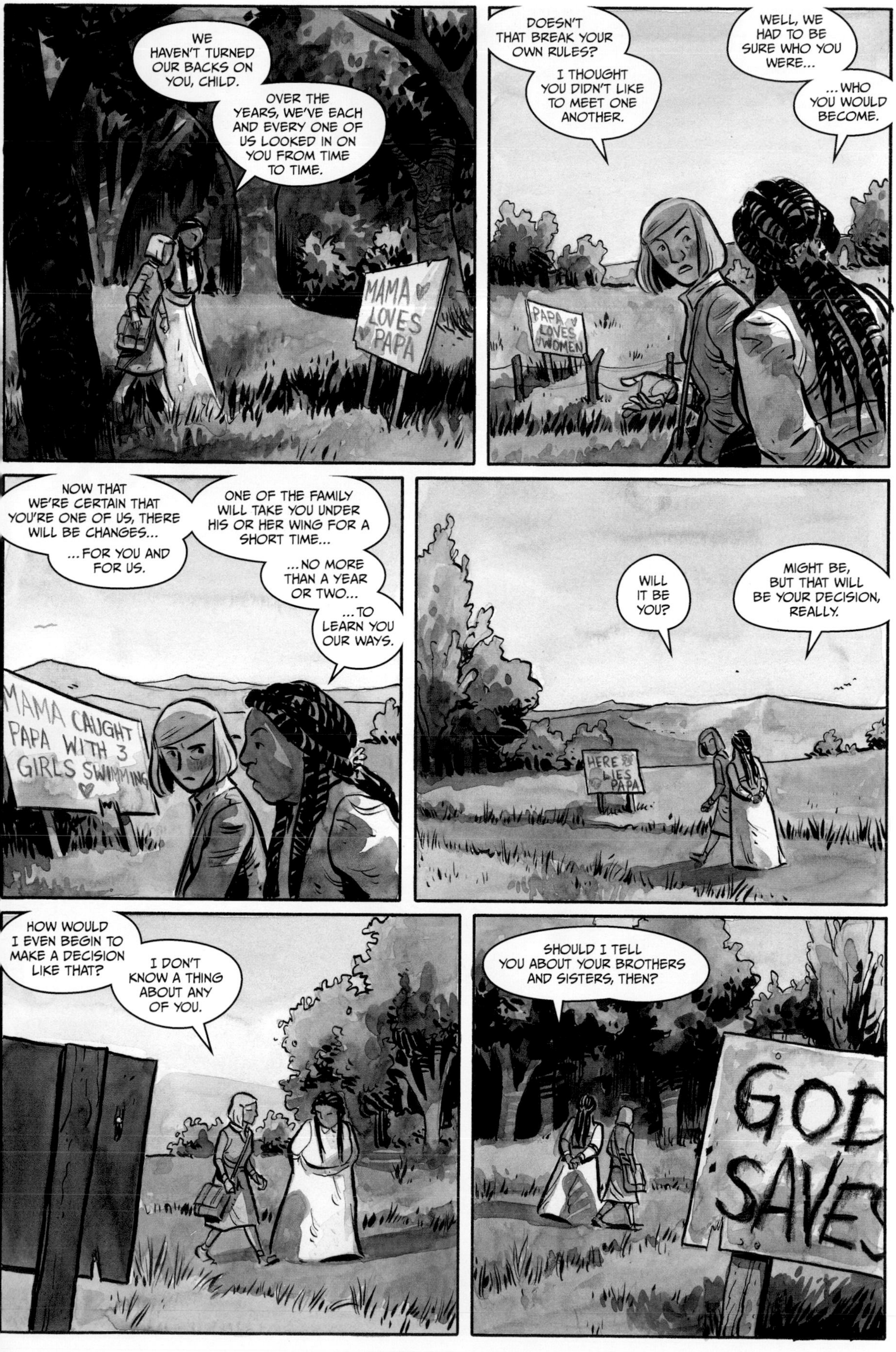
WE HAVEN'T TURNED OUR BACKS ON YOU, CHILD.
OVER THE YEARS, WE'VE EACH AND EVERY ONE OF US LOOKED IN ON YOU FROM TIME TO TIME.
MAMA LOVES PAPA
DOESN'T THAT BREAK YOUR OWN RULES?
I THOUGHT YOU DIDN'T LIKE TO MEET ONE ANOTHER.
WELL, WE HAD TO BE SURE WHO YOU WERE...
...WHO YOU WOULD BECOME.
PAPA LOVES WOMEN
NOW THAT WE'RE CERTAIN THAT YOU'RE ONE OF US, THERE WILL BE CHANGES...
...FOR YOU AND FOR US.
ONE OF THE FAMILY WILL TAKE YOU UNDER HIS OR HER WING FOR A SHORT TIME...
...NO MORE THAN A YEAR OR TWO...
...TO LEARN YOU OUR WAYS.
MAMA CAUGHT PAPA WITH 3 GIRLS SWIMMING
WILL IT BE YOU?
MIGHT BE, BUT THAT WILL BE YOUR DECISION, REALLY.
HERE LIES PAPA
HOW WOULD I EVEN BEGIN TO MAKE A DECISION LIKE THAT?
I DON'T KNOW A THING ABOUT ANY OF YOU.
SHOULD I TELL YOU ABOUT YOUR BROTHERS AND SISTERS, THEN?
GOD SAVES

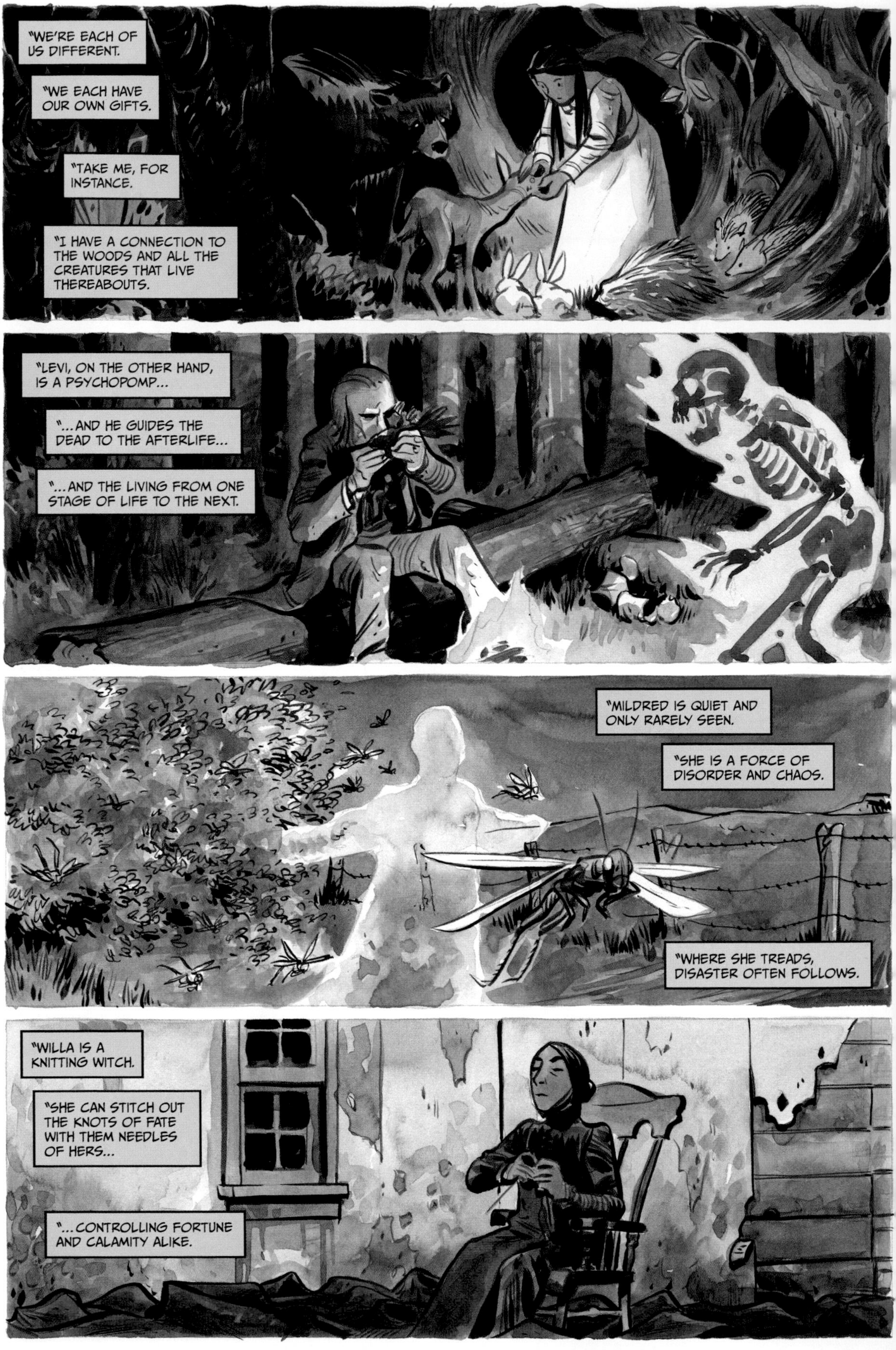
"WE'RE EACH OF US DIFFERENT.
"WE EACH HAVE OUR OWN GIFTS.
"TAKE ME, FOR INSTANCE.
"I HAVE A CONNECTION TO THE WOODS AND ALL THE CREATURES THAT LIVE THEREABOUTS.
"LEVI, ON THE OTHER HAND, IS A PSYCHOPOMP...
"...AND HE GUIDES THE DEAD TO THE AFTERLIFE...
"...AND THE LIVING FROM ONE STAGE OF LIFE TO THE NEXT.
"MILDRED IS QUIET AND ONLY RARELY SEEN.
"SHE IS A FORCE OF DISORDER AND CHAOS.
"WHERE SHE TREADS, DISASTER OFTEN FOLLOWS.
"WILLA IS A KNITTING WITCH.
"SHE CAN STITCH OUT THE KNOTS OF FATE WITH THEM NEEDLES OF HERS...
"...CONTROLLING FORTUNE AND CALAMITY ALIKE.

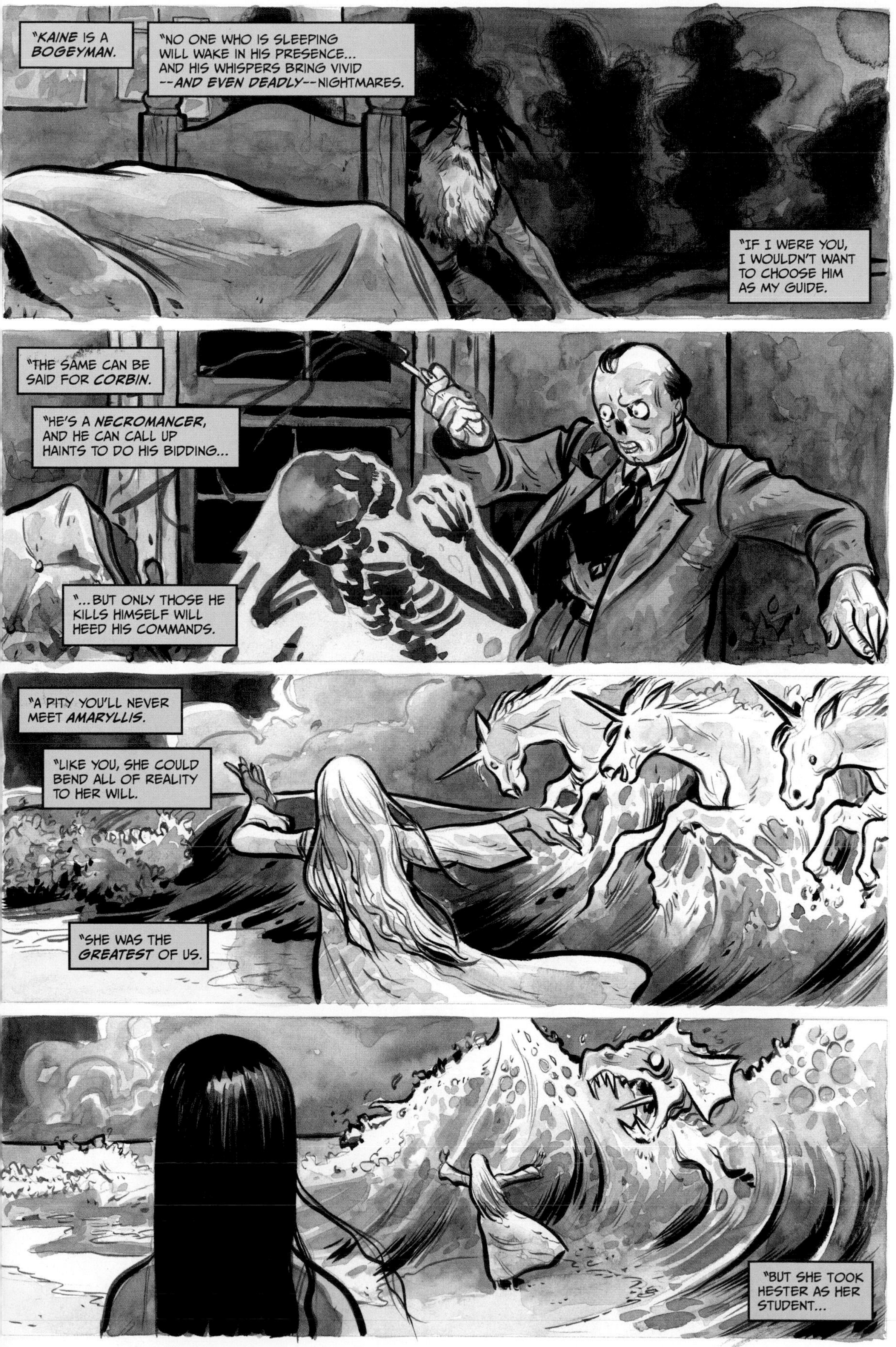
"KAINE IS A BOGEYMAN.
"NO ONE WHO IS SLEEPING WILL WAKE IN HIS PRESENCE... AND HIS WHISPERS BRING VIVID --AND EVEN DEADLY--NIGHTMARES.
"IF I WERE YOU, I WOULDN'T WANT TO CHOOSE HIM AS MY GUIDE.
"THE SAME CAN BE SAID FOR CORBIN.
"HE'S A NECROMANCER, AND HE CAN CALL UP HAINTS TO DO HIS BIDDING...
"...BUT ONLY THOSE HE KILLS HIMSELF WILL HEED HIS COMMANDS.
"A PITY YOU'LL NEVER MEET AMARYLLIS.
"LIKE YOU, SHE COULD BEND ALL OF REALITY TO HER WILL.
"SHE WAS THE GREATEST OF US.
"BUT SHE TOOK HESTER AS HER STUDENT...

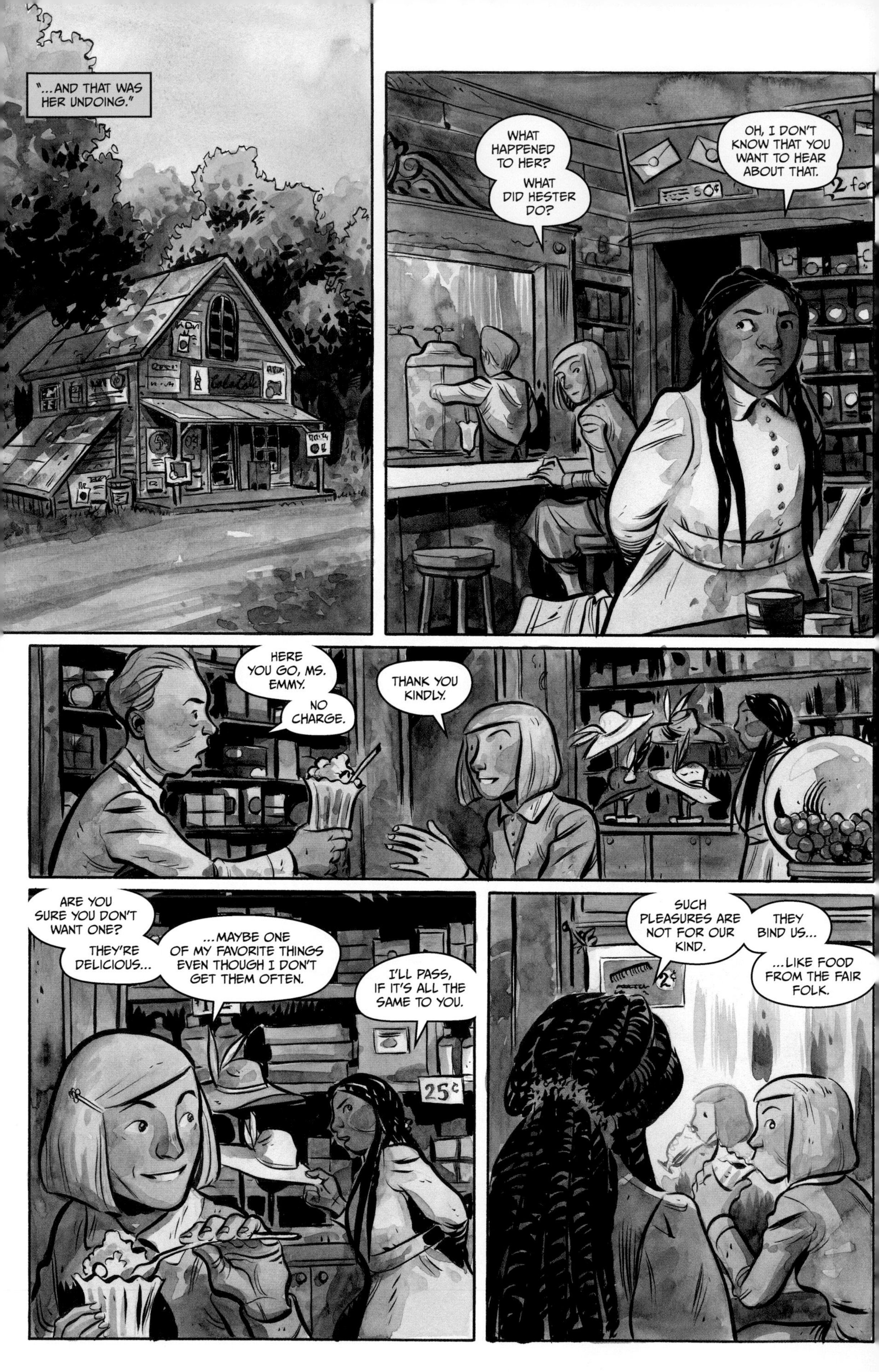
"...AND THAT WAS HER UNDOING."
WHAT HAPPENED TO HER?
WHAT DID HESTER DO?
OH, I DON'T KNOW THAT YOU WANT TO HEAR ABOUT THAT.
50¢
2 for
HERE YOU GO, MS. EMMY.
NO CHARGE.
THANK YOU KINDLY.
ARE YOU SURE YOU DON'T WANT ONE?
THEY'RE DELICIOUS...
...MAYBE ONE OF MY FAVORITE THINGS EVEN THOUGH I DON'T GET THEM OFTEN.
I'LL PASS, IF IT'S ALL THE SAME TO YOU.
25¢
SUCH PLEASURES ARE NOT FOR OUR KIND.
THEY BIND US...
...LIKE FOOD FROM THE FAIR FOLK.
2¢

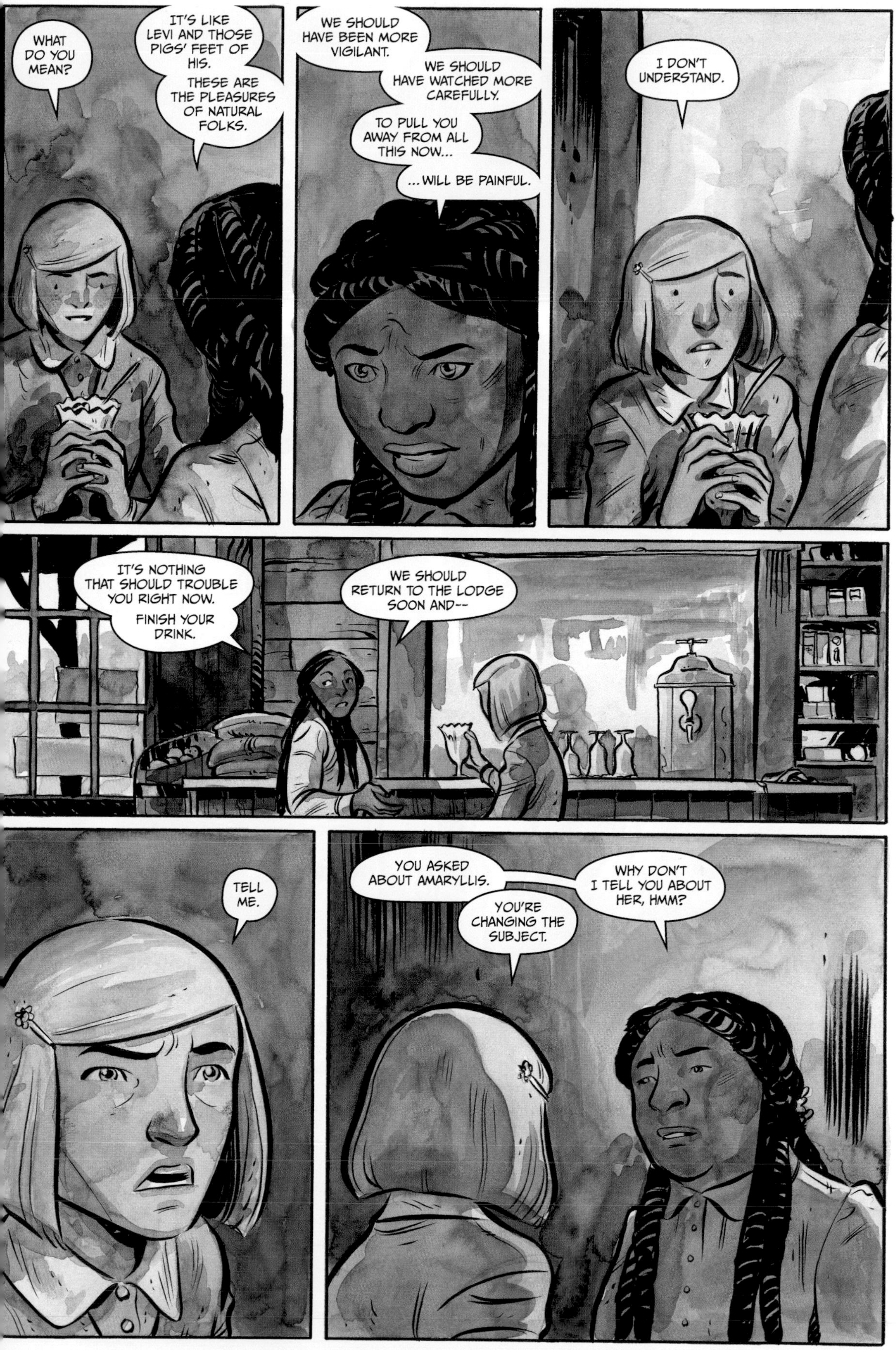
WHAT DO YOU MEAN?
IT'S LIKE LEVI AND THOSE PIGS' FEET OF HIS.
THESE ARE THE PLEASURES OF NATURAL FOLKS.
WE SHOULD HAVE BEEN MORE VIGILANT.
WE SHOULD HAVE WATCHED MORE CAREFULLY.
TO PULL YOU AWAY FROM ALL THIS NOW...
...WILL BE PAINFUL.
I DON'T UNDERSTAND.
IT'S NOTHING THAT SHOULD TROUBLE YOU RIGHT NOW.
FINISH YOUR DRINK.
WE SHOULD RETURN TO THE LODGE SOON AND--
TELL ME.
YOU ASKED ABOUT AMARYLLIS.
WHY DON'T I TELL YOU ABOUT HER, HMM?
YOU'RE CHANGING THE SUBJECT.

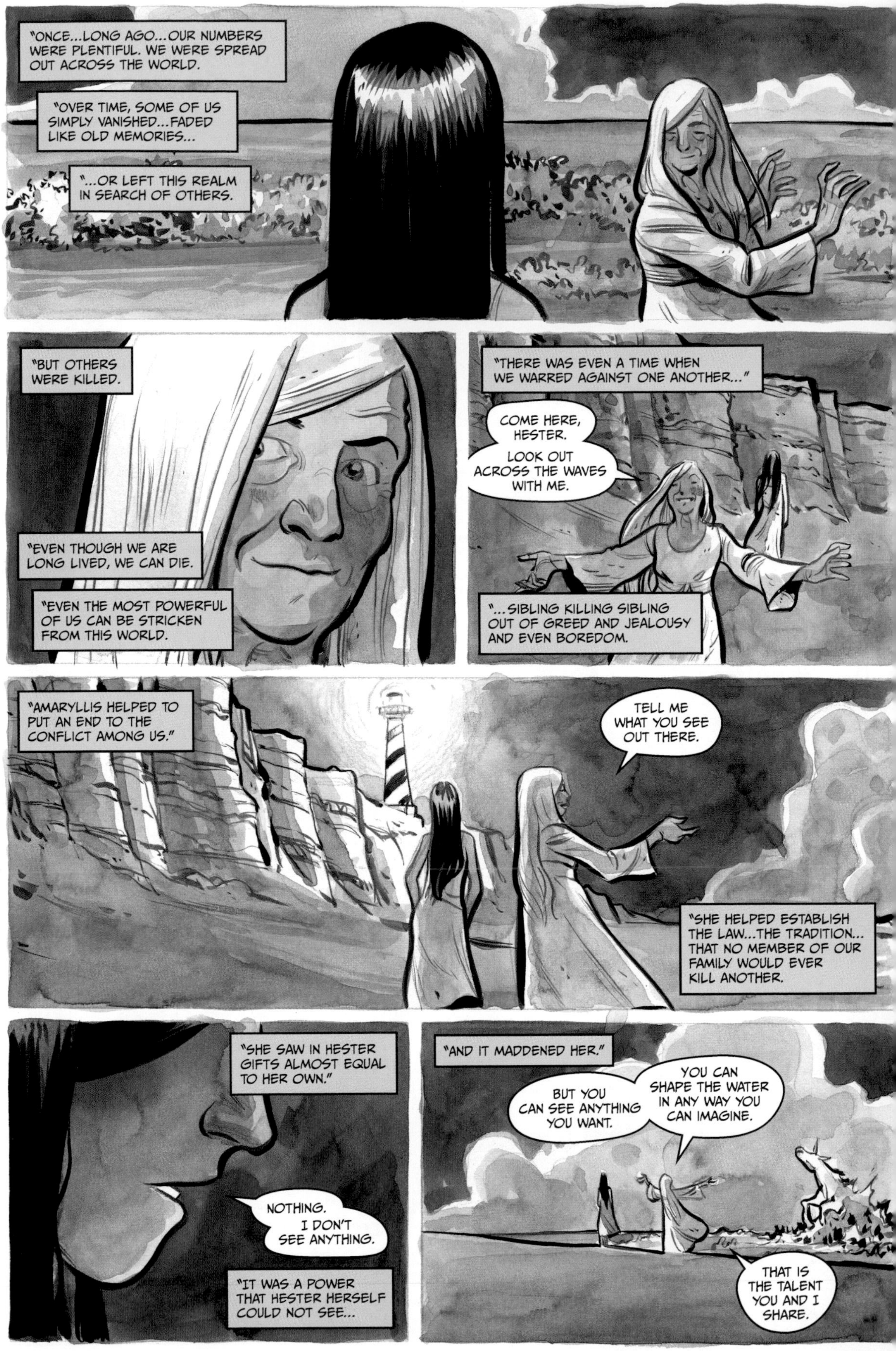
"ONCE...LONG AGO...OUR NUMBERS WERE PLENTIFUL. WE WERE SPREAD OUT ACROSS THE WORLD.
"OVER TIME, SOME OF US SIMPLY VANISHED...FADED LIKE OLD MEMORIES...
"...OR LEFT THIS REALM IN SEARCH OF OTHERS.
"BUT OTHERS WERE KILLED.
"EVEN THOUGH WE ARE LONG LIVED, WE CAN DIE.
"EVEN THE MOST POWERFUL OF US CAN BE STRICKEN FROM THIS WORLD.
"THERE WAS EVEN A TIME WHEN WE WARRED AGAINST ONE ANOTHER..."
COME HERE, HESTER.
LOOK OUT ACROSS THE WAVES WITH ME.
"...SIBLING KILLING SIBLING OUT OF GREED AND JEALOUSY AND EVEN BOREDOM.
"AMARYLLIS HELPED TO PUT AN END TO THE CONFLICT AMONG US."
TELL ME WHAT YOU SEE OUT THERE.
"SHE HELPED ESTABLISH THE LAW...THE TRADITION... THAT NO MEMBER OF OUR FAMILY WOULD EVER KILL ANOTHER.
"SHE SAW IN HESTER GIFTS ALMOST EQUAL TO HER OWN."
NOTHING. I DON'T SEE ANYTHING.
"IT WAS A POWER THAT HESTER HERSELF COULD NOT SEE...
"AND IT MADDENED HER."
BUT YOU CAN SEE ANYTHING YOU WANT.
YOU CAN SHAPE THE WATER IN ANY WAY YOU CAN IMAGINE.
THAT IS THE TALENT YOU AND I SHARE.

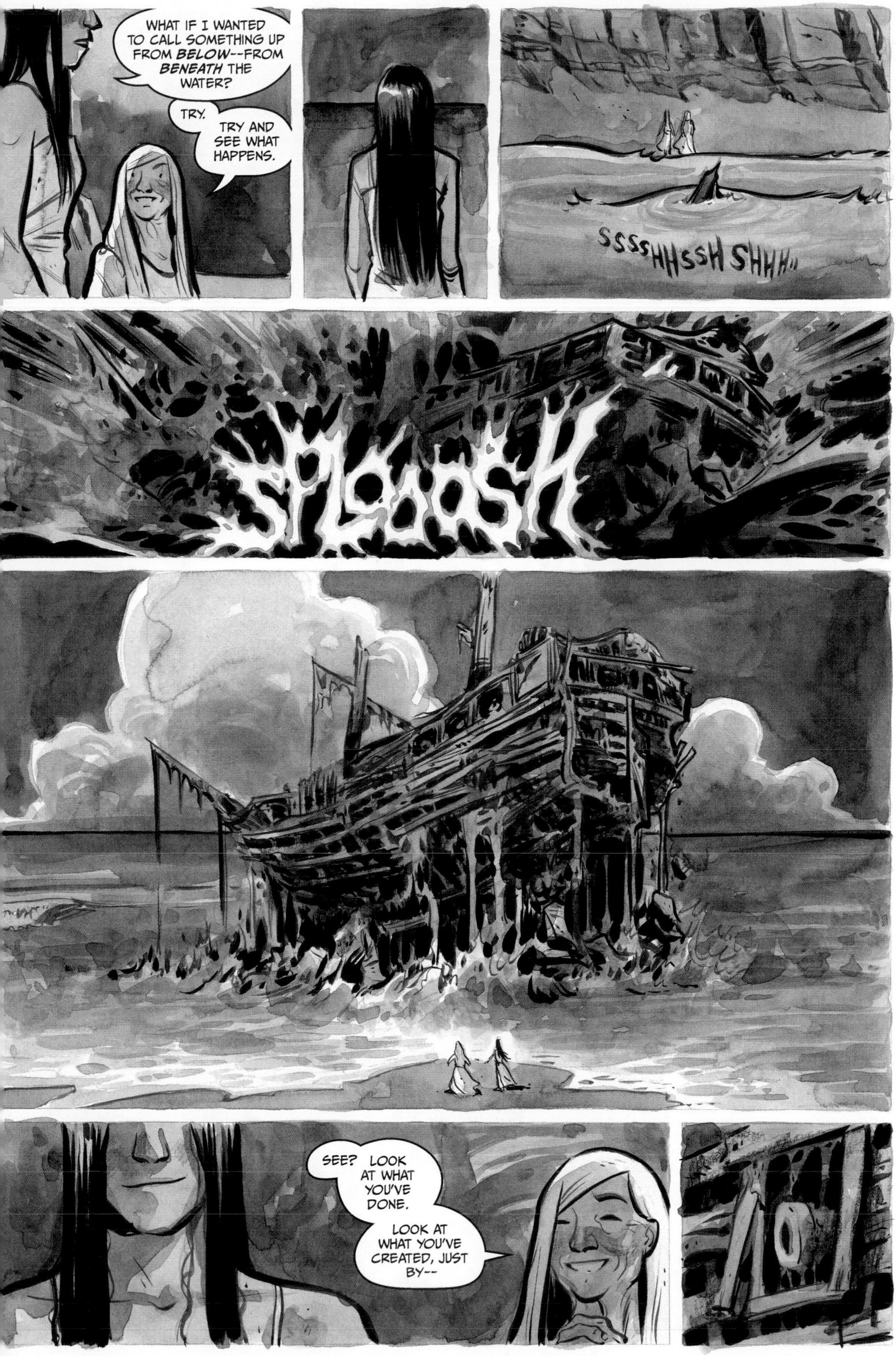

WHAT IF I WANTED TO CALL SOMETHING UP FROM *BELOW*--FROM *BENEATH* THE WATER?
TRY.
TRY AND SEE WHAT HAPPENS.
SSSSHHSSH SHHH
SPLOOOSH
SEE? LOOK AT WHAT YOU'VE DONE.
LOOK AT WHAT YOU'VE CREATED, JUST BY--

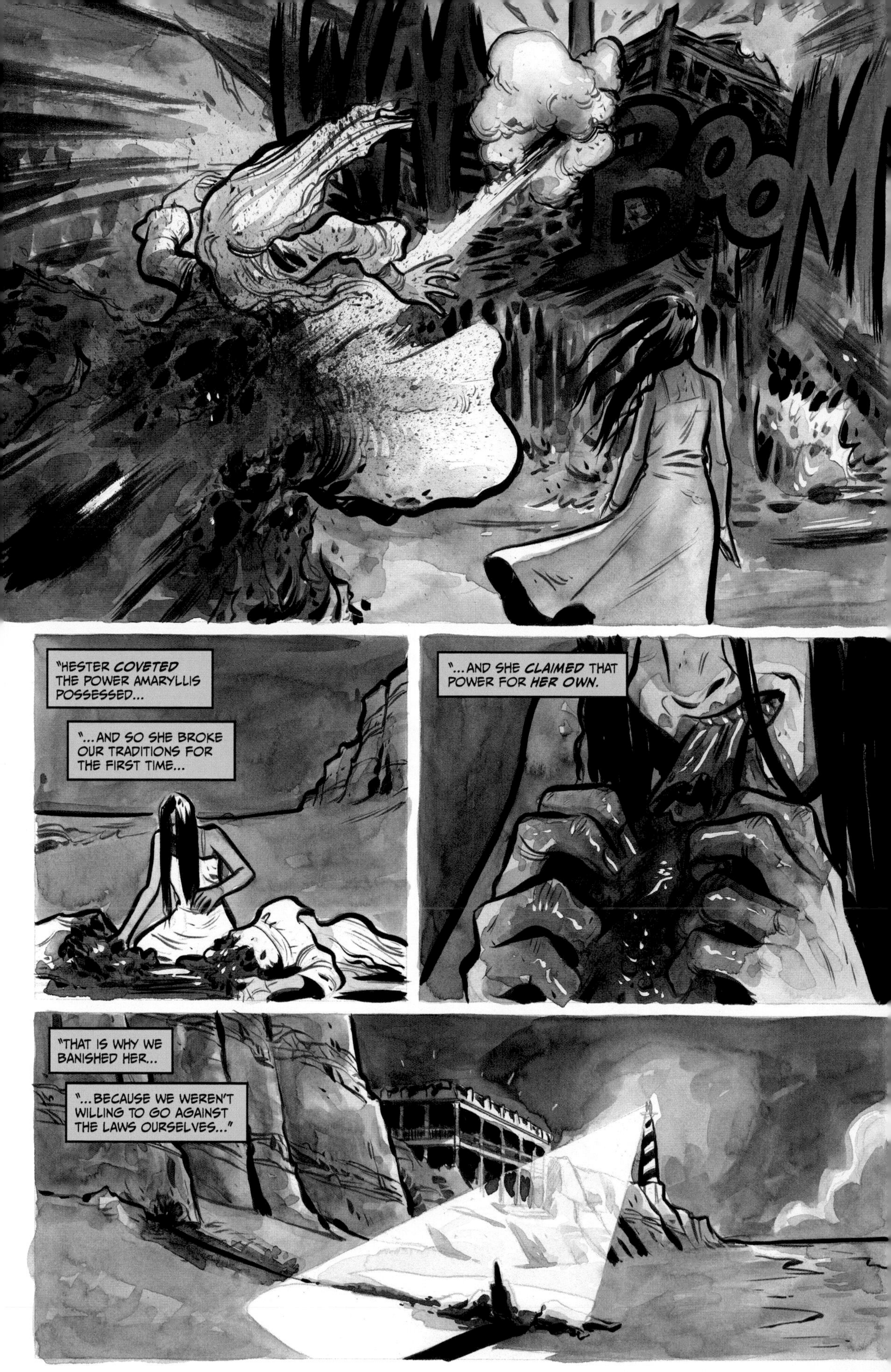
WAM
BOOM
"HESTER COVETED THE POWER AMARYLLIS POSSESSED...
"...AND SO SHE BROKE OUR TRADITIONS FOR THE FIRST TIME...
"...AND SHE CLAIMED THAT POWER FOR HER OWN.
"THAT IS WHY WE BANISHED HER...
"...BECAUSE WE WEREN'T WILLING TO GO AGAINST THE LAWS OURSELVES..."

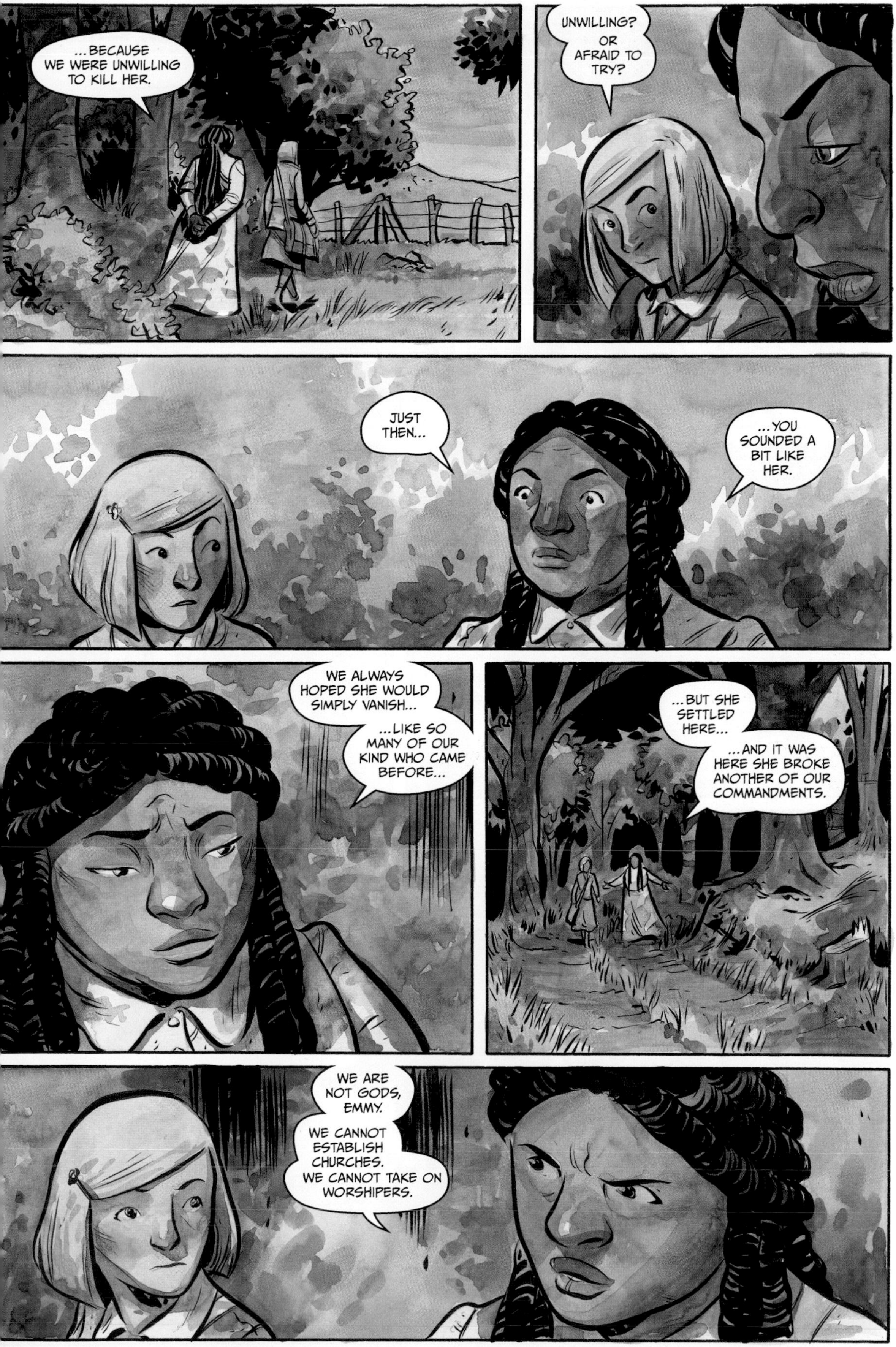
...BECAUSE WE WERE UNWILLING TO KILL HER.
UNWILLING? OR AFRAID TO TRY?
JUST THEN...
...YOU SOUNDED A BIT LIKE HER.
WE ALWAYS HOPED SHE WOULD SIMPLY VANISH...
...LIKE SO MANY OF OUR KIND WHO CAME BEFORE...
...BUT SHE SETTLED HERE...
...AND IT WAS HERE SHE BROKE ANOTHER OF OUR COMMANDMENTS.
WE ARE NOT GODS, EMMY.
WE CANNOT ESTABLISH CHURCHES. WE CANNOT TAKE ON WORSHIPERS.

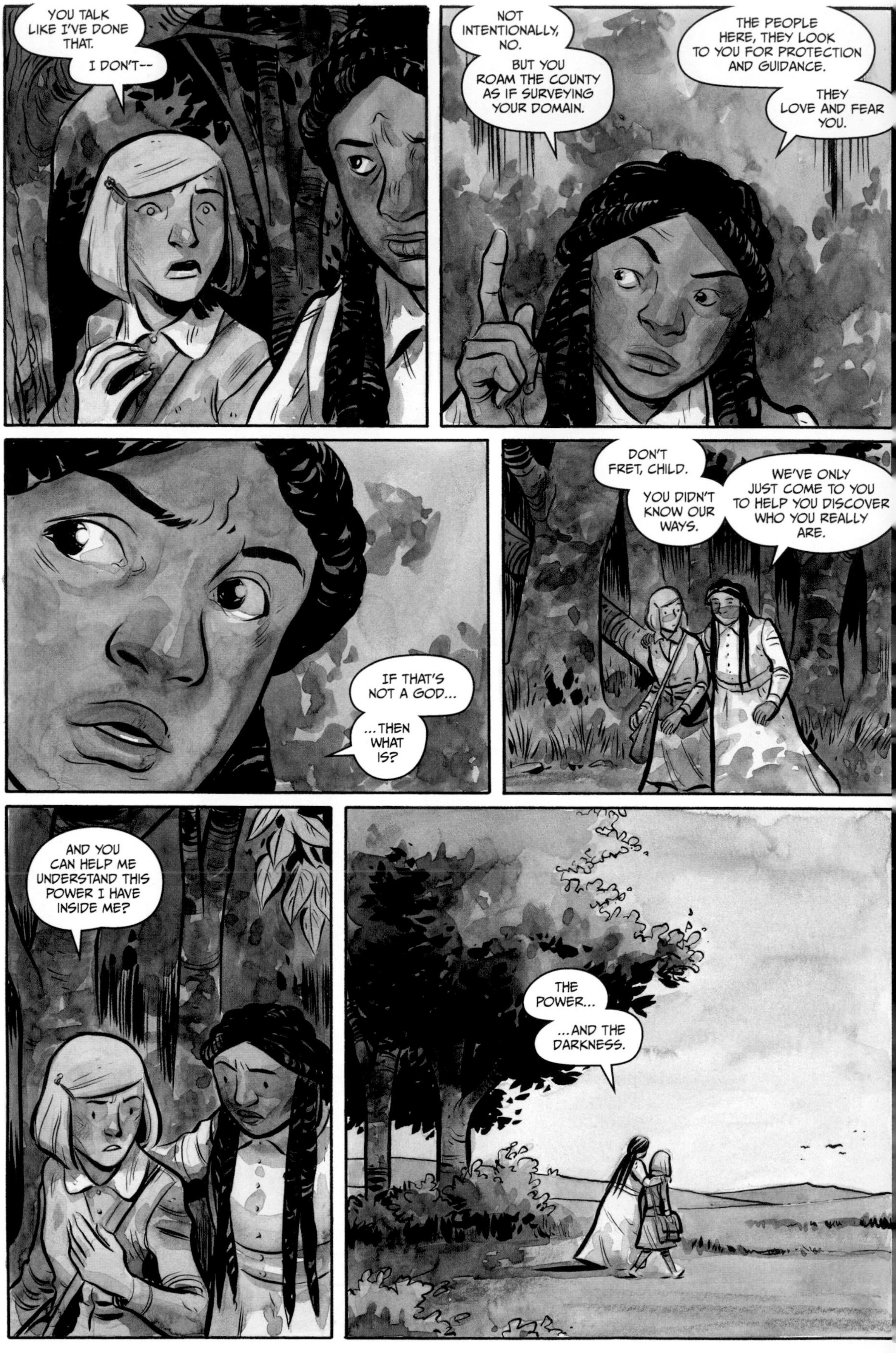
YOU TALK LIKE I'VE DONE THAT.
I DON'T--
NOT INTENTIONALLY, NO.
BUT YOU ROAM THE COUNTY AS IF SURVEYING YOUR DOMAIN.
THE PEOPLE HERE, THEY LOOK TO YOU FOR PROTECTION AND GUIDANCE.
THEY LOVE AND FEAR YOU.
IF THAT'S NOT A GOD...
...THEN WHAT IS?
DON'T FRET, CHILD.
YOU DIDN'T KNOW OUR WAYS.
WE'VE ONLY JUST COME TO YOU TO HELP YOU DISCOVER WHO YOU REALLY ARE.
AND YOU CAN HELP ME UNDERSTAND THIS POWER I HAVE INSIDE ME?
THE POWER...
...AND THE DARKNESS.

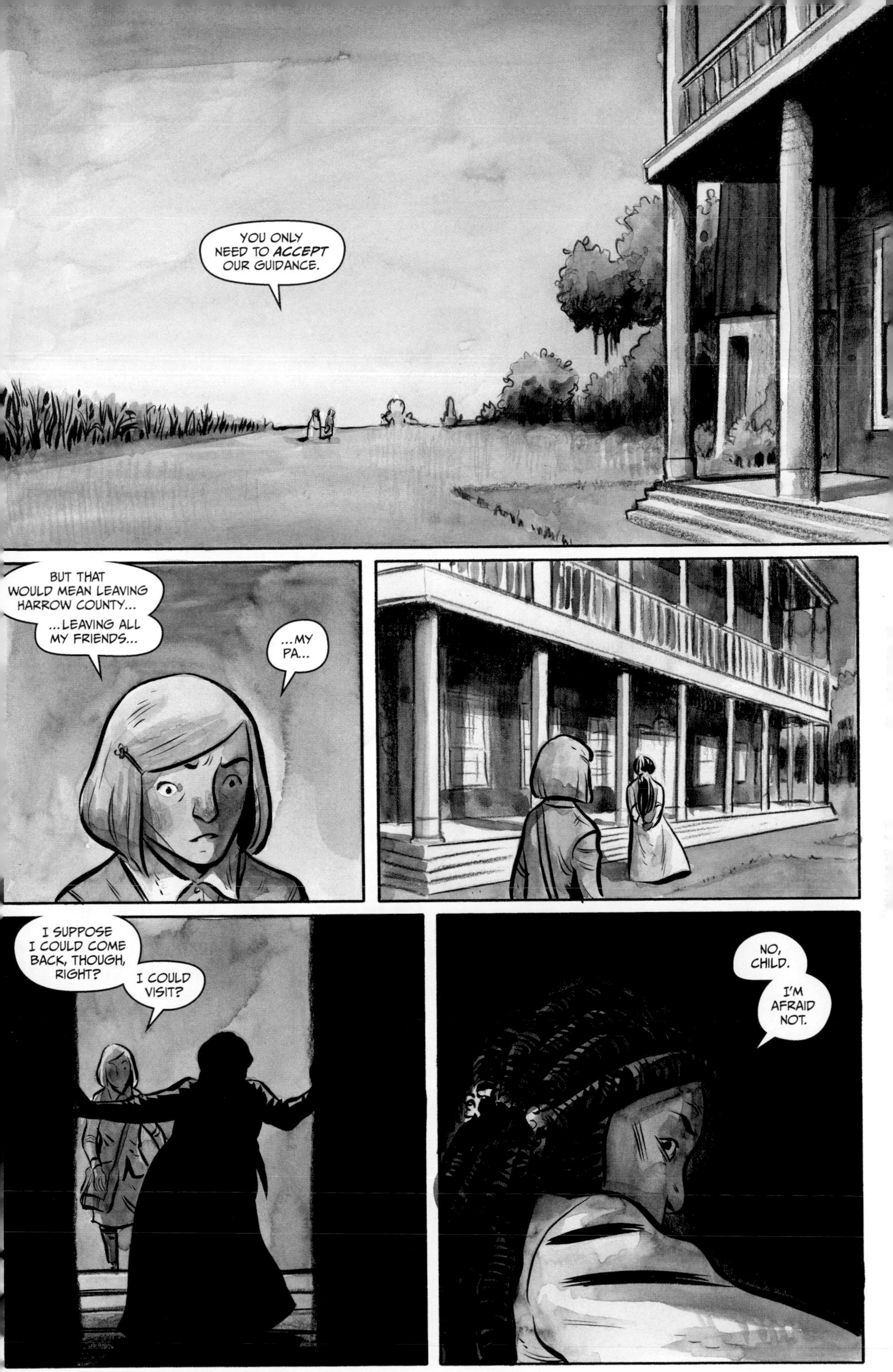
YOU ONLY NEED TO ACCEPT OUR GUIDANCE.
BUT THAT WOULD MEAN LEAVING HARROW COUNTY...
...LEAVING ALL MY FRIENDS...
...MY PA...
I SUPPOSE I COULD COME BACK, THOUGH, RIGHT?
I COULD VISIT?
NO, CHILD.
I'M AFRAID NOT.

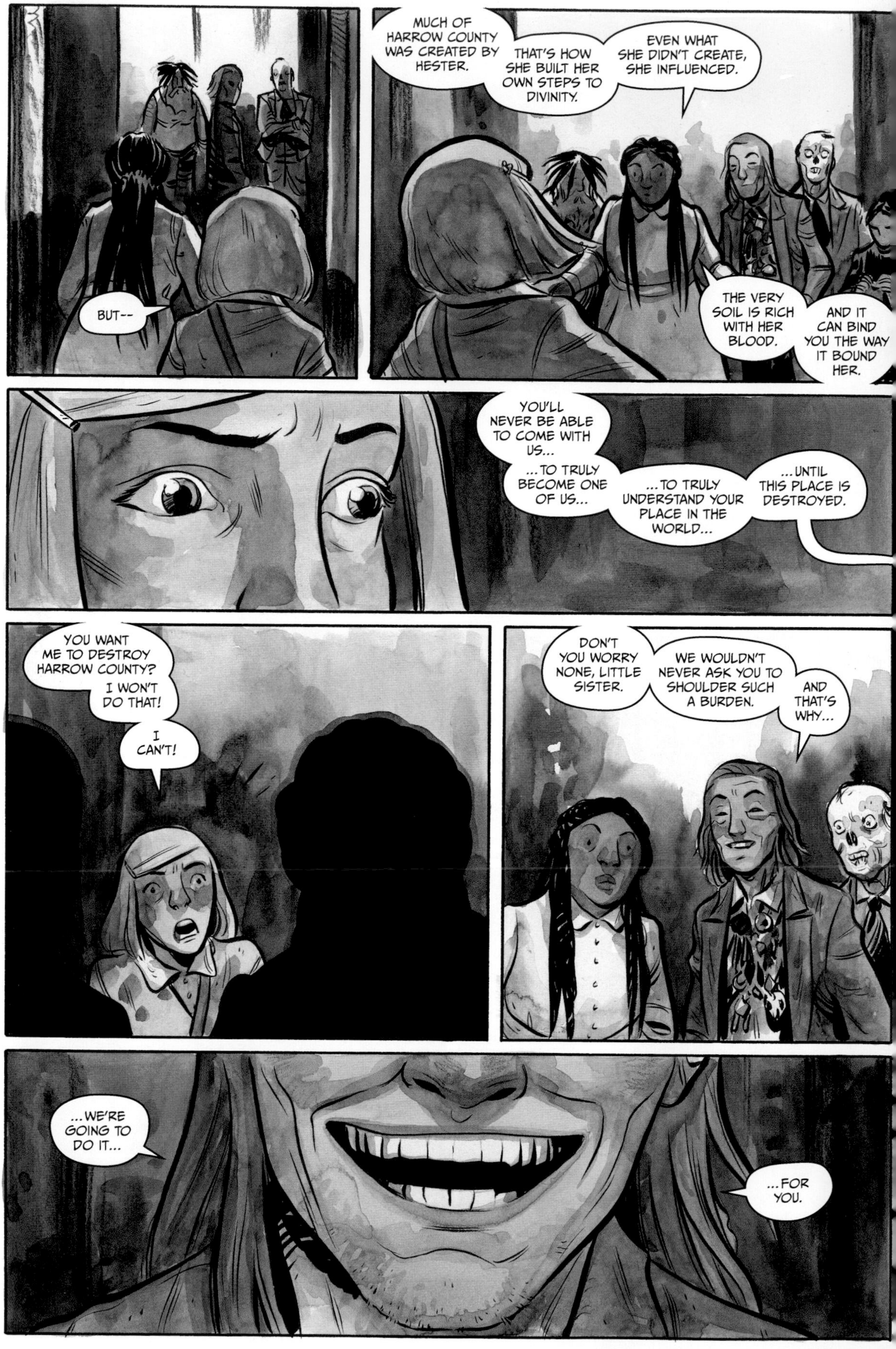
BUT--
MUCH OF HARROW COUNTY WAS CREATED BY HESTER.
THAT'S HOW SHE BUILT HER OWN STEPS TO DIVINITY.
EVEN WHAT SHE DIDN'T CREATE, SHE INFLUENCED.
THE VERY SOIL IS RICH WITH HER BLOOD.
AND IT CAN BIND YOU THE WAY IT BOUND HER.
YOU'LL NEVER BE ABLE TO COME WITH US...
...TO TRULY BECOME ONE OF US...
...TO TRULY UNDERSTAND YOUR PLACE IN THE WORLD...
...UNTIL THIS PLACE IS DESTROYED.
YOU WANT ME TO DESTROY HARROW COUNTY?
I WON'T DO THAT!
I CAN'T!
DON'T YOU WORRY NONE, LITTLE SISTER.
WE WOULDN'T NEVER ASK YOU TO SHOULDER SUCH A BURDEN.
AND THAT'S WHY...
...WE'RE GOING TO DO IT...
...FOR YOU.

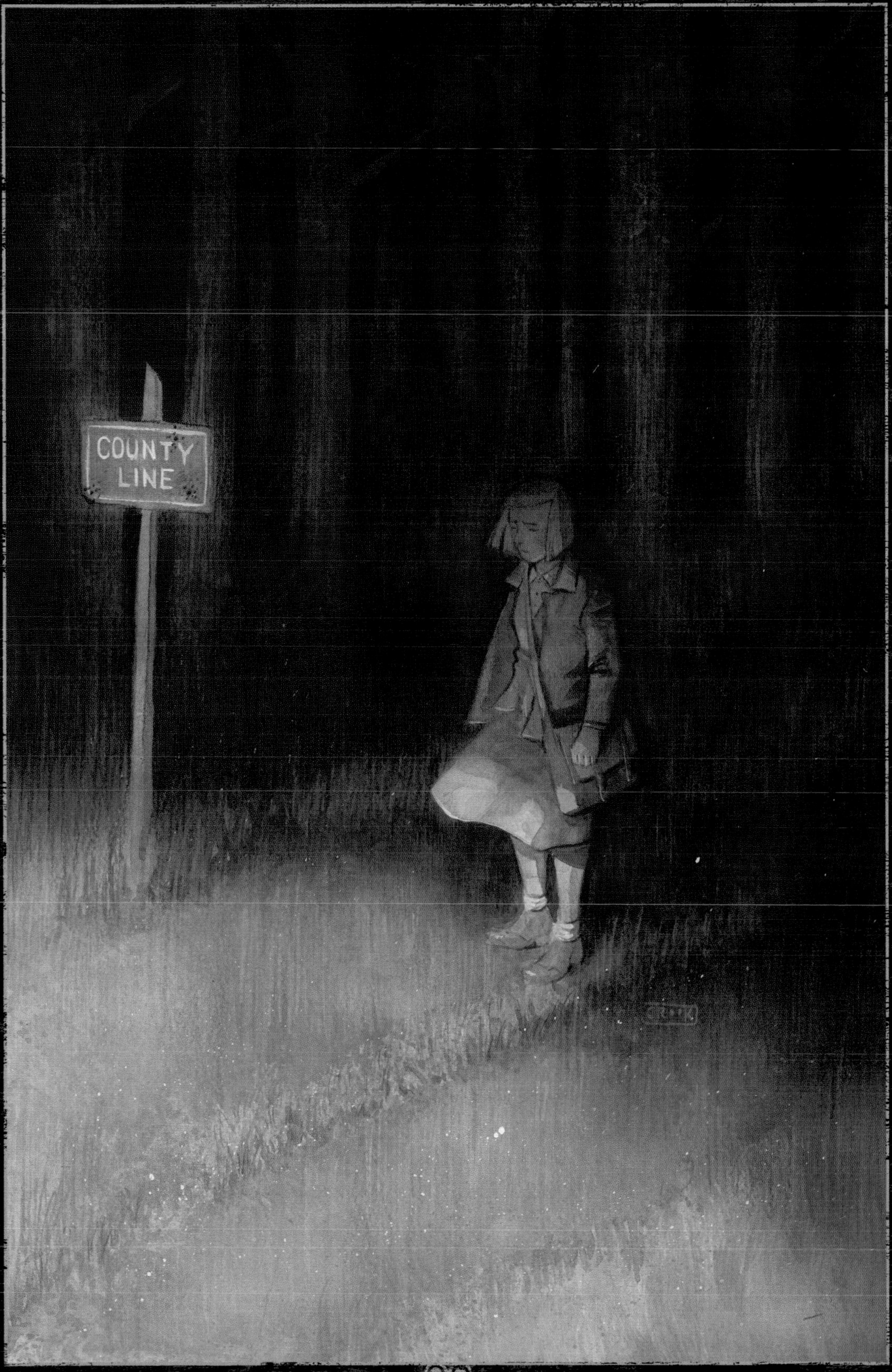
COUNTY
LINE

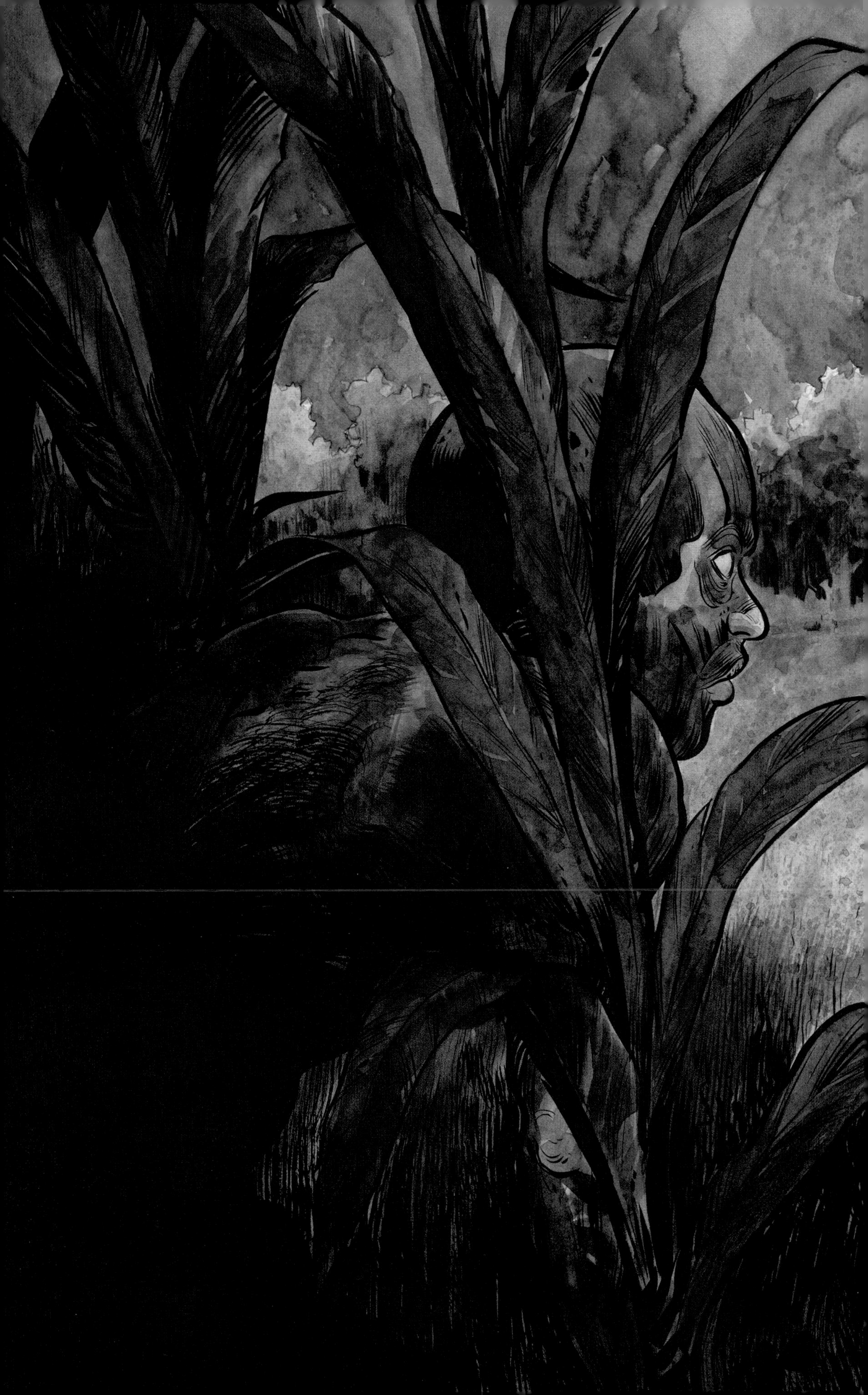

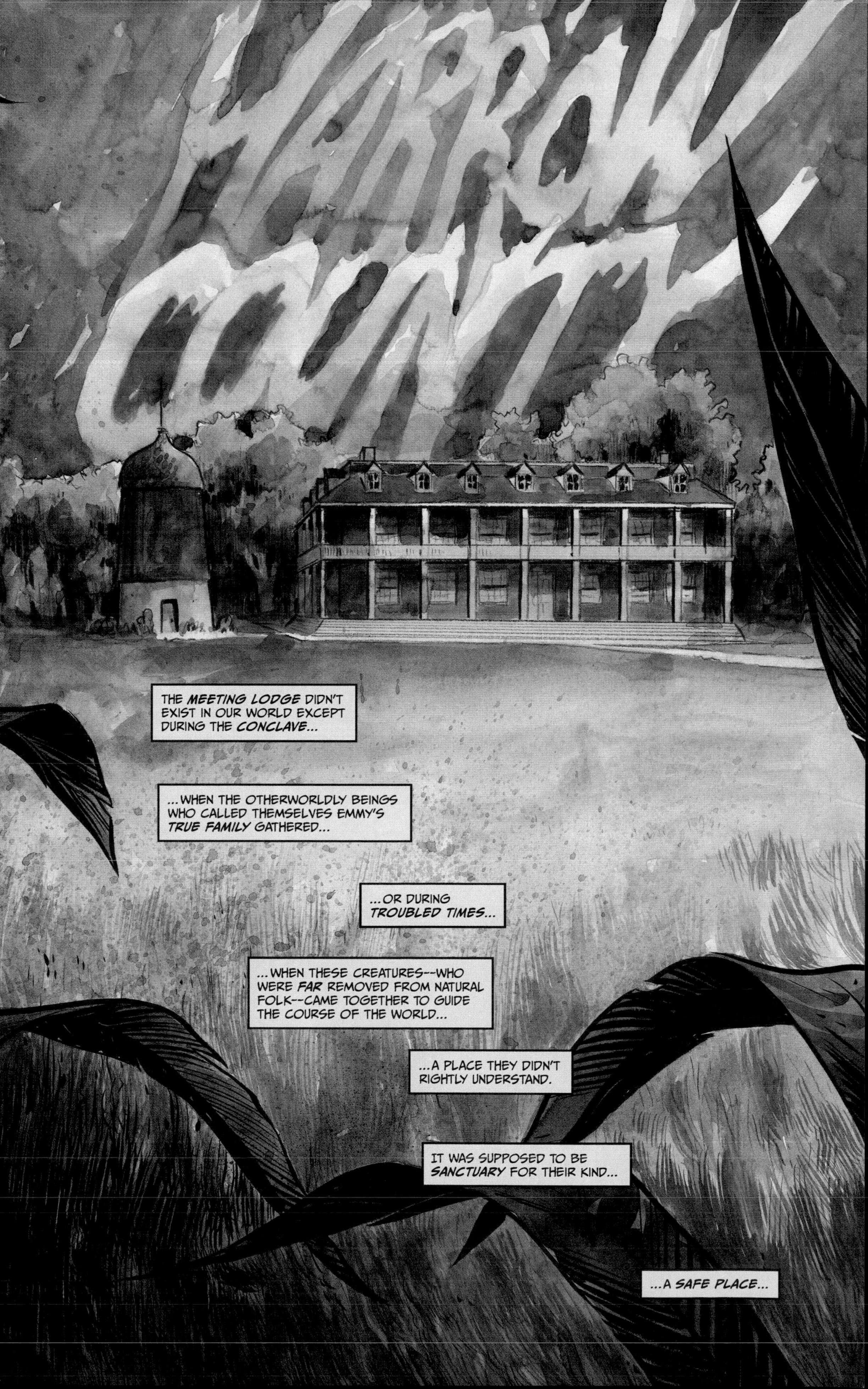
HARROW COUNTY
THE MEETING LODGE DIDN'T EXIST IN OUR WORLD EXCEPT DURING THE CONCLAVE...
...WHEN THE OTHERWORLDLY BEINGS WHO CALLED THEMSELVES EMMY'S TRUE FAMILY GATHERED...
...OR DURING TROUBLED TIMES...
...WHEN THESE CREATURES--WHO WERE FAR REMOVED FROM NATURAL FOLK--CAME TOGETHER TO GUIDE THE COURSE OF THE WORLD...
...A PLACE THEY DIDN'T RIGHTLY UNDERSTAND.
IT WAS SUPPOSED TO BE SANCTUARY FOR THEIR KIND...
...A SAFE PLACE...

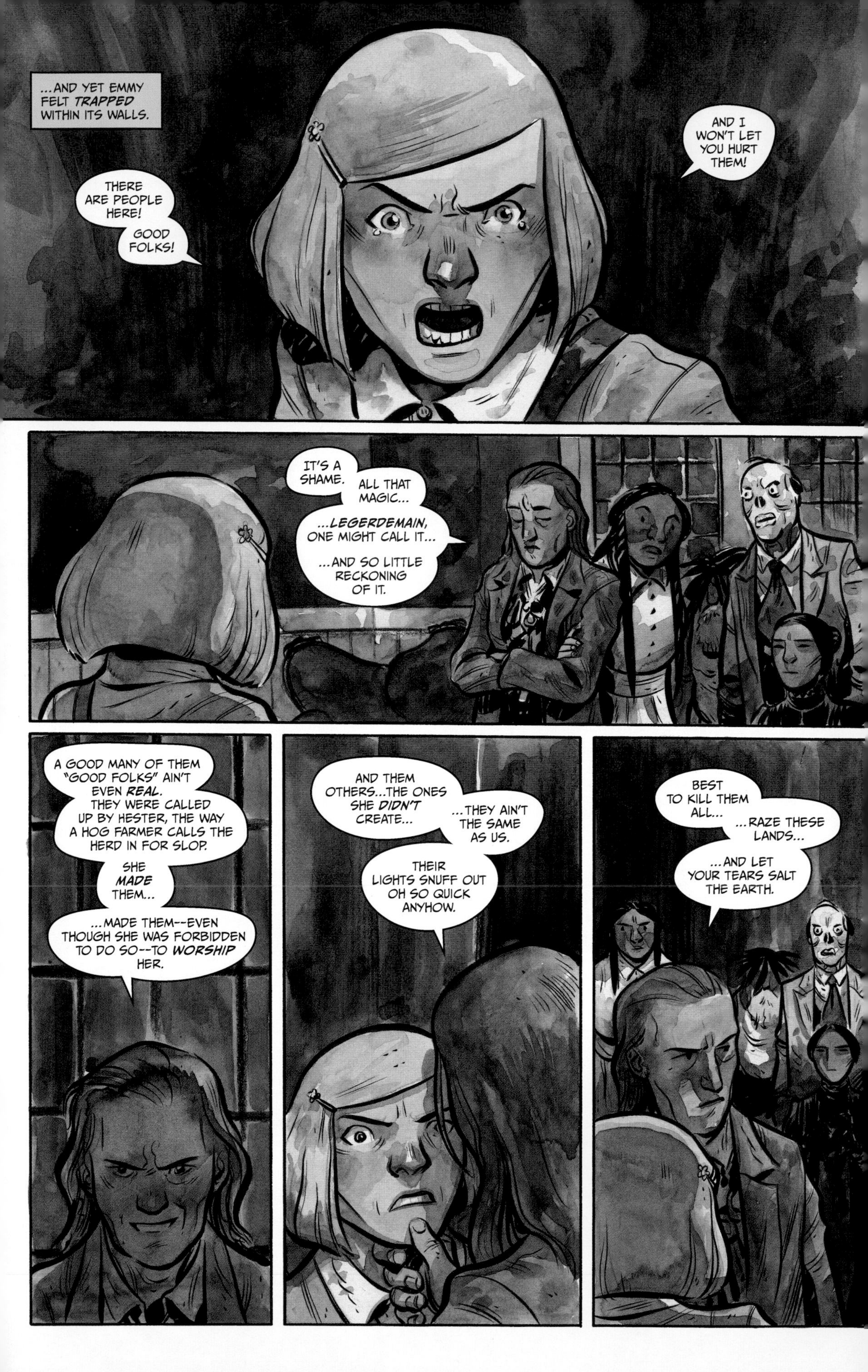
...AND YET EMMY FELT TRAPPED WITHIN ITS WALLS.
THERE ARE PEOPLE HERE!
GOOD FOLKS!
AND I WON'T LET YOU HURT THEM!
IT'S A SHAME.
ALL THAT MAGIC...
...LEGERDEMAIN, ONE MIGHT CALL IT...
...AND SO LITTLE RECKONING OF IT.
A GOOD MANY OF THEM "GOOD FOLKS" AIN'T EVEN REAL.
THEY WERE CALLED UP BY HESTER, THE WAY A HOG FARMER CALLS THE HERD IN FOR SLOP.
SHE MADE THEM...
...MADE THEM--EVEN THOUGH SHE WAS FORBIDDEN TO DO SO--TO WORSHIP HER.
AND THEM OTHERS...THE ONES SHE DIDN'T CREATE...
...THEY AIN'T THE SAME AS US.
THEIR LIGHTS SNUFF OUT OH SO QUICK ANYHOW.
BEST TO KILL THEM ALL...
...RAZE THESE LANDS...
...AND LET YOUR TEARS SALT THE EARTH.

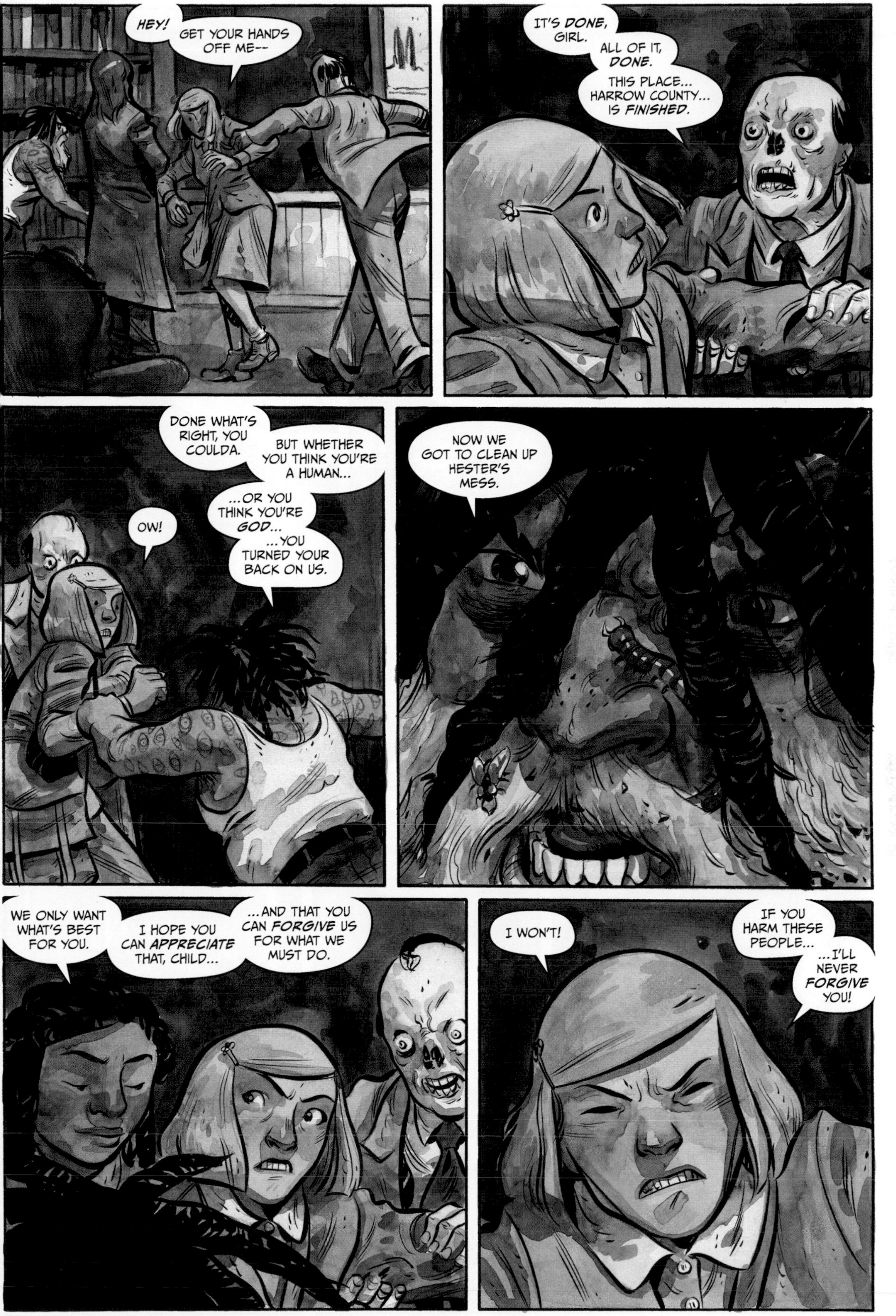
HEY!
GET YOUR HANDS OFF ME--
IT'S DONE, GIRL.
ALL OF IT, DONE.
THIS PLACE... HARROW COUNTY... IS FINISHED.
DONE WHAT'S RIGHT, YOU COULDA.
BUT WHETHER YOU THINK YOU'RE A HUMAN...
...OR YOU THINK YOU'RE GOD...
...YOU TURNED YOUR BACK ON US.
OW!
NOW WE GOT TO CLEAN UP HESTER'S MESS.
WE ONLY WANT WHAT'S BEST FOR YOU.
I HOPE YOU CAN APPRECIATE THAT, CHILD...
...AND THAT YOU CAN FORGIVE US FOR WHAT WE MUST DO.
I WON'T!
IF YOU HARM THESE PEOPLE...
...I'LL NEVER FORGIVE YOU!

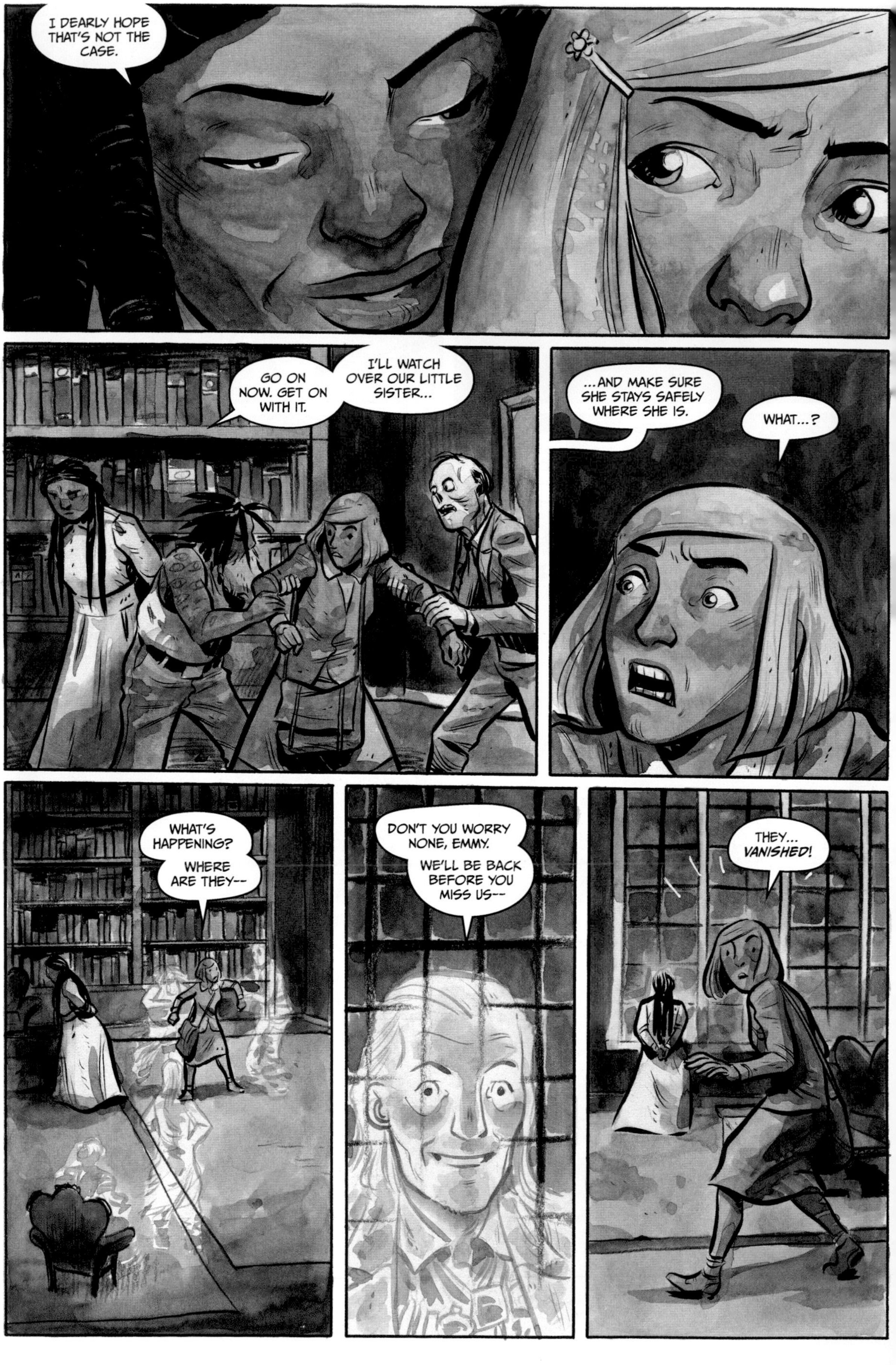
I DEARLY HOPE THAT'S NOT THE CASE.
GO ON NOW. GET ON WITH IT.
I'LL WATCH OVER OUR LITTLE SISTER...
...AND MAKE SURE SHE STAYS SAFELY WHERE SHE IS.
WHAT...?
WHAT'S HAPPENING?
WHERE ARE THEY--
DON'T YOU WORRY NONE, EMMY.
WE'LL BE BACK BEFORE YOU MISS US--
THEY... *VANISHED!*

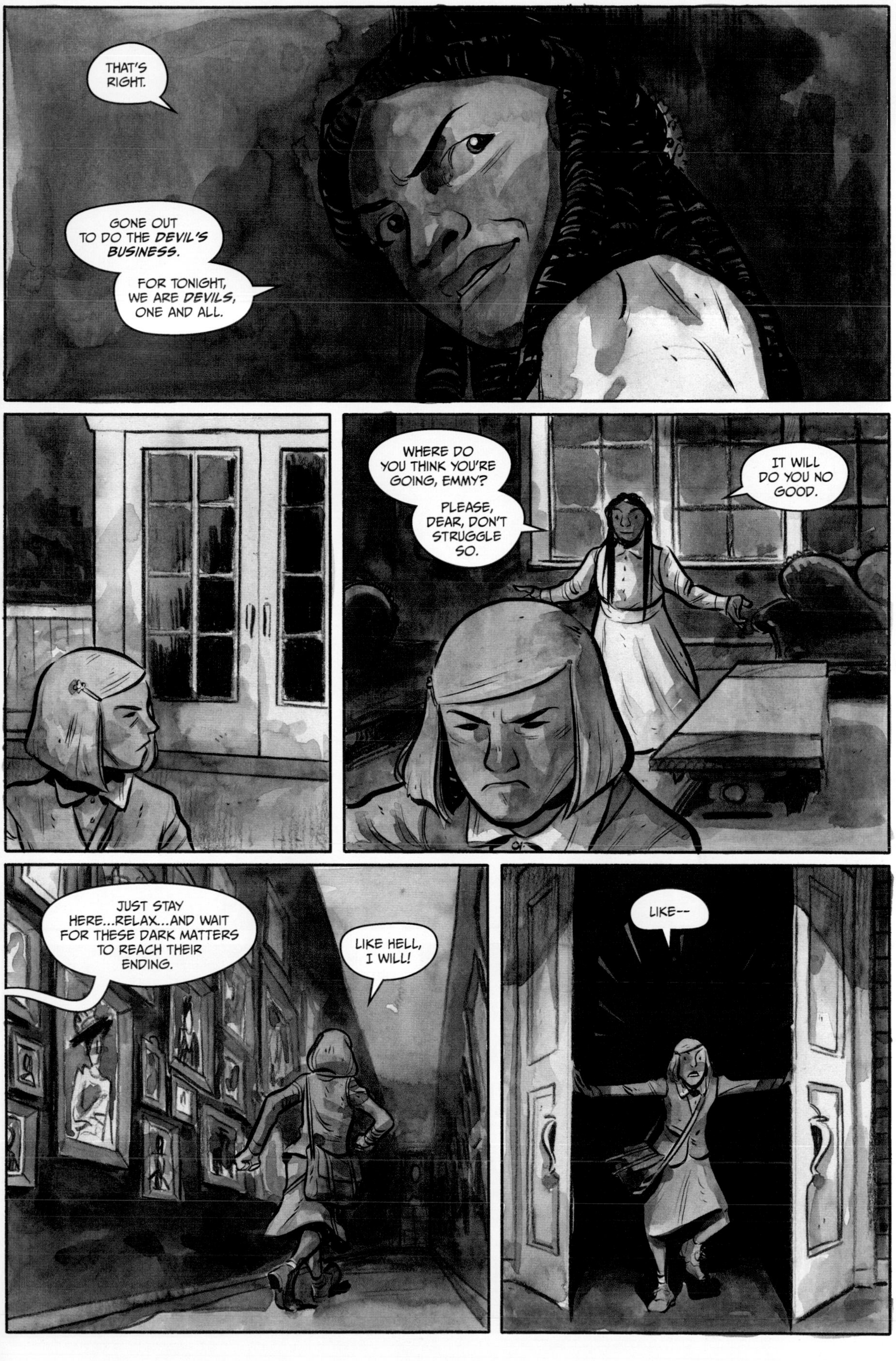
THAT'S RIGHT.
GONE OUT TO DO THE *DEVIL'S BUSINESS.*
FOR TONIGHT, WE ARE *DEVILS,* ONE AND ALL.
WHERE DO YOU THINK YOU'RE GOING, EMMY?
PLEASE, DEAR, DON'T STRUGGLE SO.
IT WILL DO YOU NO GOOD.
JUST STAY HERE...RELAX...AND WAIT FOR THESE DARK MATTERS TO REACH THEIR ENDING.
LIKE HELL, I WILL!
LIKE--

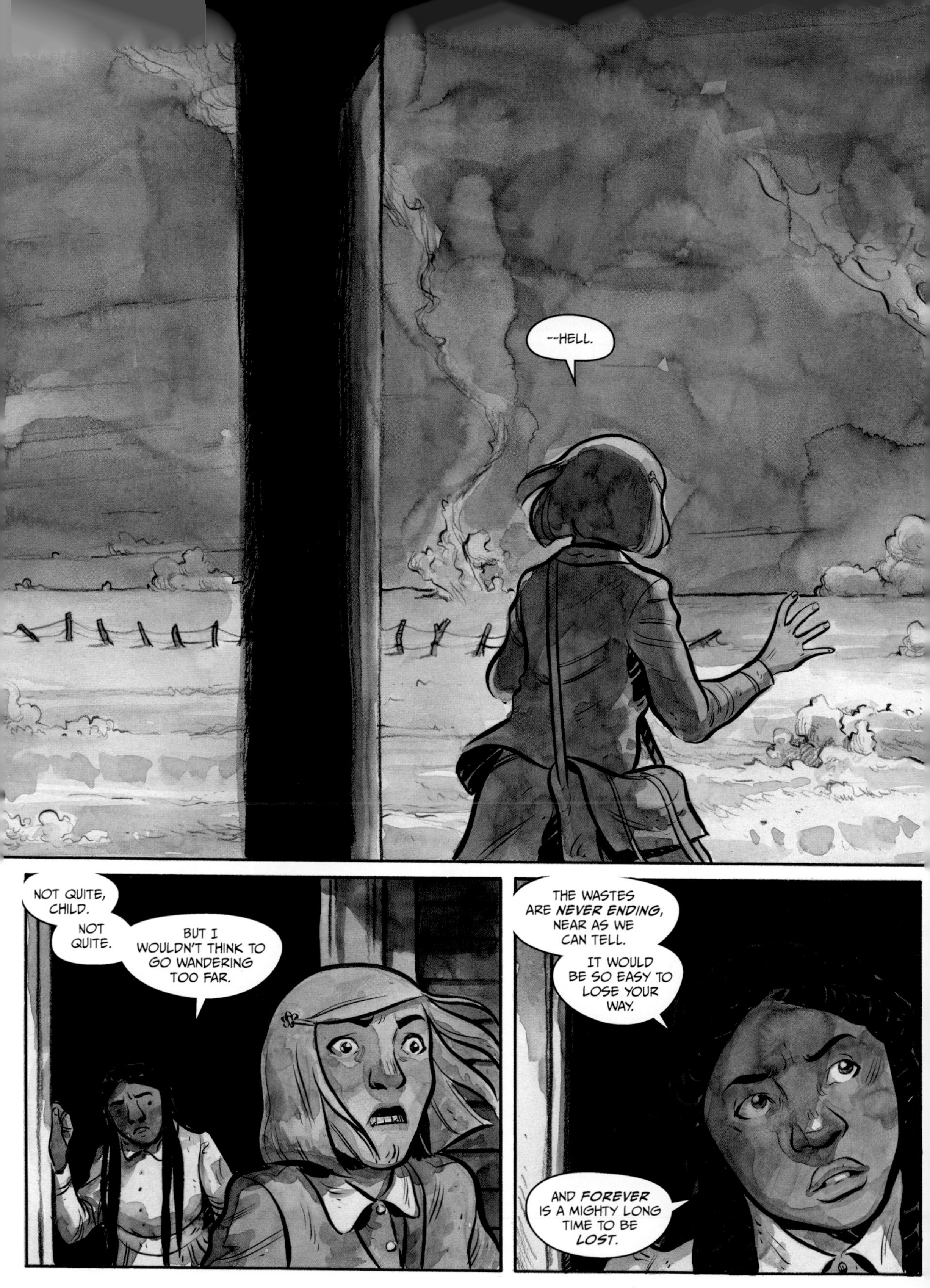
--HELL.
NOT QUITE, CHILD.
NOT QUITE.
BUT I WOULDN'T THINK TO GO WANDERING TOO FAR.
THE WASTES ARE *NEVER ENDING*, NEAR AS WE CAN TELL.
IT WOULD BE SO EASY TO LOSE YOUR WAY.
AND *FOREVER* IS A MIGHTY LONG TIME TO BE *LOST*.

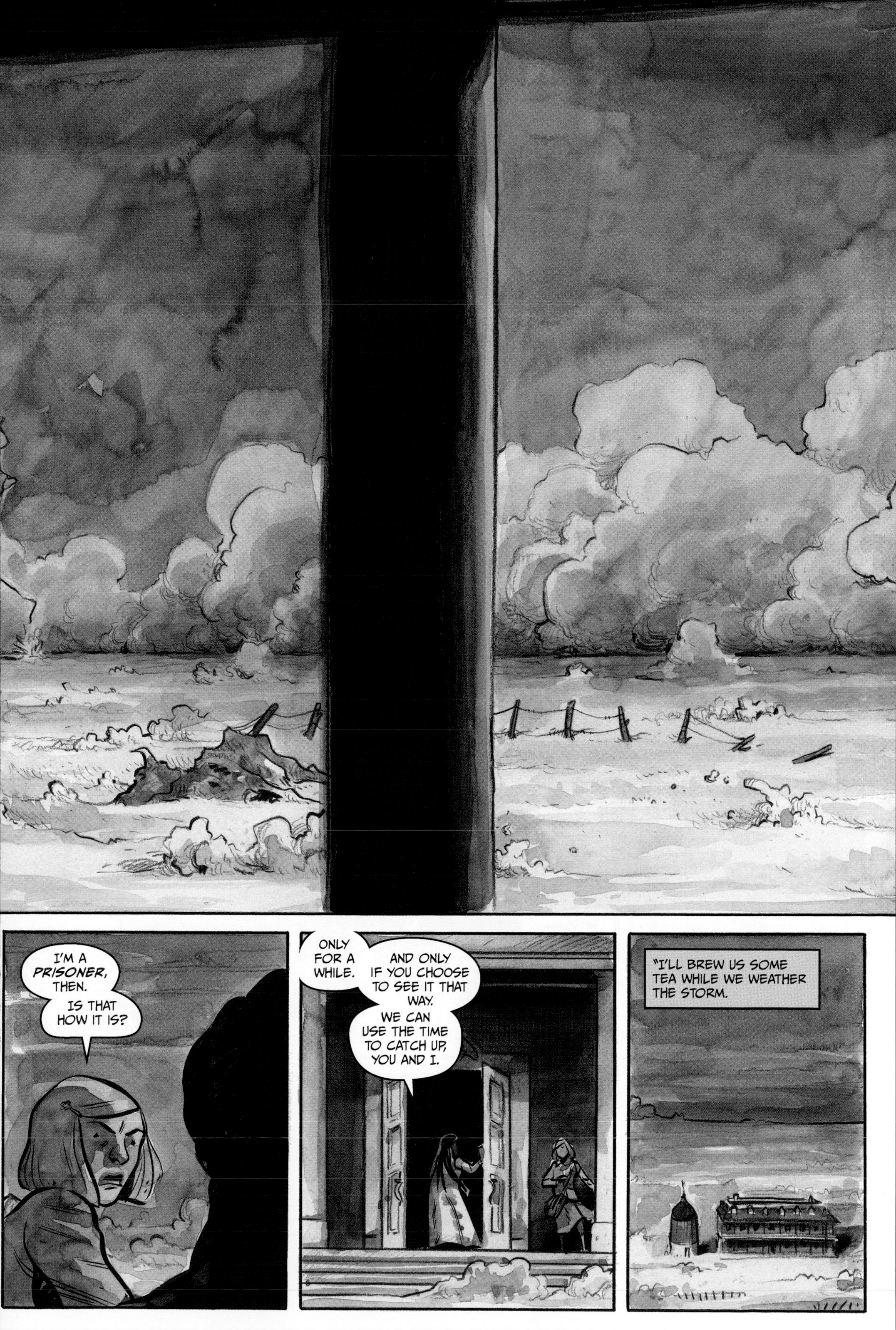
I'M A *PRISONER*, THEN.
IS THAT HOW IT IS?
ONLY FOR A WHILE.
AND ONLY IF YOU CHOOSE TO SEE IT THAT WAY.
WE CAN USE THE TIME TO CATCH UP, YOU AND I.
"I'LL BREW US SOME TEA WHILE WE WEATHER THE STORM.

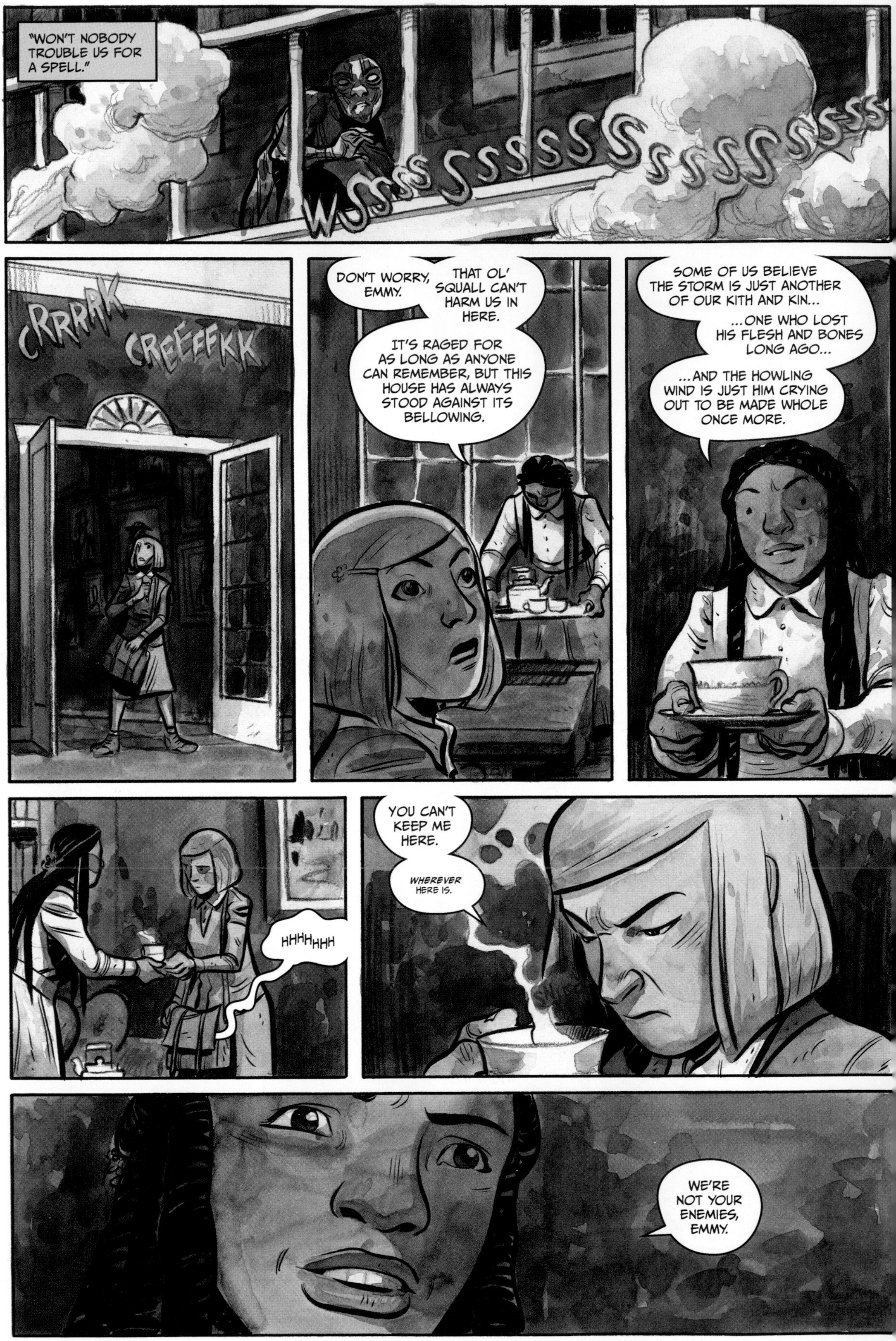
"WON'T NOBODY TROUBLE US FOR A SPELL."
WSSSSSSSSSSSSSSSSSSS
CRRRRK
CREEEFKK
DON'T WORRY, EMMY.
THAT OL' SQUALL CAN'T HARM US IN HERE.
IT'S RAGED FOR AS LONG AS ANYONE CAN REMEMBER, BUT THIS HOUSE HAS ALWAYS STOOD AGAINST ITS BELLOWING.
SOME OF US BELIEVE THE STORM IS JUST ANOTHER OF OUR KITH AND KIN...
...ONE WHO LOST HIS FLESH AND BONES LONG AGO...
...AND THE HOWLING WIND IS JUST HIM CRYING OUT TO BE MADE WHOLE ONCE MORE.
HHHHHHH
YOU CAN'T KEEP ME HERE.
WHEREVER HERE IS.
WE'RE NOT YOUR ENEMIES, EMMY.

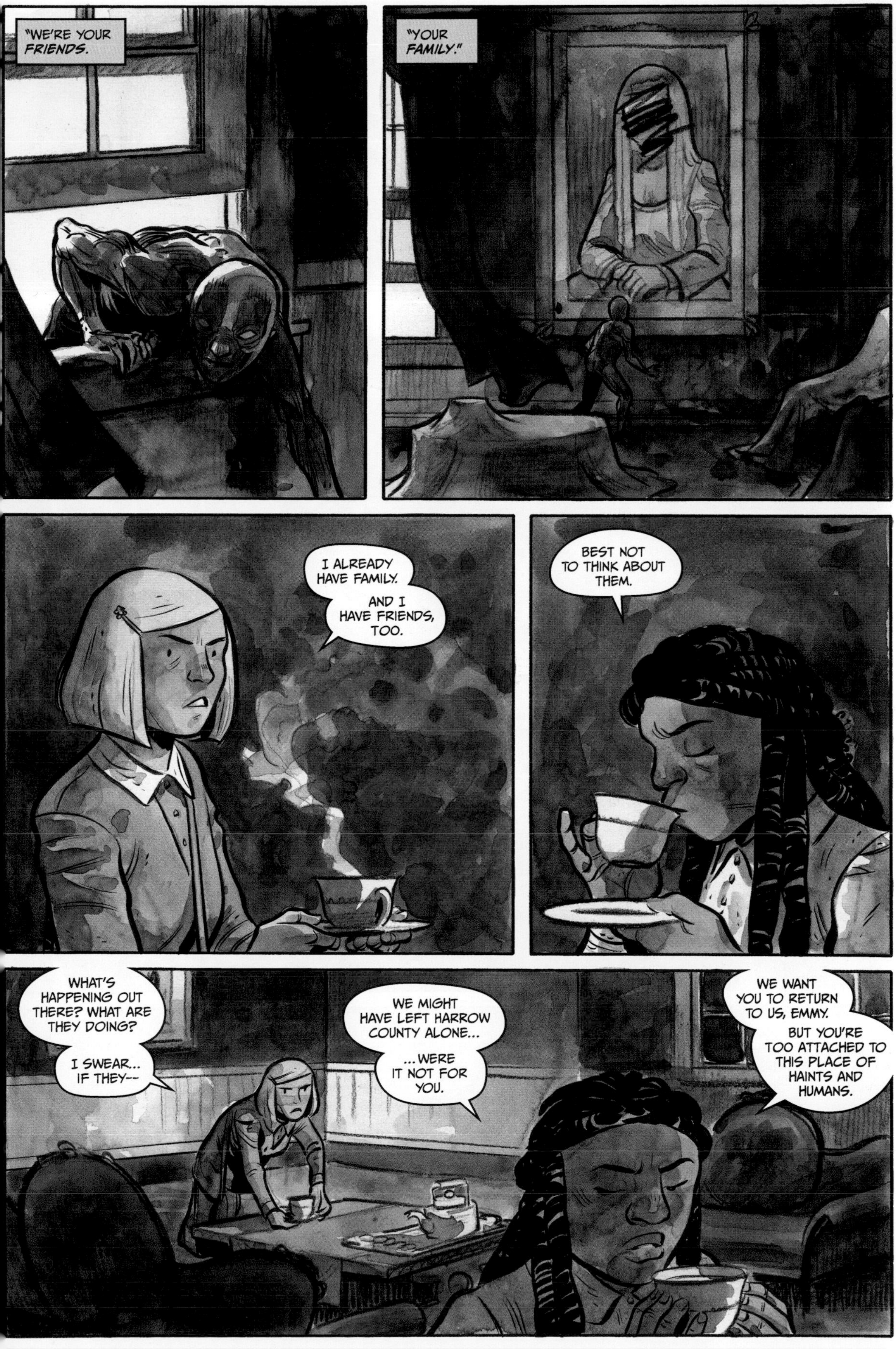
"WE'RE YOUR FRIENDS.
"YOUR FAMILY."
I ALREADY HAVE FAMILY.
AND I HAVE FRIENDS, TOO.
BEST NOT TO THINK ABOUT THEM.
WHAT'S HAPPENING OUT THERE? WHAT ARE THEY DOING?
I SWEAR... IF THEY--
WE MIGHT HAVE LEFT HARROW COUNTY ALONE...
...WERE IT NOT FOR YOU.
WE WANT YOU TO RETURN TO US, EMMY.
BUT YOU'RE TOO ATTACHED TO THIS PLACE OF HAINTS AND HUMANS.

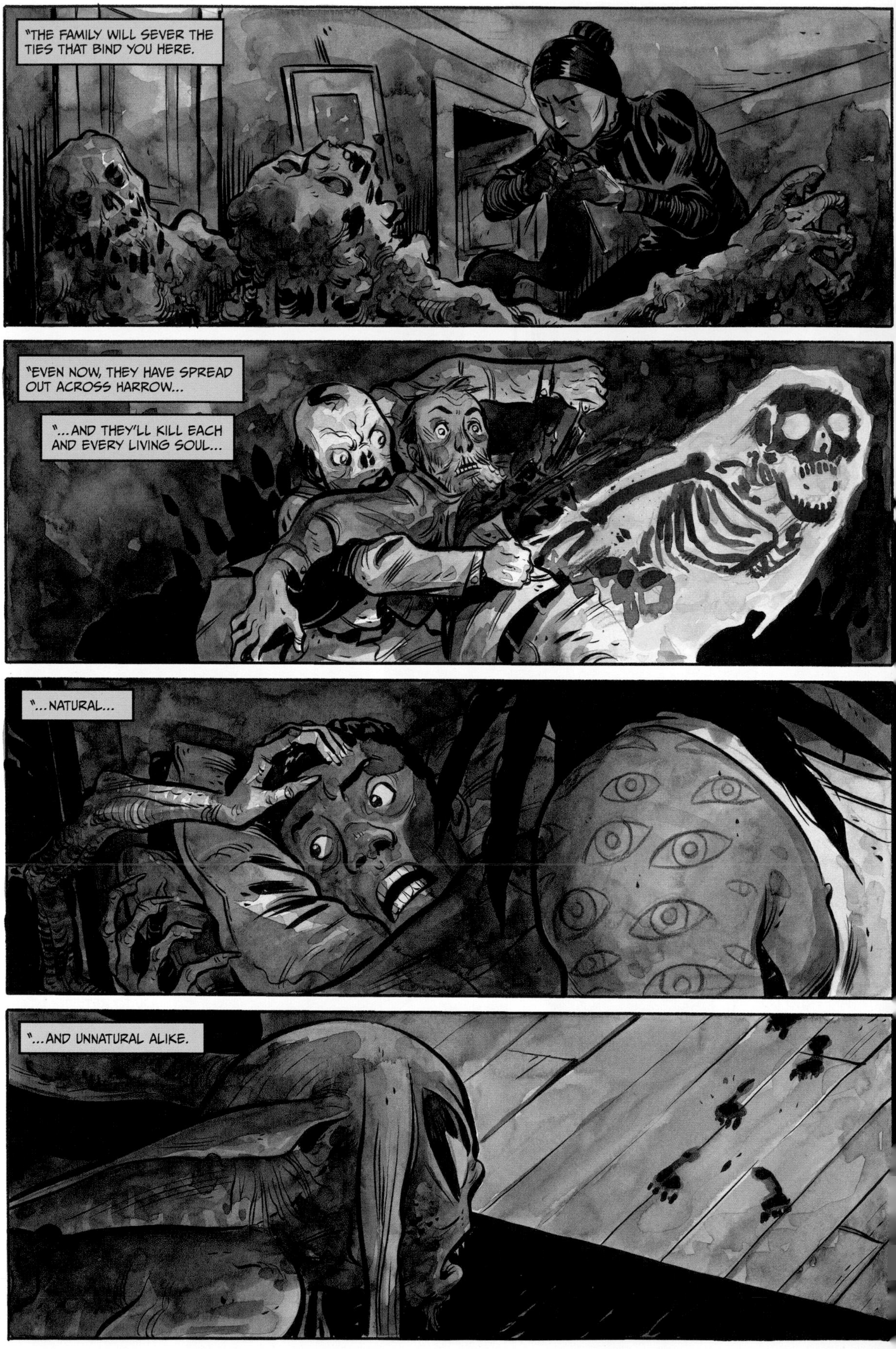
"THE FAMILY WILL SEVER THE TIES THAT BIND YOU HERE.
"EVEN NOW, THEY HAVE SPREAD OUT ACROSS HARROW...
"...AND THEY'LL KILL EACH AND EVERY LIVING SOUL...
"...NATURAL...
"...AND UNNATURAL ALIKE.

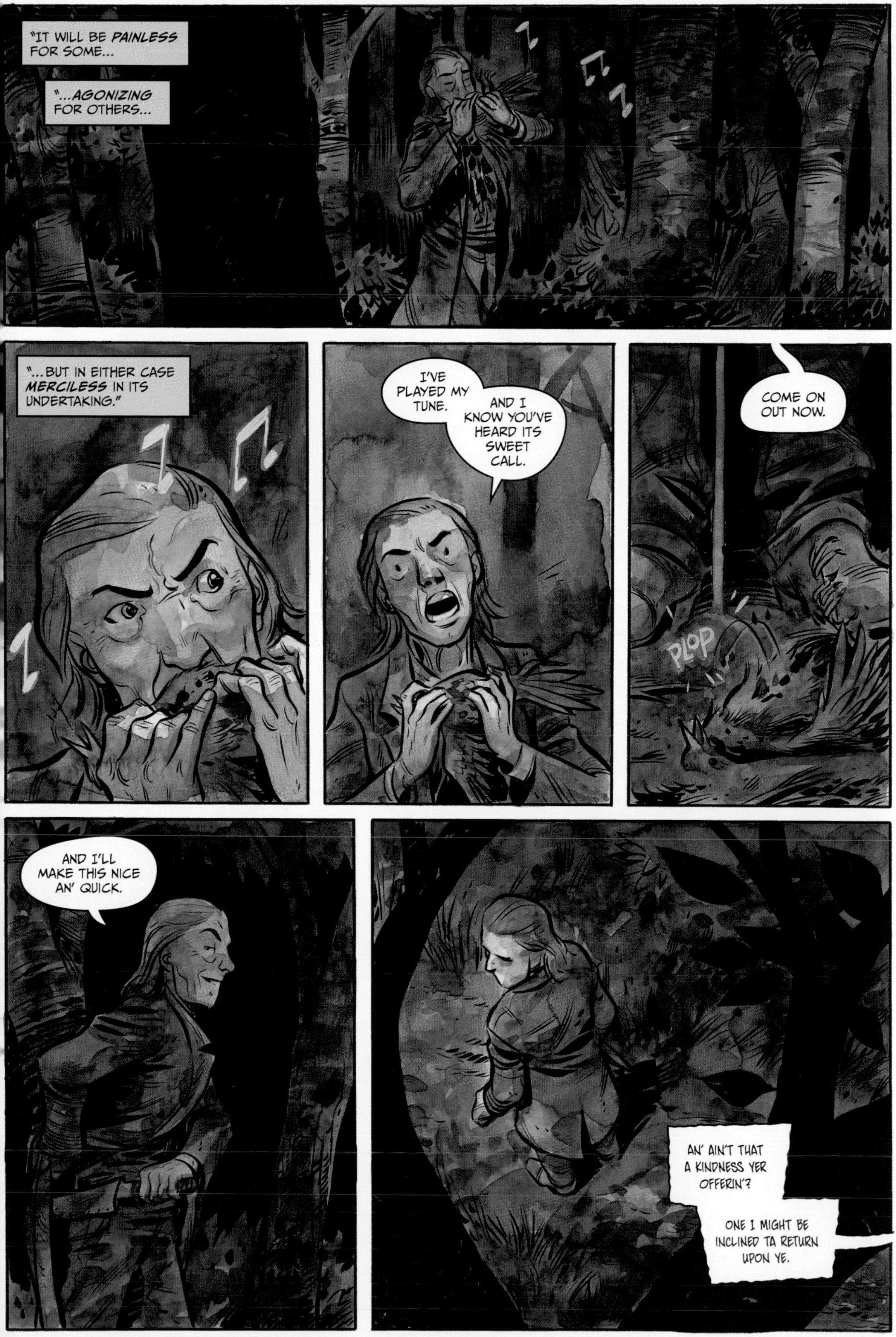
"IT WILL BE *PAINLESS* FOR SOME...
"...*AGONIZING* FOR OTHERS...
"...BUT IN EITHER CASE *MERCILESS* IN ITS UNDERTAKING."
I'VE PLAYED MY TUNE.
AND I KNOW YOU'VE HEARD ITS SWEET CALL.
COME ON OUT NOW.
PLOP
AND I'LL MAKE THIS NICE AN' QUICK.
AN' AIN'T THAT A KINDNESS YER OFFERIN'?
ONE I MIGHT BE INCLINED TA RETURN UPON YE.

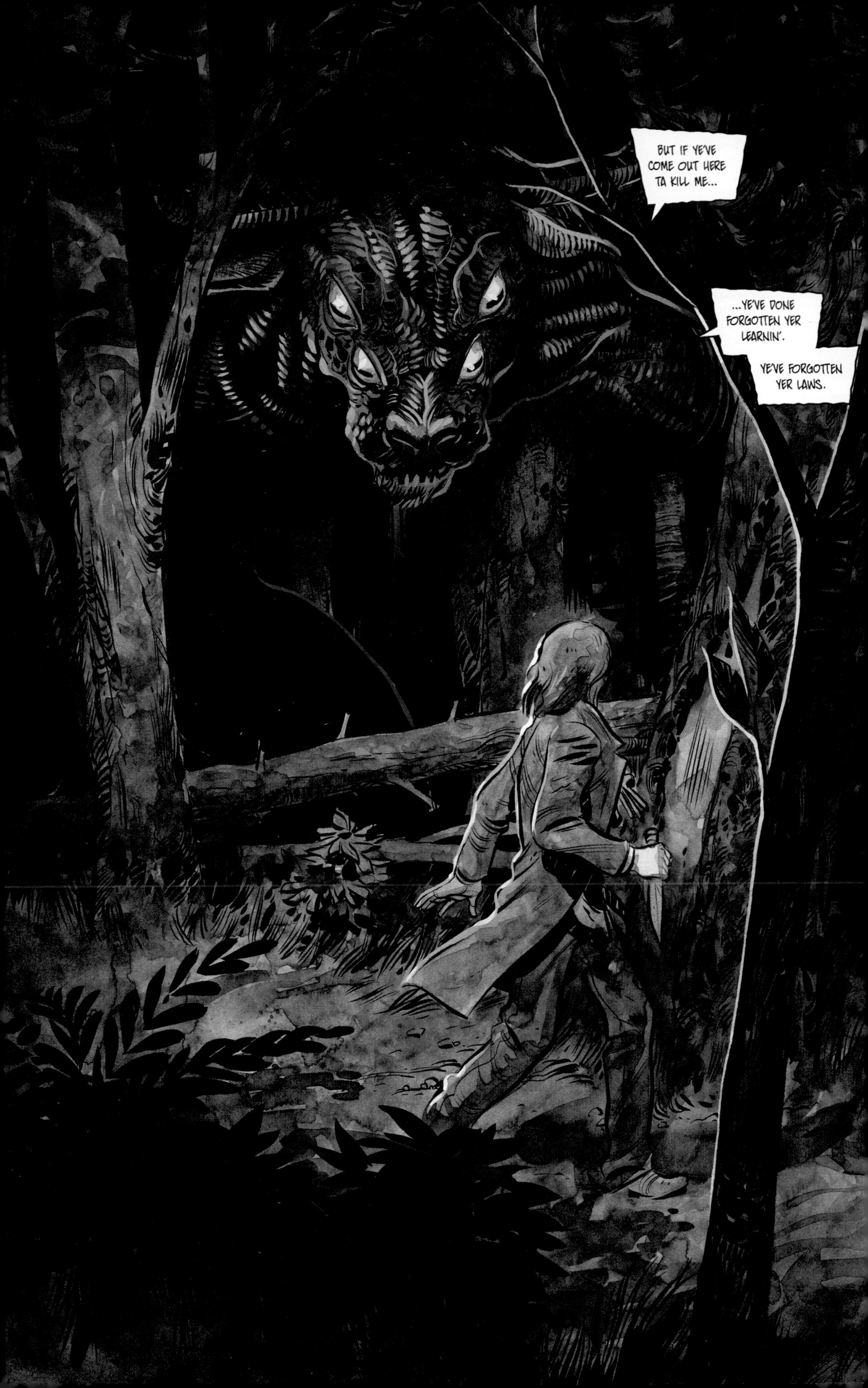
BUT IF YE'VE COME OUT HERE TA KILL ME...
...YE'VE DONE FORGOTTEN YER LEARNIN'.
YE'VE FORGOTTEN YER LAWS.

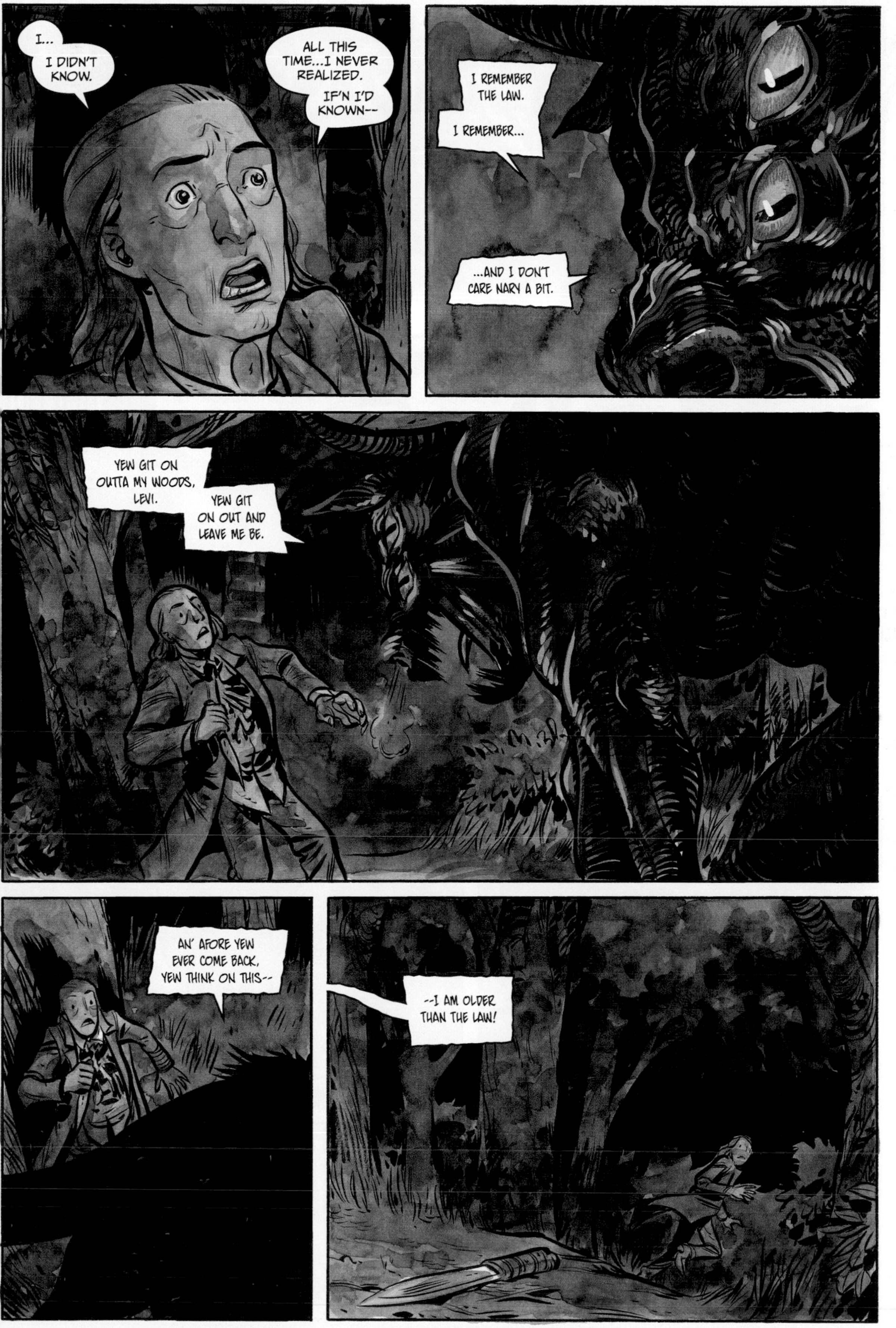
I...
I DIDN'T KNOW.
ALL THIS TIME...I NEVER REALIZED.
IF'N I'D KNOWN--
I REMEMBER THE LAW.
I REMEMBER...
...AND I DON'T CARE NARY A BIT.
YEW GIT ON OUTTA MY WOODS, LEVI.
YEW GIT ON OUT AND LEAVE ME BE.
AN' AFORE YEW EVER COME BACK, YEW THINK ON THIS--
--I AM OLDER THAN THE LAW!

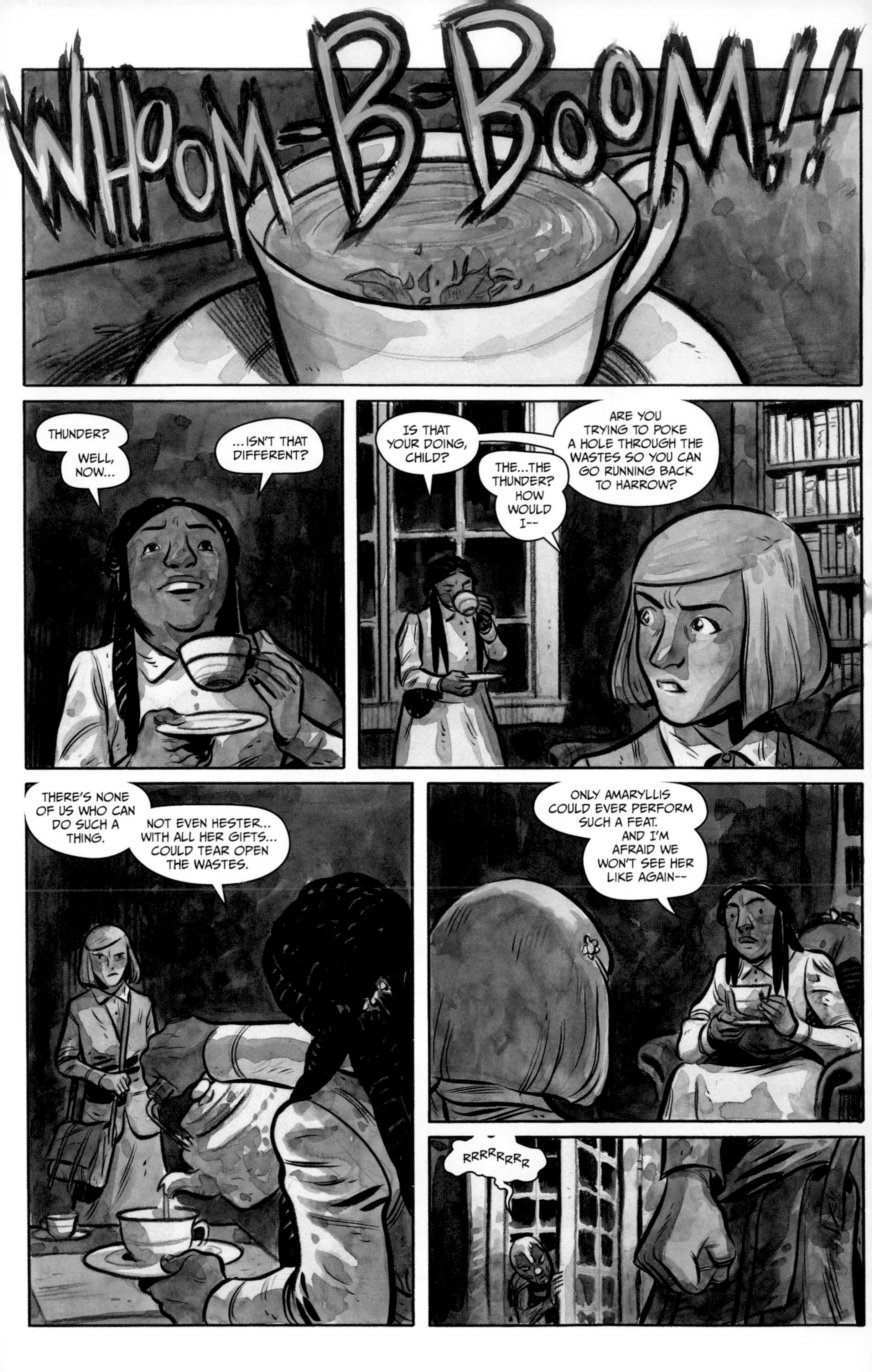
WHOOM-B-BOOM!!
THUNDER? WELL, NOW...
...ISN'T THAT DIFFERENT?
IS THAT YOUR DOING, CHILD?
ARE YOU TRYING TO POKE A HOLE THROUGH THE WASTES SO YOU CAN GO RUNNING BACK TO HARROW?
THE...THE THUNDER? HOW WOULD I--
THERE'S NONE OF US WHO CAN DO SUCH A THING.
NOT EVEN HESTER... WITH ALL HER GIFTS... COULD TEAR OPEN THE WASTES.
ONLY AMARYLLIS COULD EVER PERFORM SUCH A FEAT.
AND I'M AFRAID WE WON'T SEE HER LIKE AGAIN--
RRRRRRRR

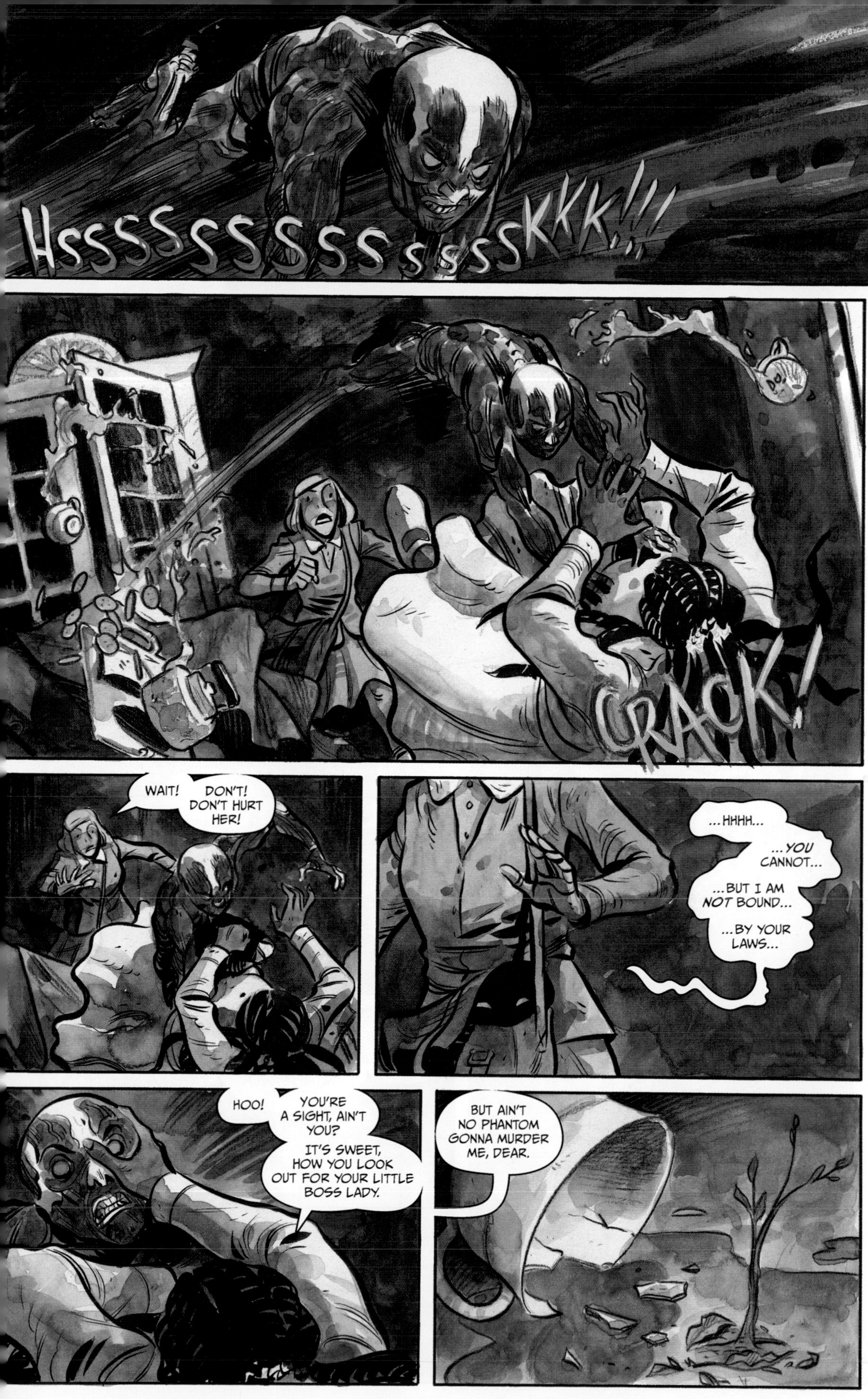
HSSSSSSSSSSSSKKK!!!
CRACK!
WAIT!
DON'T! DON'T HURT HER!
...HHHH...
...YOU CANNOT...
...BUT I AM NOT BOUND...
...BY YOUR LAWS...
HOO!
YOU'RE A SIGHT, AIN'T YOU?
IT'S SWEET, HOW YOU LOOK OUT FOR YOUR LITTLE BOSS LADY.
BUT AIN'T NO PHANTOM GONNA MURDER ME, DEAR.

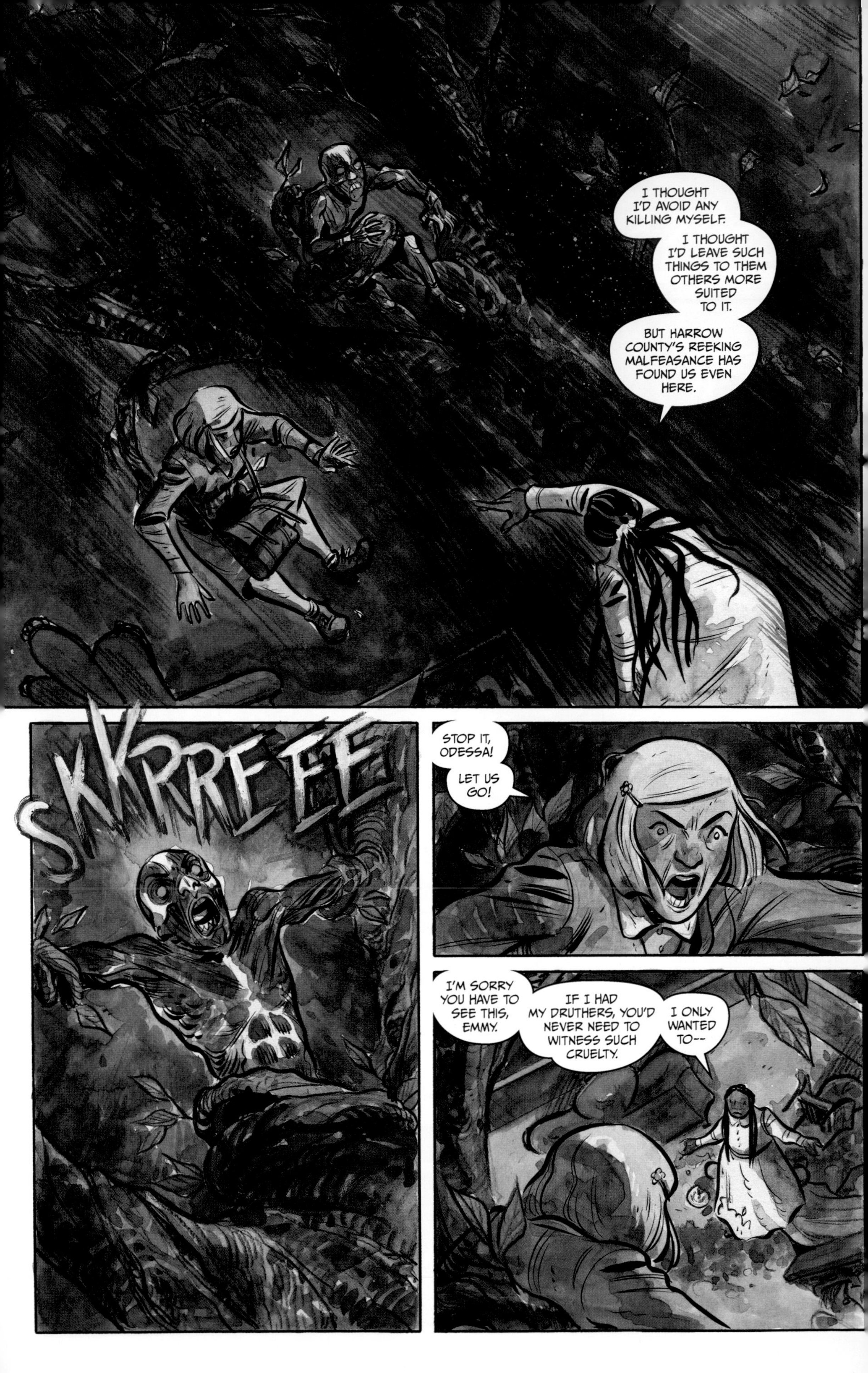
I THOUGHT I'D AVOID ANY KILLING MYSELF.
I THOUGHT I'D LEAVE SUCH THINGS TO THEM OTHERS MORE SUITED TO IT.
BUT HARROW COUNTY'S REEKING MALFEASANCE HAS FOUND US EVEN HERE.
SKKRRFEEE
STOP IT, ODESSA!
LET US GO!
I'M SORRY YOU HAVE TO SEE THIS, EMMY.
IF I HAD MY DRUTHERS, YOU'D NEVER NEED TO WITNESS SUCH CRUELTY.
I ONLY WANTED TO--

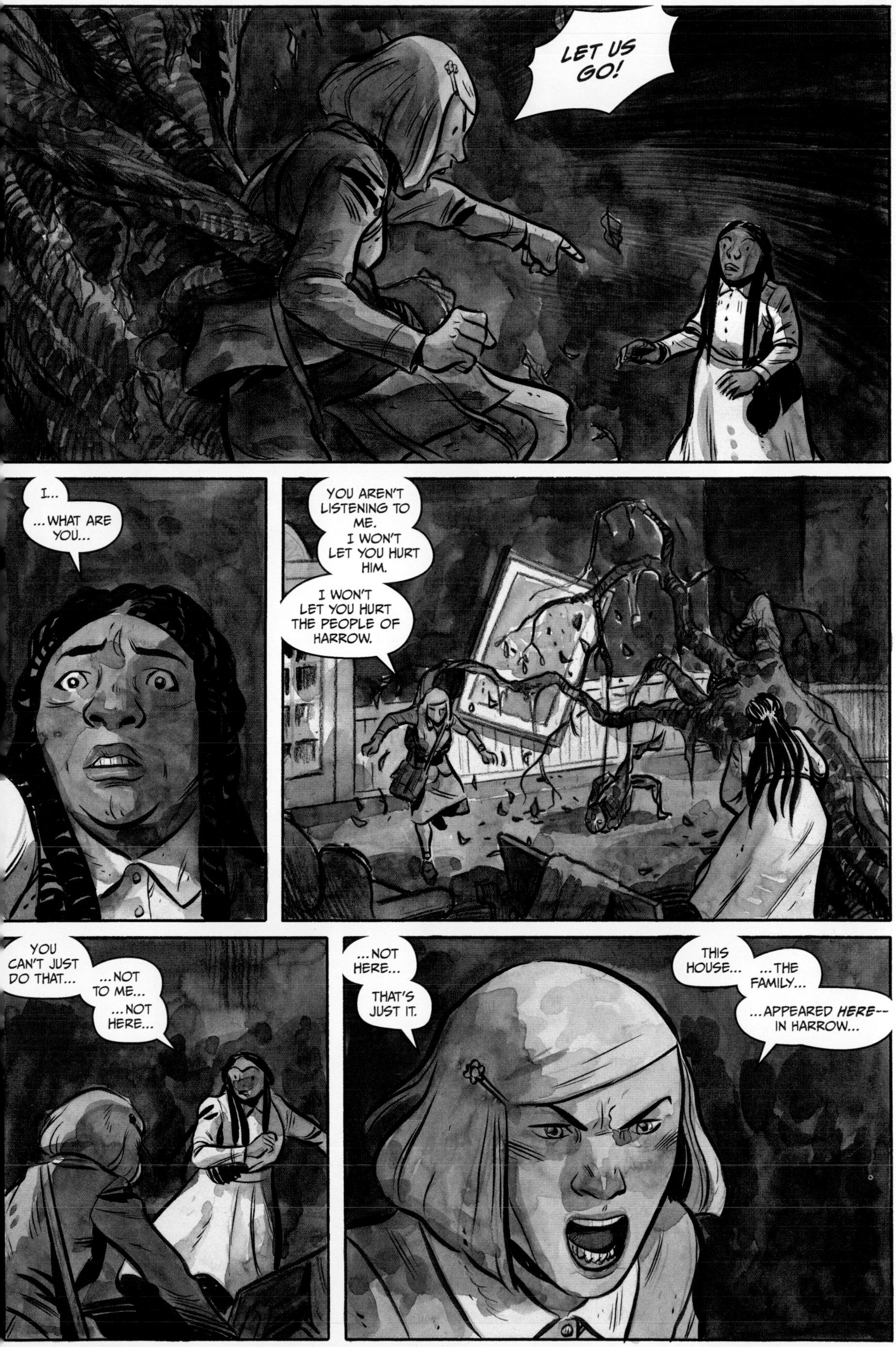
LET US GO!
I...
...WHAT ARE YOU...
YOU AREN'T LISTENING TO ME.
I WON'T LET YOU HURT HIM.
I WON'T LET YOU HURT THE PEOPLE OF HARROW.
YOU CAN'T JUST DO THAT...
...NOT TO ME...
...NOT HERE...
...NOT HERE...
THAT'S JUST IT.
THIS HOUSE...
...THE FAMILY...
...APPEARED *HERE*-- IN HARROW...

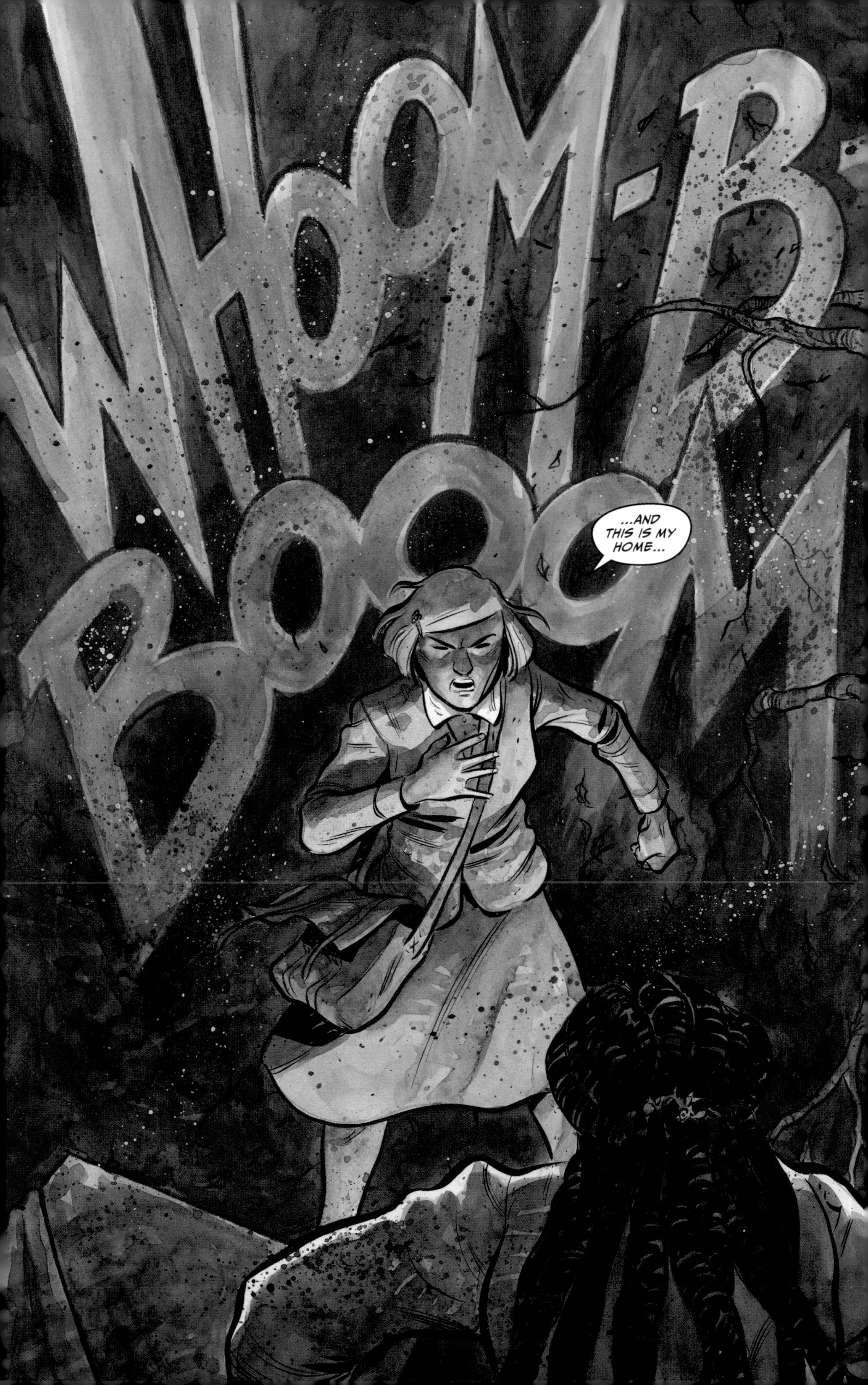
WHOOM-B-
BOOOM
...AND THIS IS MY HOME...

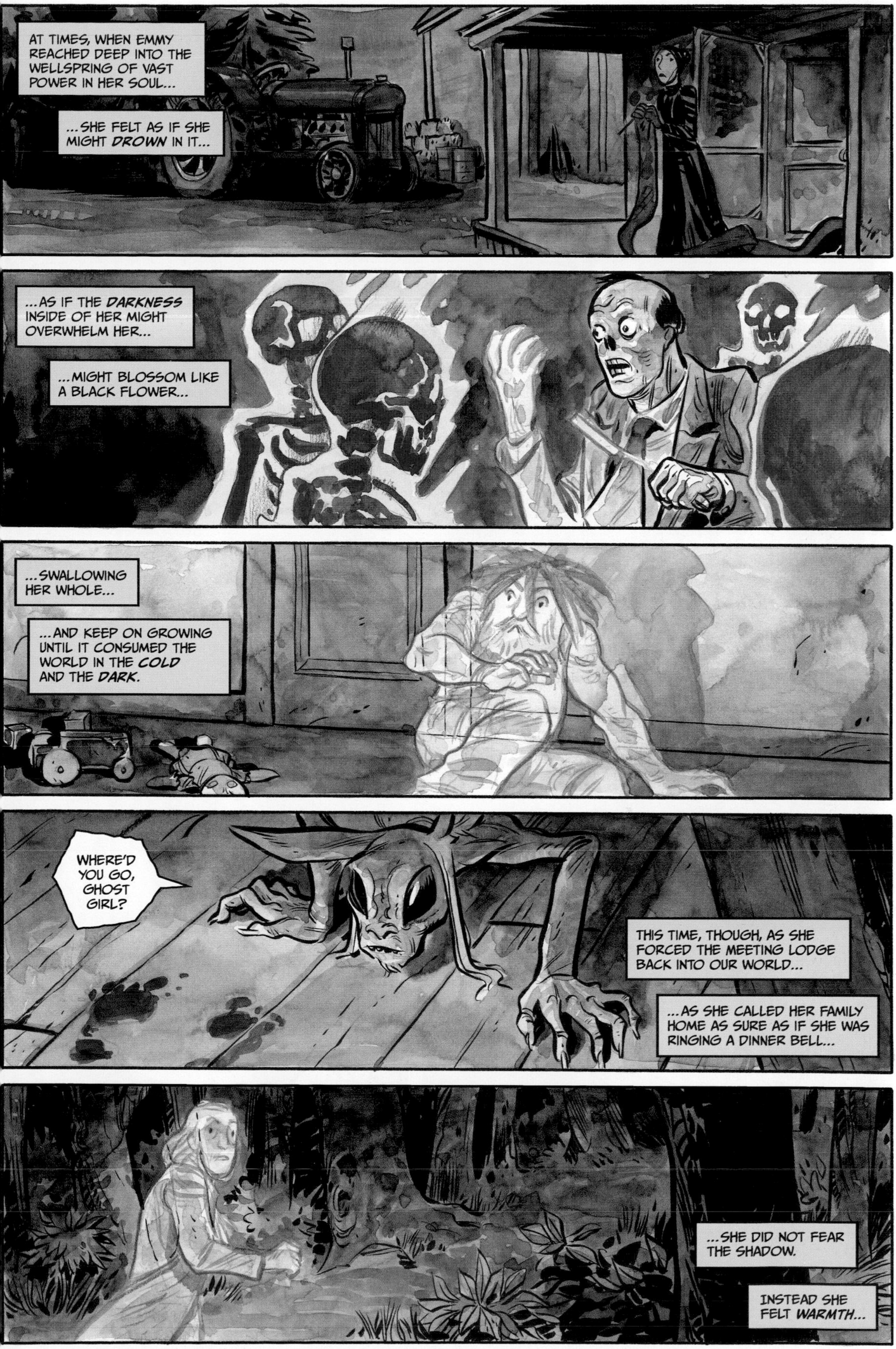
AT TIMES, WHEN EMMY REACHED DEEP INTO THE WELLSPRING OF VAST POWER IN HER SOUL...
...SHE FELT AS IF SHE MIGHT *DROWN* IN IT...
...AS IF THE *DARKNESS* INSIDE OF HER MIGHT OVERWHELM HER...
...MIGHT BLOSSOM LIKE A BLACK FLOWER...
...SWALLOWING HER WHOLE...
...AND KEEP ON GROWING UNTIL IT CONSUMED THE WORLD IN THE *COLD* AND THE *DARK*.
WHERE'D YOU GO, GHOST GIRL?
THIS TIME, THOUGH, AS SHE FORCED THE MEETING LODGE BACK INTO OUR WORLD...
...AS SHE CALLED HER FAMILY HOME AS SURE AS IF SHE WAS RINGING A DINNER BELL...
...SHE DID NOT FEAR THE SHADOW.
INSTEAD SHE FELT *WARMTH*...

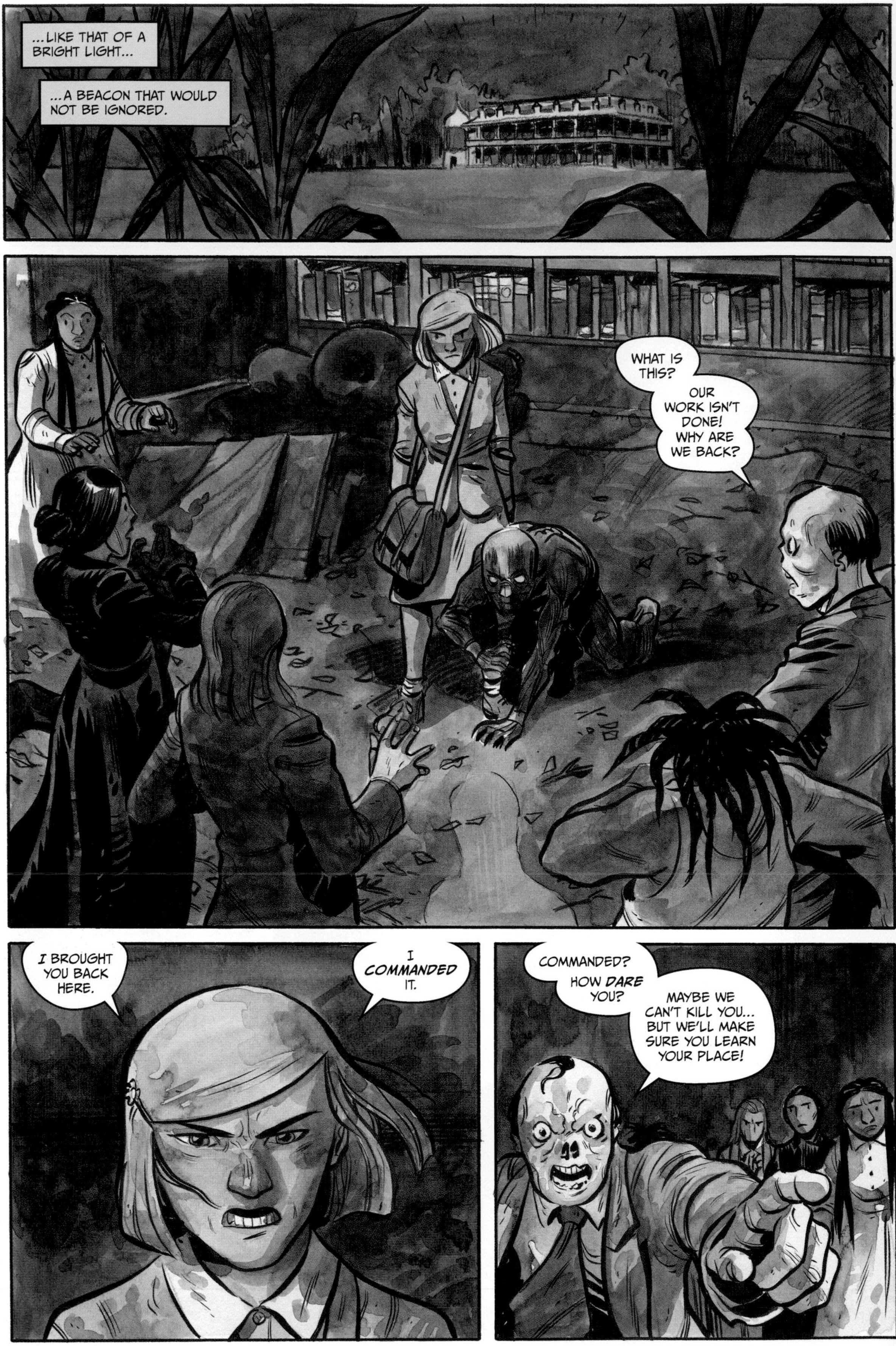
...LIKE THAT OF A BRIGHT LIGHT...
...A BEACON THAT WOULD NOT BE IGNORED.
WHAT IS THIS?
OUR WORK ISN'T DONE! WHY ARE WE BACK?
I BROUGHT YOU BACK HERE.
I *COMMANDED* IT.
COMMANDED?
HOW *DARE* YOU?
MAYBE WE CAN'T KILL YOU... BUT WE'LL MAKE SURE YOU LEARN YOUR PLACE!

RAAAGH!

SNAP!

THAT'S JUST IT. THAT'S WHAT NONE OF YOU SEEMS TO COMPREHEND.

THIS IS MY PLACE.

HARROW IS MY PLACE.

AND YOU'RE NOT WELCOME HERE.

ARE WE GOING TO LET HER TALK TO US THAT WAY?

YOU'RE NOT ALL COWARDS, ARE YOU?

OH, CORBIN... JUST HUSH NOW.

DON'T YOU SEE?

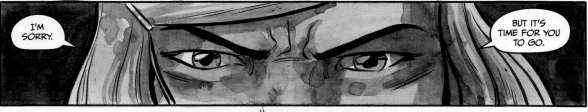

I'M SORRY.

BUT IT'S TIME FOR YOU TO GO.

WA-THROOMBOOM

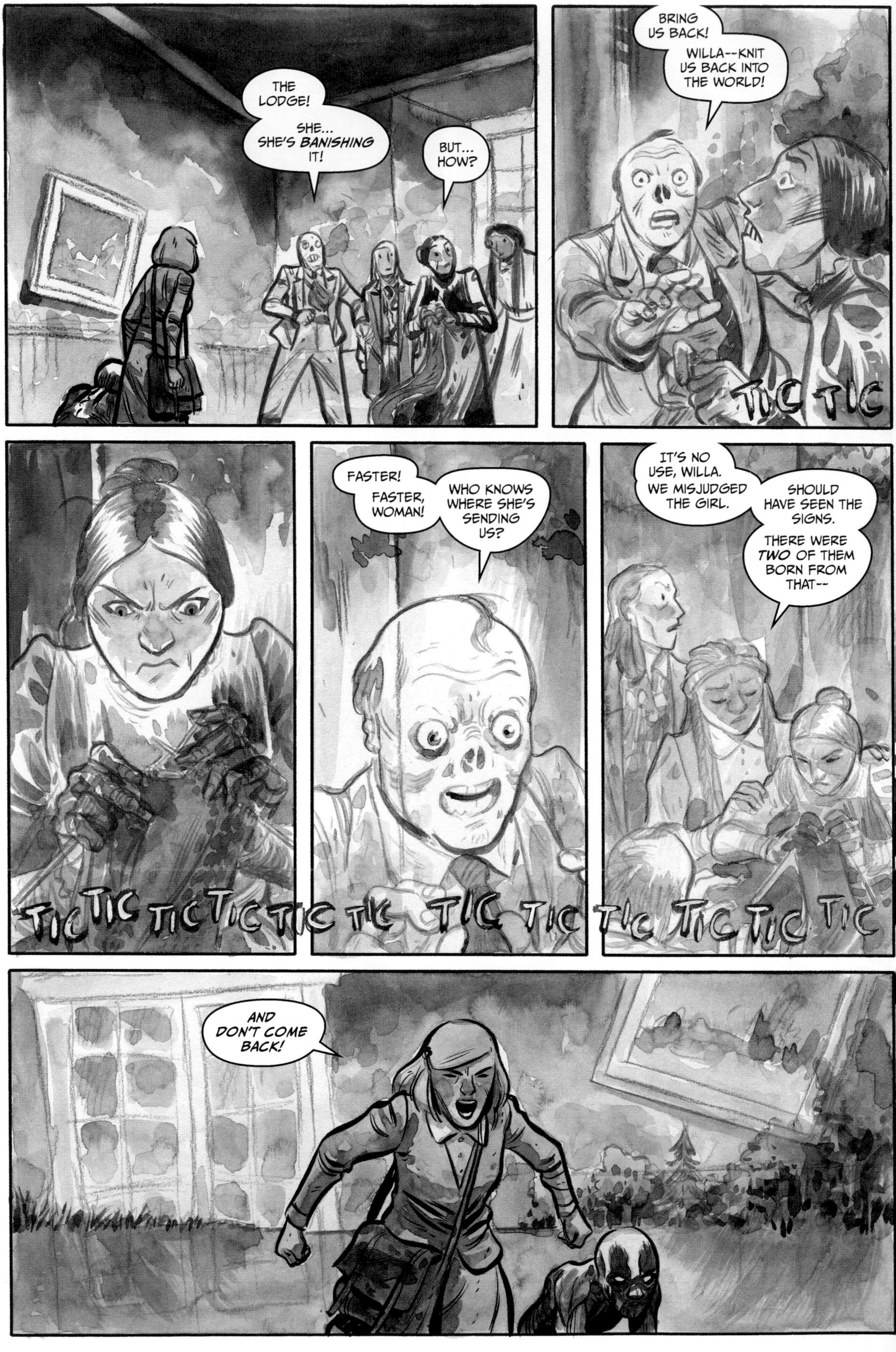
THE LODGE!
SHE... SHE'S BANISHING IT!
BUT... HOW?
BRING US BACK!
WILLA--KNIT US BACK INTO THE WORLD!
TIC TIC
TIC TIC TIC TIC TIC TIC
FASTER! FASTER, WOMAN!
WHO KNOWS WHERE SHE'S SENDING US?
TIC TIC TIC
IT'S NO USE, WILLA. WE MISJUDGED THE GIRL.
SHOULD HAVE SEEN THE SIGNS.
THERE WERE TWO OF THEM BORN FROM THAT--
TIC TIC TIC TIC TIC
AND DON'T COME BACK!

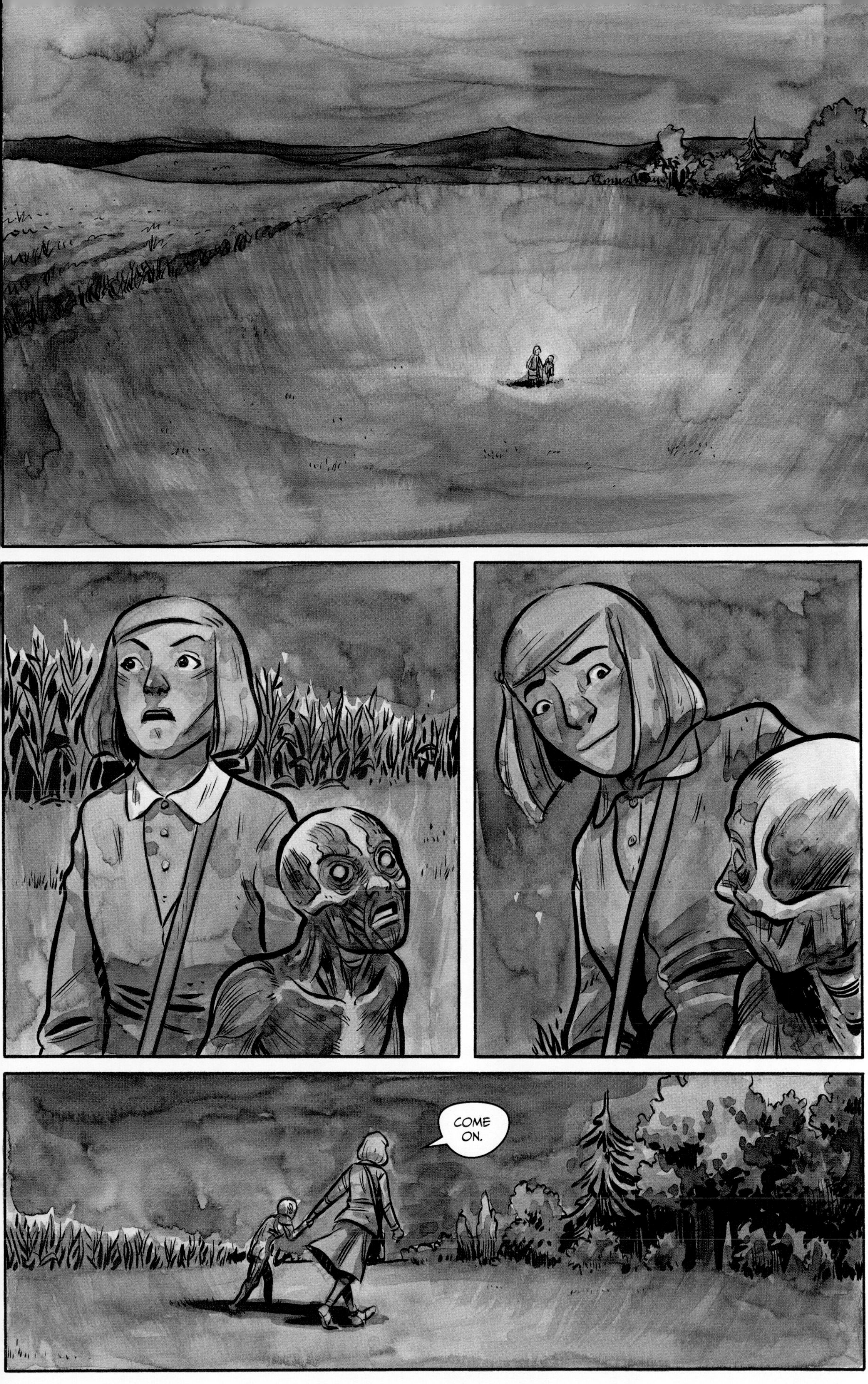
COME ON.

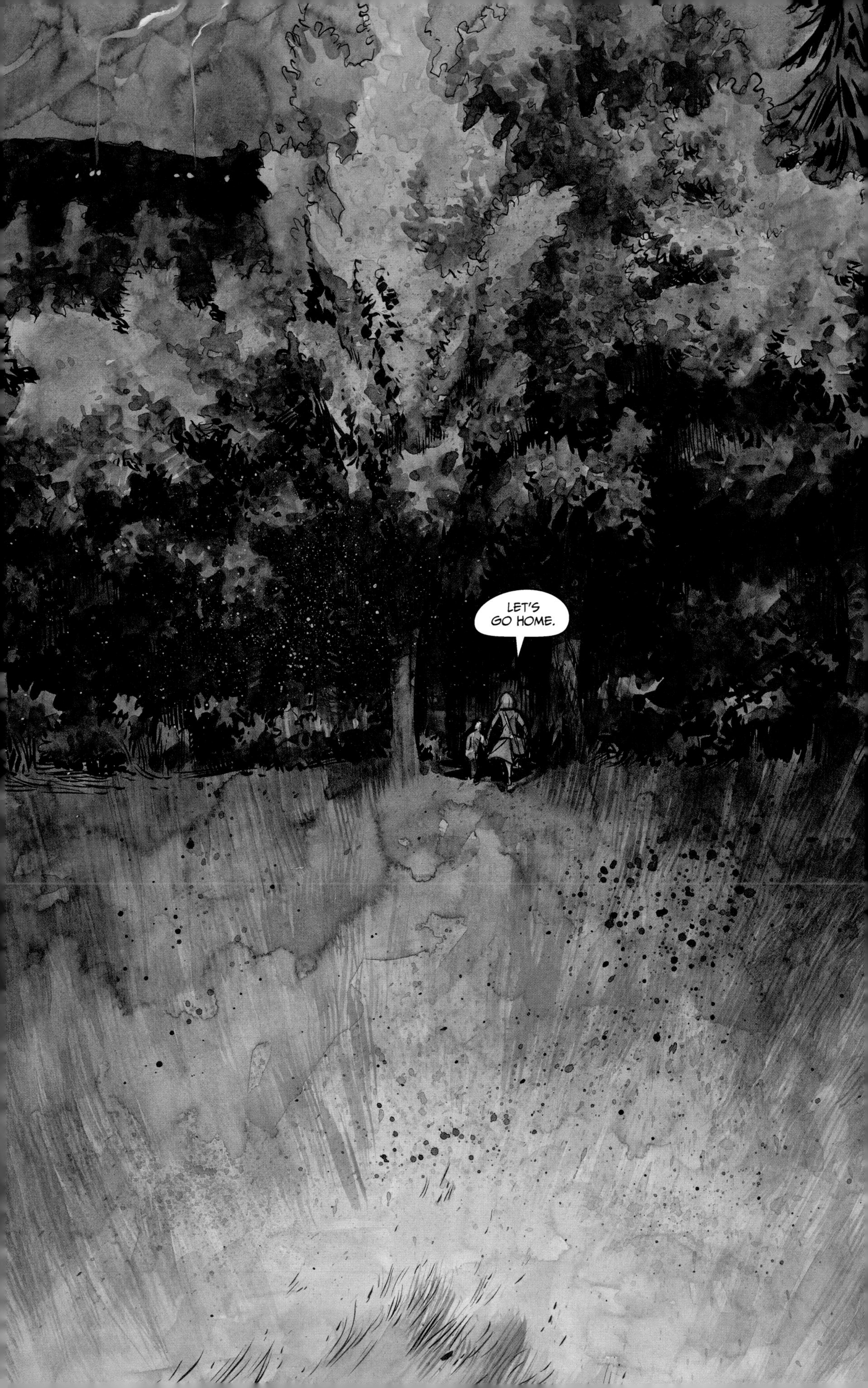
LET'S GO HOME.

HARROW
◄ SKETCHBOOK ►
COUNTY ™

NOTES BY
TYLER CROOK

ODESSA
V.01

• LONG HAIR TWISTS.
• DRESSES IN ALL WHITE
• ALWAYS HAS AT LEAST
  ONE ANIMAL BUDDY
  WITH HER.

I ended up not giving Odessa animal buddies. Mostly because it would have been kind of hard to manage from scene to scene. But I kind of wish I'd stuck with the idea.

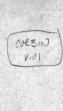

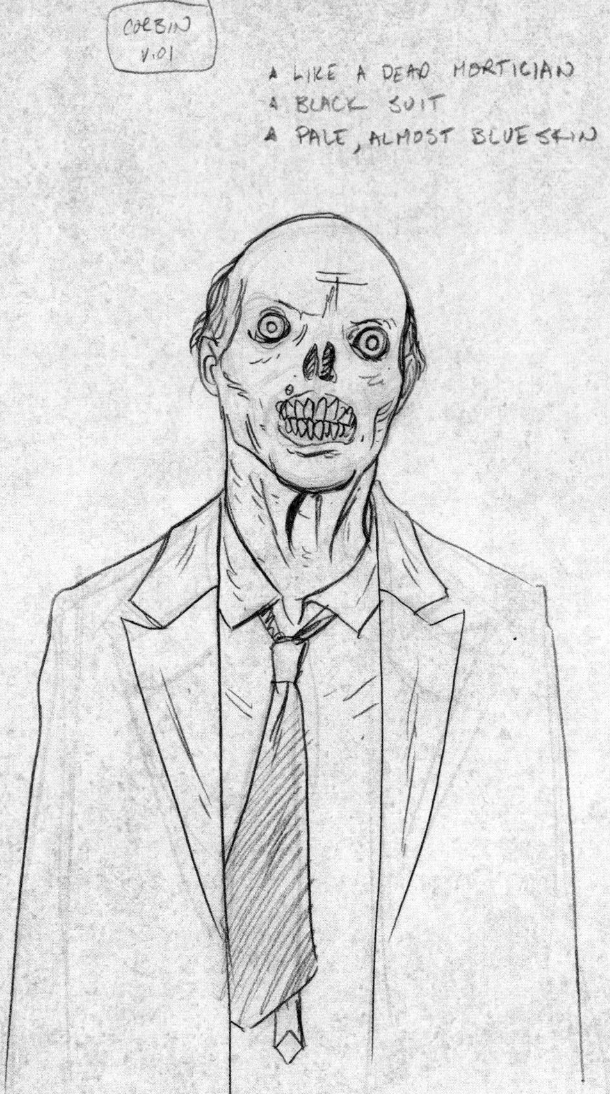
CORBIN V.01
LIKE A DEAD MORTICIAN
BLACK SUIT
PALE, ALMOST BLUE SKIN

Cullen's notes on Corbin said that he tried to make himself look more like the dead. So I put him in a suit as if that was what he was buried in. But by the end I started thinking of it as more of a business suit, and his business is being the world's whiniest necromancer. Good work if you can get it, I guess.

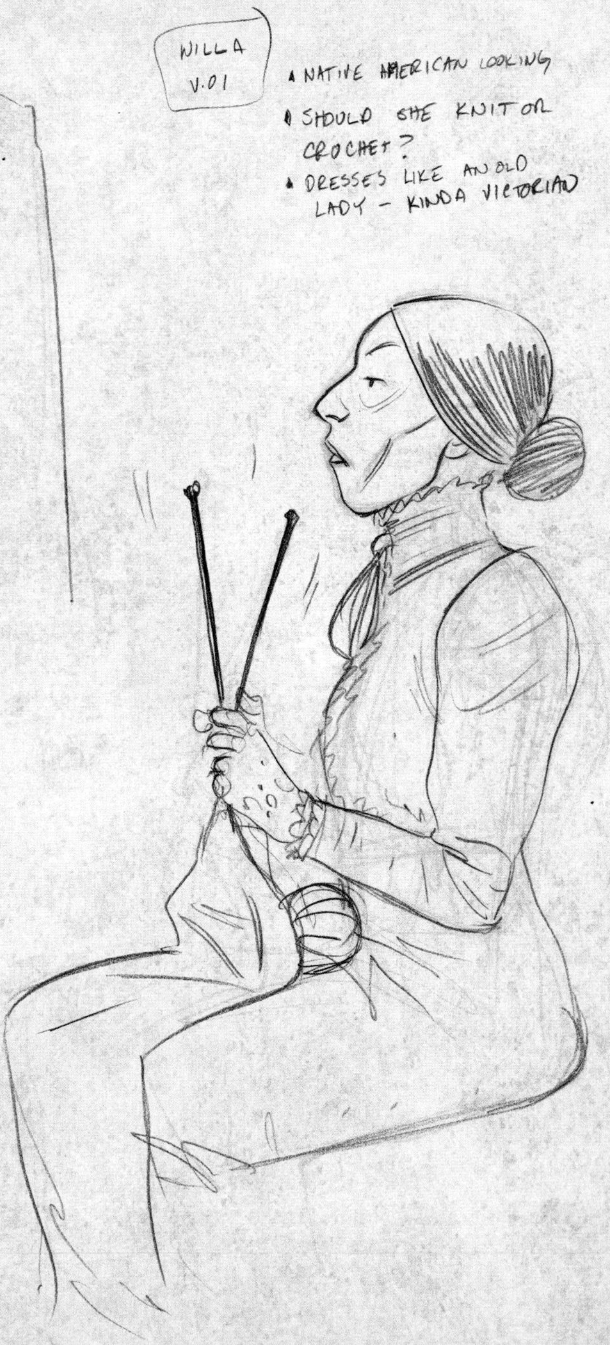
WILLA V.01
NATIVE AMERICAN LOOKING
SHOULD SHE KNIT OR CROCHET?
DRESSES LIKE AN OLD LADY - KINDA VICTORIAN

The way Willa tries to knit fate to her will made me think that she'd be all prim and proper—wanting everything in its place. So I dressed her like a Victorian nanny. I'm still a little embarrassed that I drew her holding the knitting needles like that. I'm also pretty sure I forgot to give her bloody fingers a couple of times.

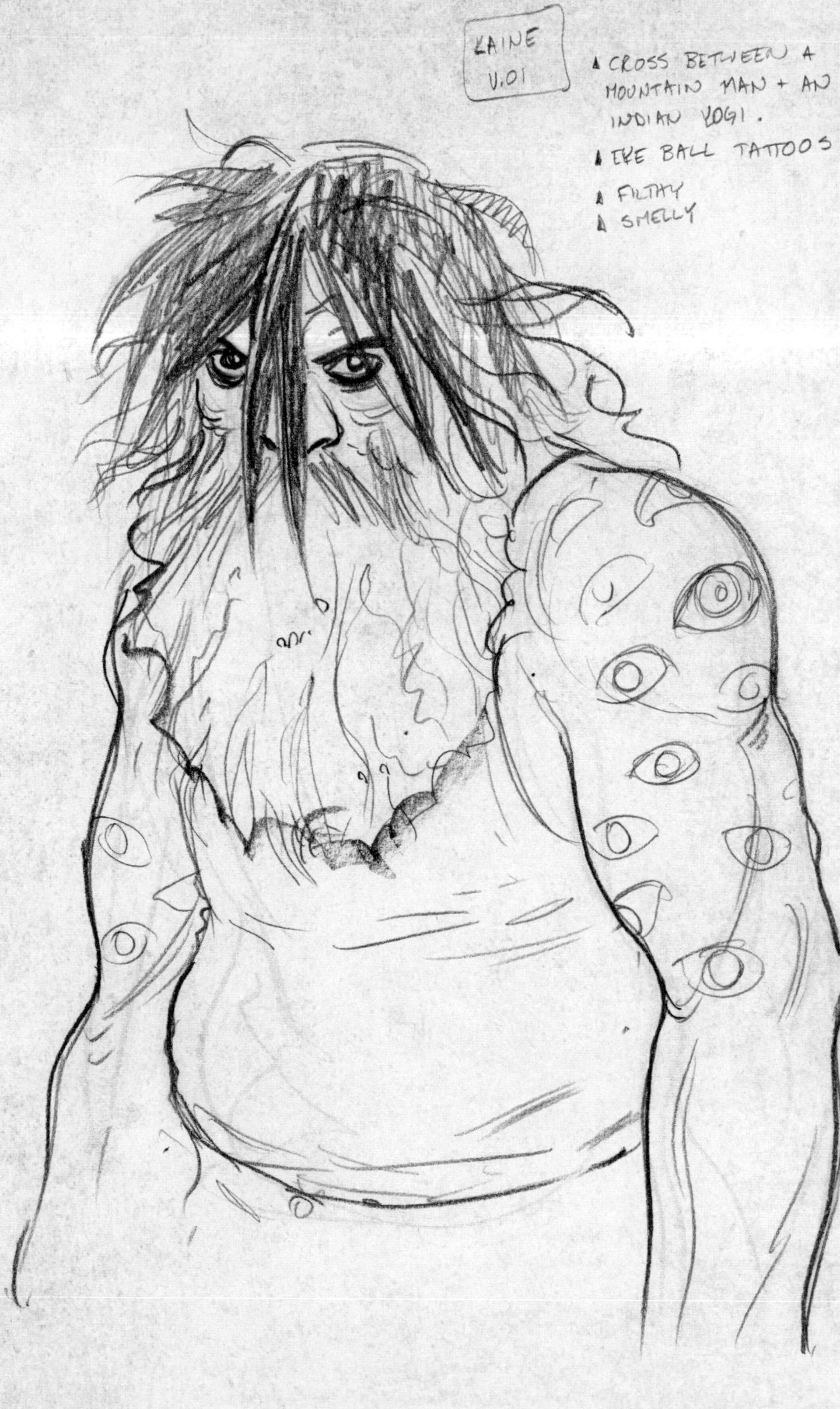
KAINE
V.01
▲ CROSS BETWEEN A MOUNTAIN MAN + AN INDIAN YOGI.
▲ EYE BALL TATTOOS
▲ FILTHY
▲ SMELLY

I thought of Kaine as an ascetic who came out of his filthy cave just to scare children. His tank top and grungy pants were basically his sleep clothes and he'd been wearing them for decades. Initially I was going to make his clothes more like pajamas but that was too gross for me.

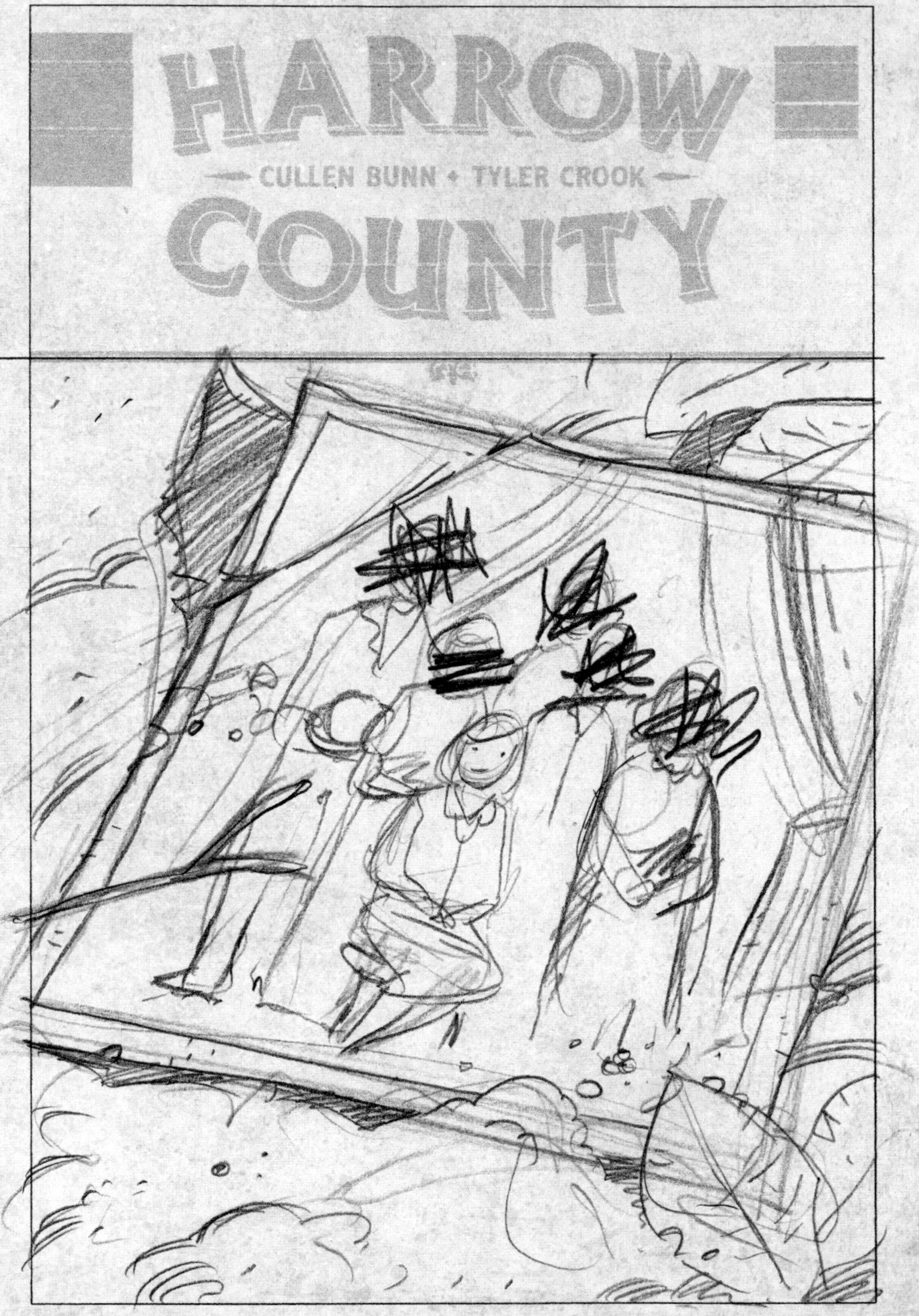
HARROW
CULLEN BUNN + TYLER CROOK
COUNTY

I usually draw the covers three or four months before I draw the interior art. This was the first time I had to draw a cover before the script was done. That's been the case for pretty much every cover since this one. So without having the script, we had to get the idea of what was going on without being too specific. I don't remember who came up with the family portrait but I sure like the idea. We stuck it in the mud to get across the idea that this family portrait is lost and forgotten—and also so it could have a splash of color.

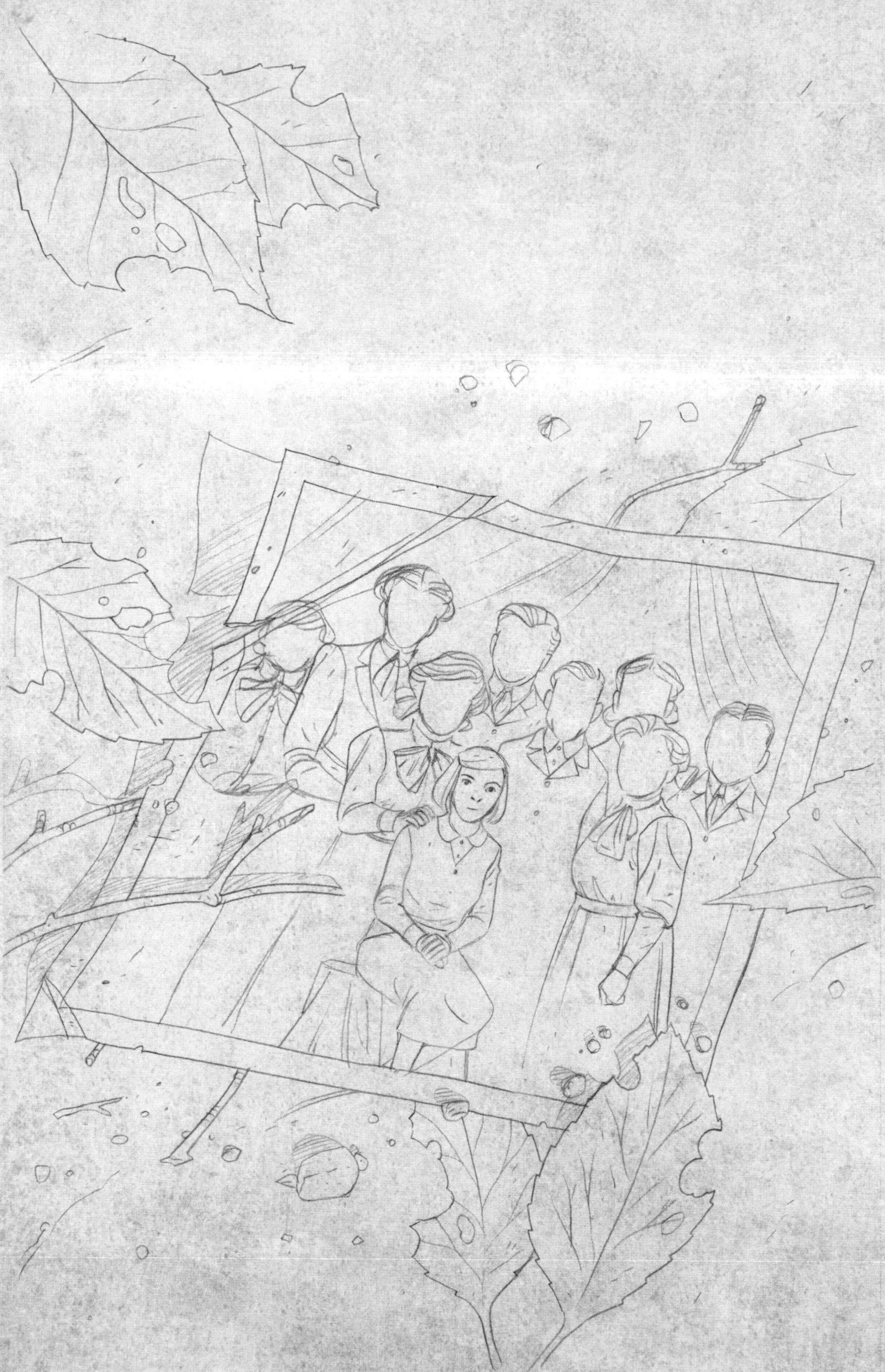

This is one of those covers where most of the work is in the painting. The pencils look almost barren. I didn't bother drawing the faces for anyone but Emmy because I knew I'd be scratching them out anyway.

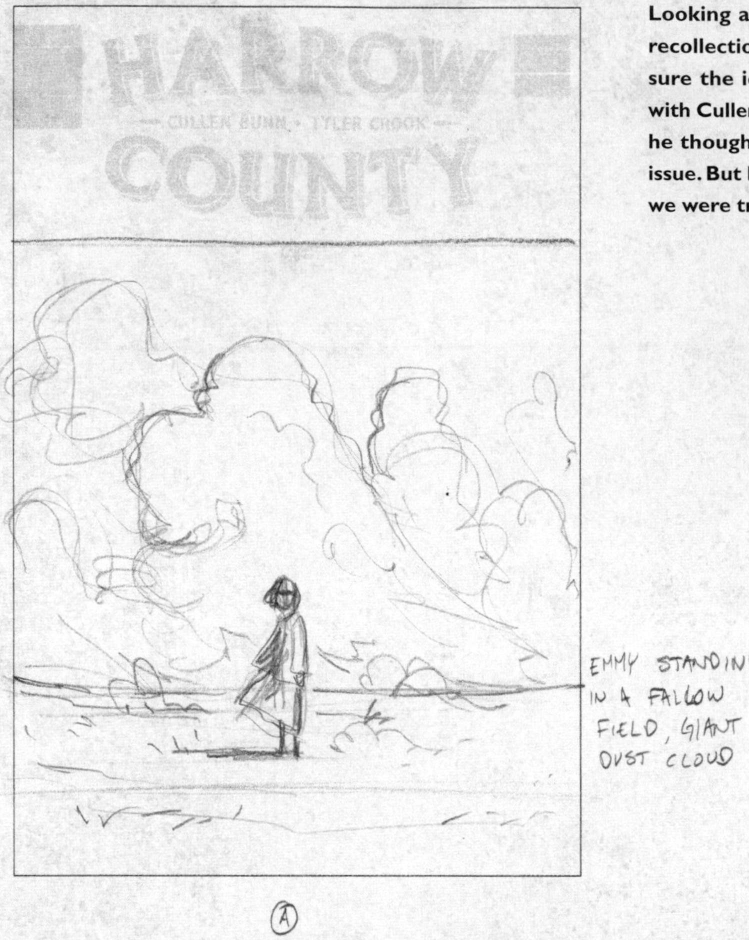
HARROW
CULLEN BUNN • TYLER CROOK
COUNTY
EMMY STANDING IN A FALLOW FIELD, GIANT DUST CLOUD
A

Looking at this sketch now, I have zero recollection of why we thought of it. I'm sure the idea came out of a phone call with Cullen where he was telling me what he thought was going to happen in this issue. But I don't remember what exactly we were trying to get across.

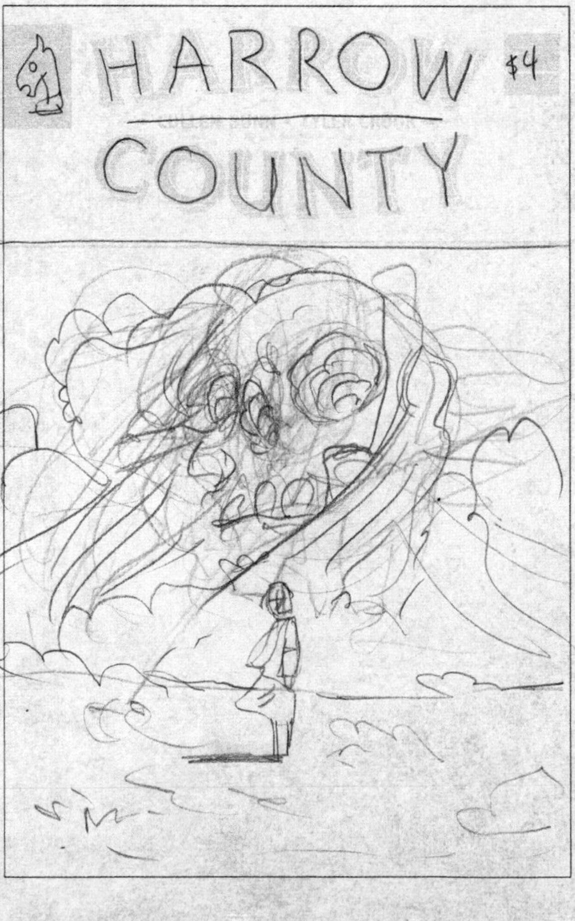
HARROW
$4
CULLEN BUNN • TYLER CROOK
COUNTY

I do remember that our editor Daniel recommended that I do something to make the clouds more interesting, so I added Hester's skull. I think it made the cover more striking and more story relevant as well because Emmy starts learning about her connections to the past in this issue.

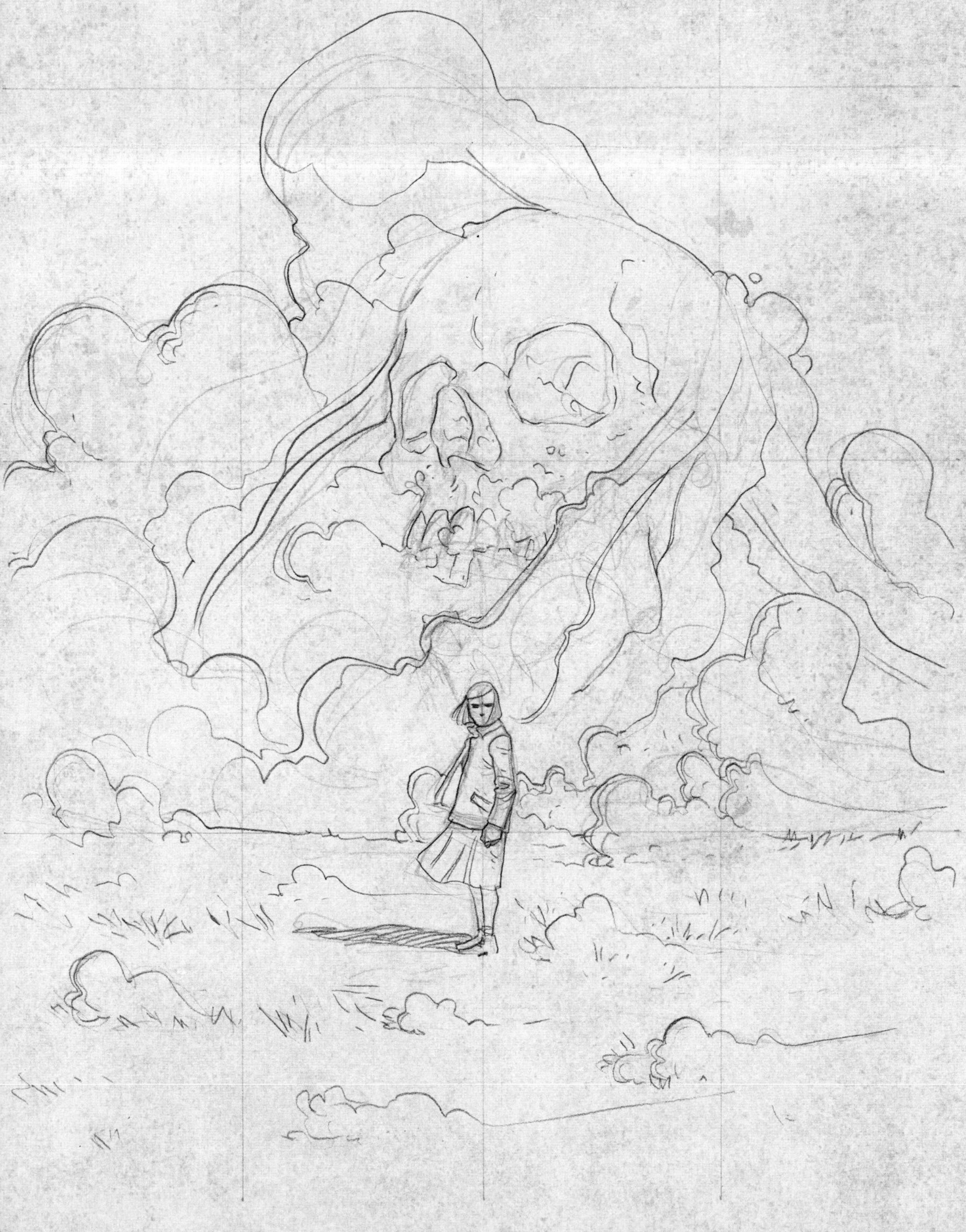

This is another one where the pencils feel very minimal. All the focus and interest come from the color and texture. I just need the pencils as a framework to build the painting on.

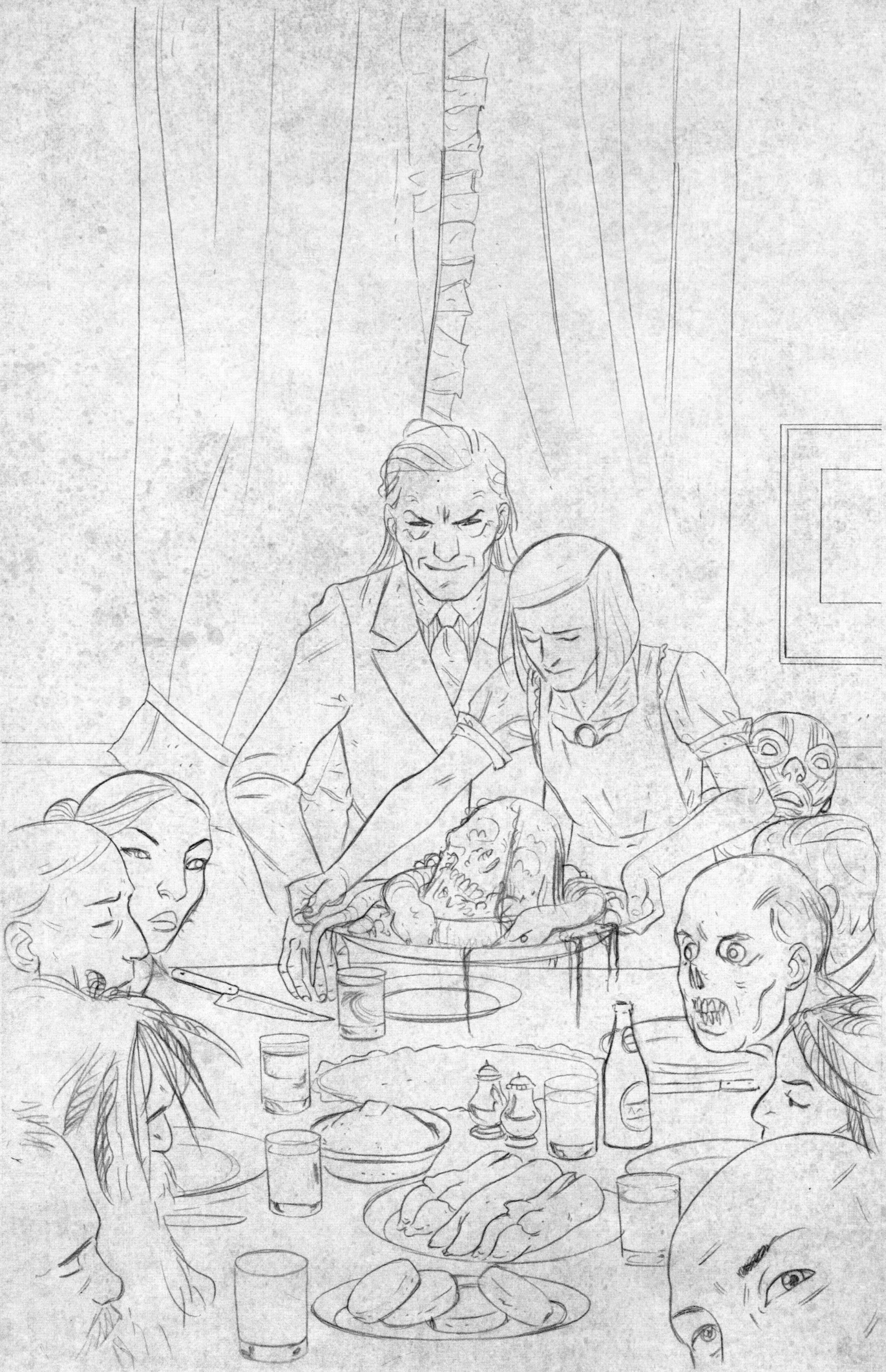

Here's a hot tip: If you ever need a cover idea, just steal one from Norman Rockwell. That's supposed to be me in the lower left and Cullen gleefully peeking back at us on the lower right.

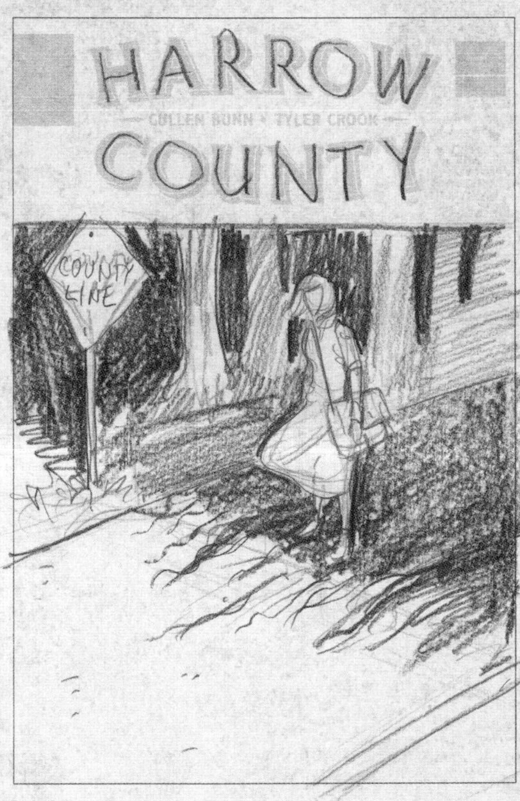
HARROW
CULLEN BUNN • TYLER CROOK
COUNTY
COUNTY LINE

A

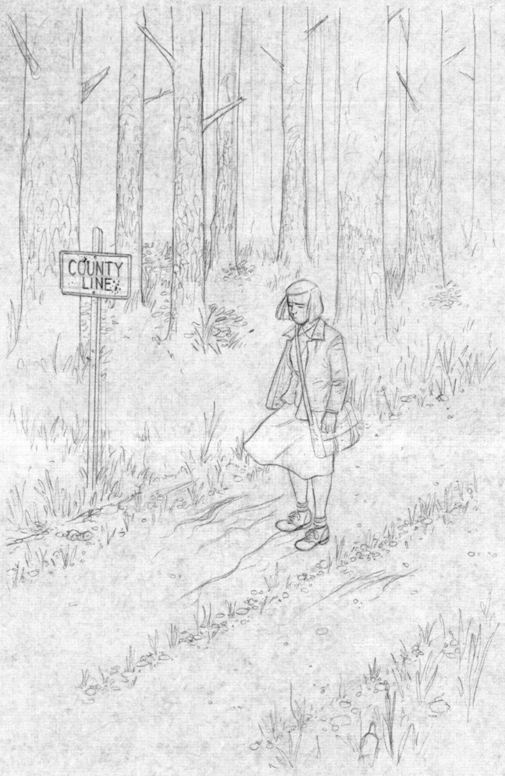
COUNTY LINE

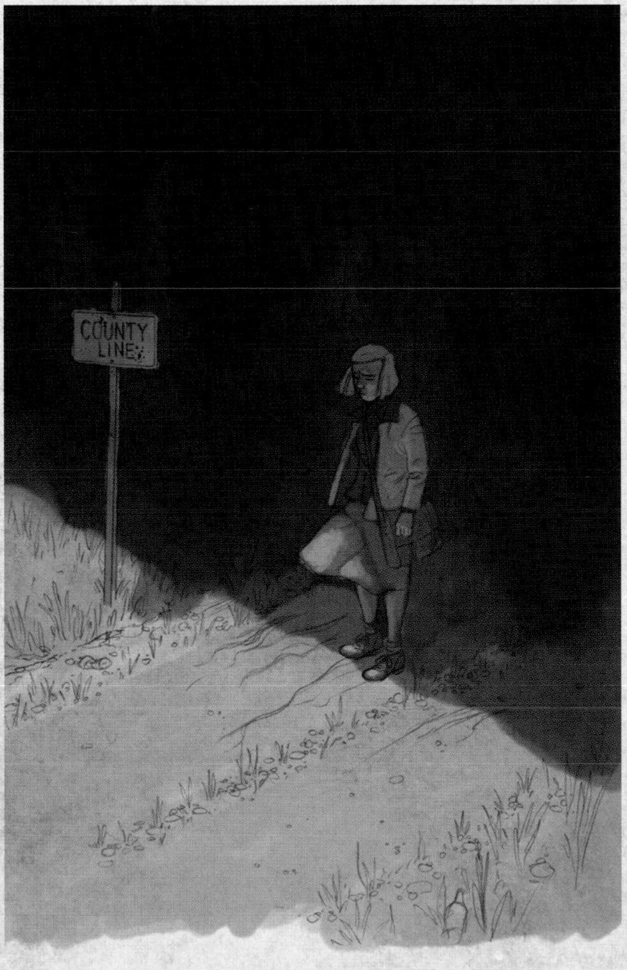
COUNTY LINE

The idea behind this cover is that Emmy was going to be asked to leave Harrow County and she had to decide how she was going to react. The cover seems a little heavy handed, but I still like it. This is one of those times where I penciled all those trees and then carefully painted them all black and then completely covered them with a logo.

HARROW

— CULLEN BUNN ◆ TYLER CROOK —

COUNTY

Layouts are hard, and that makes them hard to talk about. Turning words and ideas into a well-functioning comic book page is surprisingly complex. You have to balance the page with the pages before and after it. You have to lay out the panels so that they flow and read easily while giving room for dialogue and also accentuating the important elements of the story. Each panel needs to be composed so that it reads well but also looks good and doesn't interrupt the flow of the dialogue or the panel flow that you've established. You have to work out the staging, action, and emotions of the characters. Everything has to be clear and expressive, and it always feels like every choice is a compromise, taking from one column to add to another column. It's probably the most important part of the comics-making process, and it's exhausting, but because of the challenges, it's also a lot of fun.

In the next few pages you can see how I interpreted Cullen's script. There are things that I add and things I take away and things that I switch up. It's a fluid process, and I think this is where the artist and the writer are truly collaborating.

HARROW COUNTY

ISSUE #15 SCRIPT

<u>PAGE 1 (Splash Page)</u>

As seen in previous issues, this book starts with a double-page splash, running across the inside front cover. The HARROW COUNTY logo should appear somewhere in the artwork for the panel.

First four pages are a FLASHBACK.

A shot of the muddy banks of a river on a stormy night. Hester Beck stands in the rain, her clothing soaked and sticking to her pale form, the hem of her dress covered in mud. Her arms are covered in mud and blood to the elbows. She holds her arms out, as if welcoming guests. We probably don't see it from this angle, but there is a large clay bowl on the ground. Blood slicks the inside of the bowl, and tiny dribbles of blood ooze down the outer side. A knife is propped in the bowl. All around her, crawling out of the mud, are the townsfolk of Harrow County. Lightning flickers across the cloudy night sky.

CAPTION (Odessa):

"It was Hester who broke the **law**…

"…who broke from **our traditions**…

"…when she took it upon herself to become a **god**.

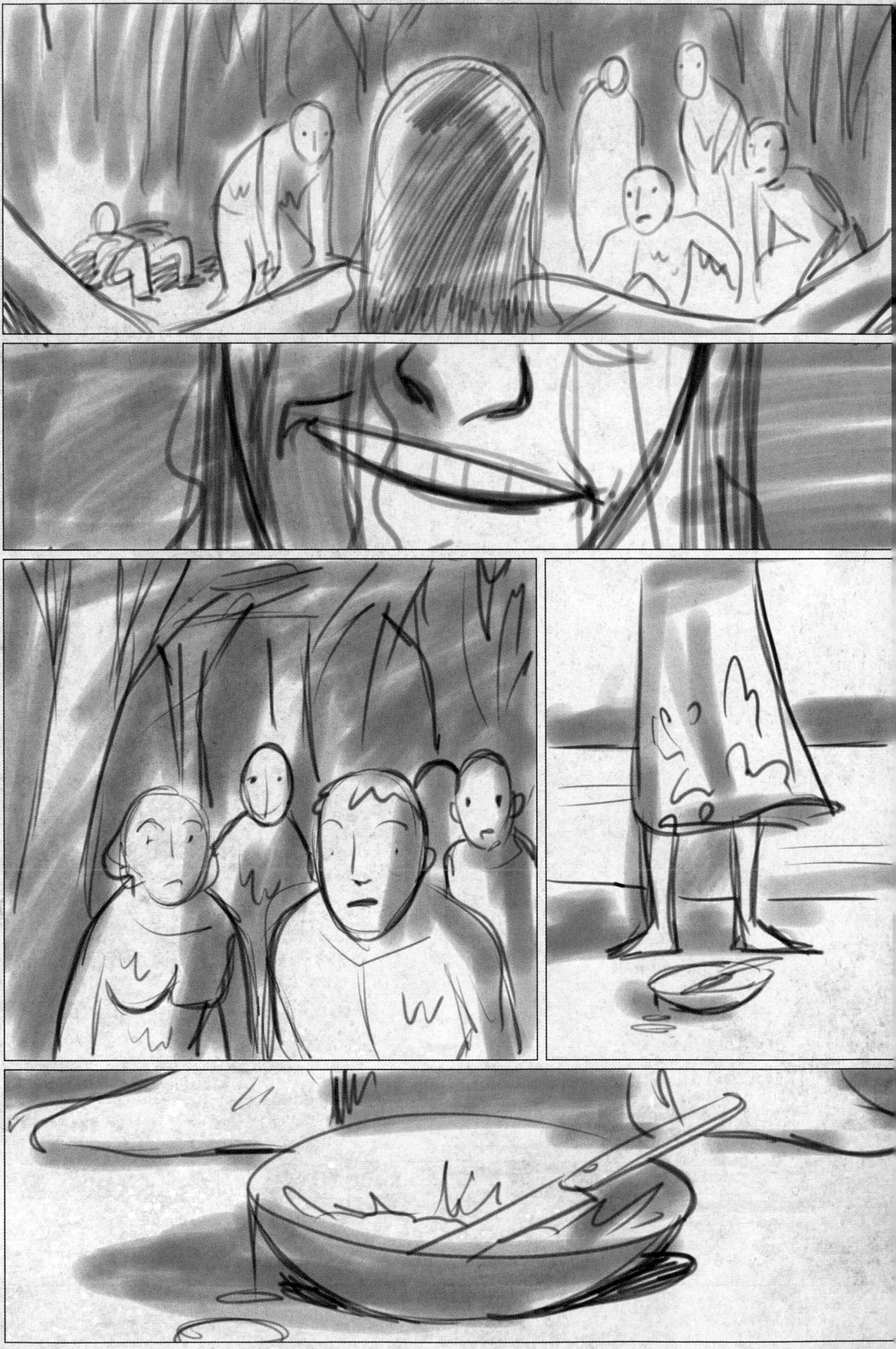

PANEL 1
Behind Hester as she looks out across the mud-covered faces of the people of Harrow. We might see some we recognize, but the mud obscures most of their features. They all wear expressions of bewilderment.

CAPTION (Odessa):

"She was always making trouble, though.

"That's why we cast her out in the first place.

PANEL 2
Close on Hester, a slight smile on her wet face.

CAPTION (Odessa):

"That might have been where we went wrong...

"...in distancing ourselves from our kin.

PANEL 3
Close on the muddy faces of the newborn Harrow County folks, still bewildered.

CAPTION (Odessa):

"Hester never did like being alone...

"...and in **loneliness**, her thoughts turned to **mischief**.

PANEL 4
Angle from below, past the bloody bowl at Hester's feet. She stands tall before it, and she looks down toward it.

CAPTION (Odessa):

"She called forth others to keep her company...

"...shaped them out of the mud...

PANEL 5
On the bowl, the inside red with blood (just slicking the sides, though. The bowl was filled with blood, but it has been poured out), a knife propped inside it.

CAPTION (Odessa):

"...and **her blood**.

PANEL I
Angle past the muddy townsfolk. Hester stands before them, reaching out to take the hand of one of the people who reaches out for her. In the background, staring out from the trees, we might see the hulking, shadowy faces of several monstrous haints, their eyes gleaming.

CAPTION (Odessa):

"Her blood…

"…and **ours**.

PANEL 2
On the shadowy shapes of the haints, watching with their glowing eyes. Still dark here.

CAPTION (Odessa):

"Oh, how she **tested** us…

"…even in the early days of her exile…

PANEL 3
As previous, but a lightning flash lights the hideous faces of the watching haints.

CAPTION (Odessa):

"…creating unnatural beasts, just to see if she could do it…

"…just to see if we were a-watching."

SFX (Thunder):

SHRRR-B-BOOM!

PANEL 4
Hester walks through the crowd of the newly created people in the mud. The mud is starting to wash off of them in the rain. They part to let her pass, and they watch her lovingly.

CAPTION (Odessa):

"And when we didn't react in the way she wanted…

"…she once more done what was **expressly forbidden**.

PANEL 5
On the newly created faces, the mud washing off of them.

CAPTION (Odessa):

"Where she had once committed murder in defiance of our ways…

"…now she breathed life into the lifeless.

PANEL 6
On Hester, turning, as if she senses someone behind her.

CAPTION (Odessa):

"That, of course, summoned us…

"…brought us from the **far places** to visit our estranged sister once more."

LEVI (OP):

Lookit what you done, girl.

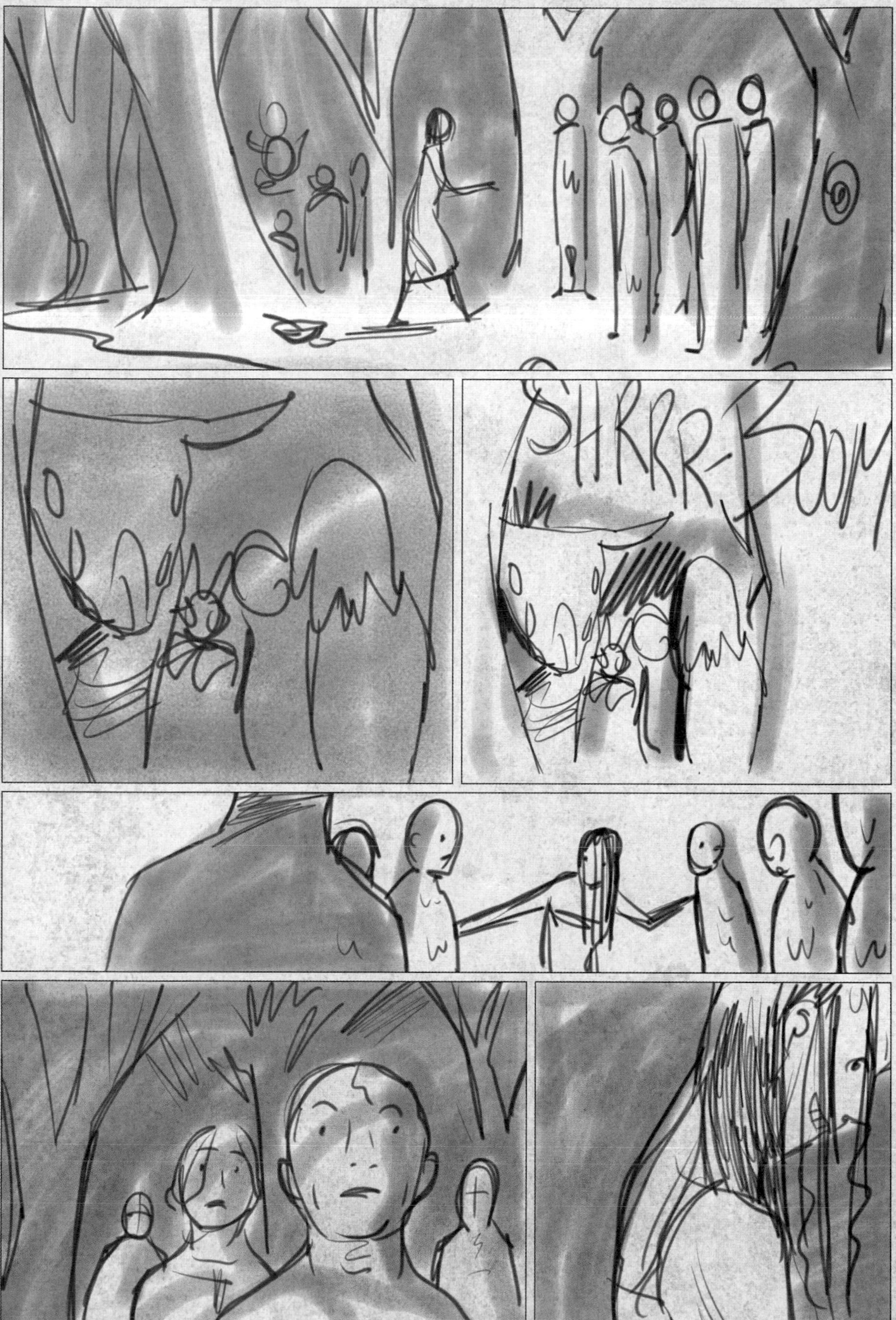
SHRR-BOOM

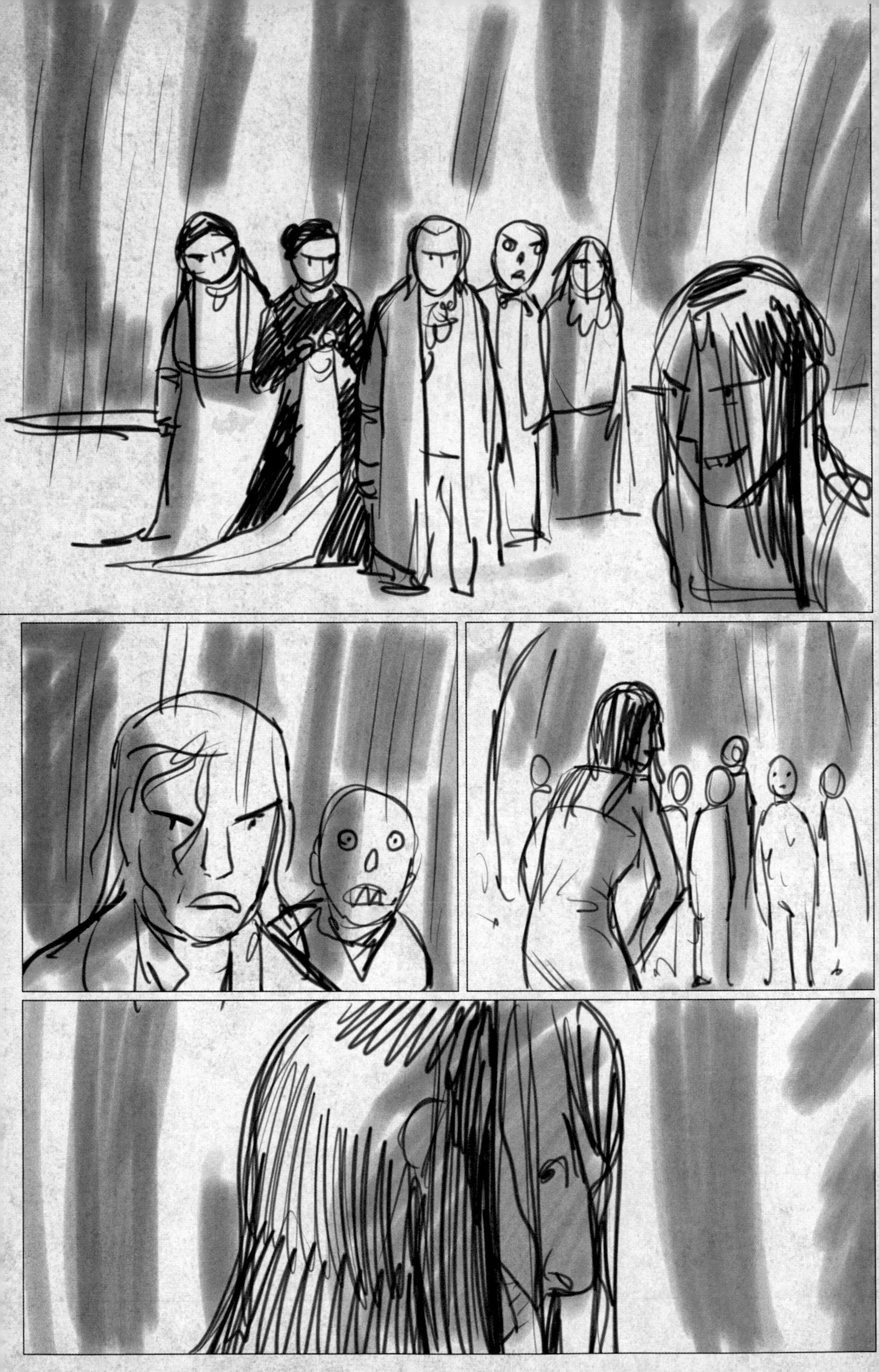

PANEL 1
Big panel. From behind Hester as she turns to face the Family. They stand before her in the rain, ghoulish figures wearing disapproving glares. Shadows fall across their faces, making them all the more menacing.

LEVI:

You done wrong and you know it.

And you must've known we couldn't let this stand.

Yet here we are.

PANEL 2
Close on Levi, water dripping off his face, looking cold and menacing.

LEVI:

Ain't you got nothin' to say?

PANEL 3
Close on Hester, head tilted just slightly, as if regarding her family curiously.

NO COPY.

PANEL 4
As previous, but Hester's lips twitch into a smile.

HESTER:

What are you going to do about it?

CAPTION (Odessa):

"There weren't much more we could say…

"…seeing as we had already learned her the extent of the punishment we could mete out."

PANEL 1
Now we cut to the HERE AND NOW. It is day, not a cloud in the sky. We see Emmy walking along with Odessa, a stroll through the woods.

ODESSA:

After all, as far as Hester was concerned, we had already done the **very worst** we could to her.

EMMY:

If you don't mind my asking, Odessa...

...why didn't you do something more?

PANEL 2
Close on Emmy and Odessa. Emmy glances at Odessa curiously. Odessa has a content look on her face as she looks straight ahead.

EMMY:

You and your family--

ODESSA:

Your family, too, dear.

EMMY:

So you say.

But you all seem...more than human.

So why didn't you do something to stop Hester all those years ago?

PANEL 3
Angle past Emmy as Odessa looks at her, still seemingly content.

ODESSA:

As I mentioned...

...there are traditions that **even we** must revere.

PANEL 4
Pull back, seeing Emmy and Odessa from behind as they walk along the path.

ODESSA:

Besides...

...if we had done away with Hester back then...

...**you** might not be with us right now.

PANEL 5
Close on Emmy and Odessa. Emmy looks down, a little sad. Odessa looks at her with a bit of shock.

EMMY:

Maybe...

...that would have been for the best.

ODESSA:

Don't talk such nonsense, girl.

I don't believe that and neither do you.

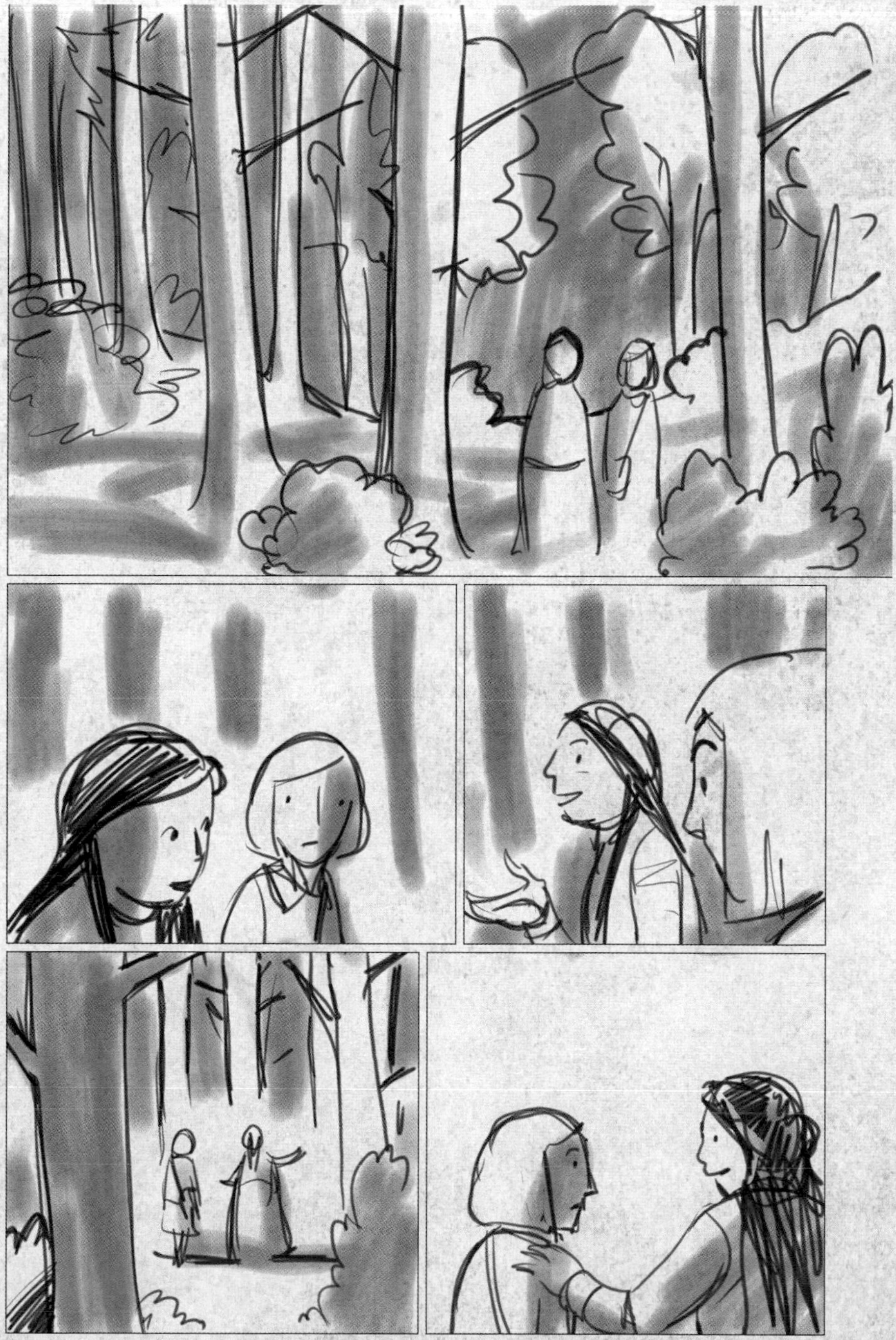

PANEL 1
In the foreground, we see the old bowl that Hester used in the flashback. It is sticking up out of the dirt here, forgotten and half-submerged, rusted and covered in weeds. Emmy and Odessa are walking along the banks of the creek in the background.

ODESSA:

The world is better with you in it.

PANEL 2
On Odessa and Emmy, walking along the banks of the creek. Odessa looks over at the girl. A friendly smile on Odessa's lips.

ODESSA:

Better...

...and **much bigger** than you have ever imagined.

PANEL 3
From behind Emmy and Odessa. They are looking down into the water of the creek, their marbled reflections looking back at them.

EMMY:

It's true, though, isn't it?

I'm her...

...Hester...

...returned from the grave.

ODESSA:

That's near enough to the truth, I suppose.

PANEL 4
Close on Emmy's reflection in the water.

EMMY (OP):

You said yourself...

...Hester was trouble.

You even said she was a **killer**.

PANEL 5
Emmy looks at Odessa, who places a comforting hand on the girl's shoulder.

ODESSA:

That don't have to be you, though.

You don't have to do things the way Hester did.

Fact of the matter is, we're hoping you won't.

PANEL 6
Angle past Emmy and Hester. In the distance, we see the rickety wooden bridge spanning the river. (They aren't going to cross it…but they see it spanning the water.) Emmy is hesitating.

EMMY:

Uh--

ODESSA:

What is it, child?

Is something troubling you?

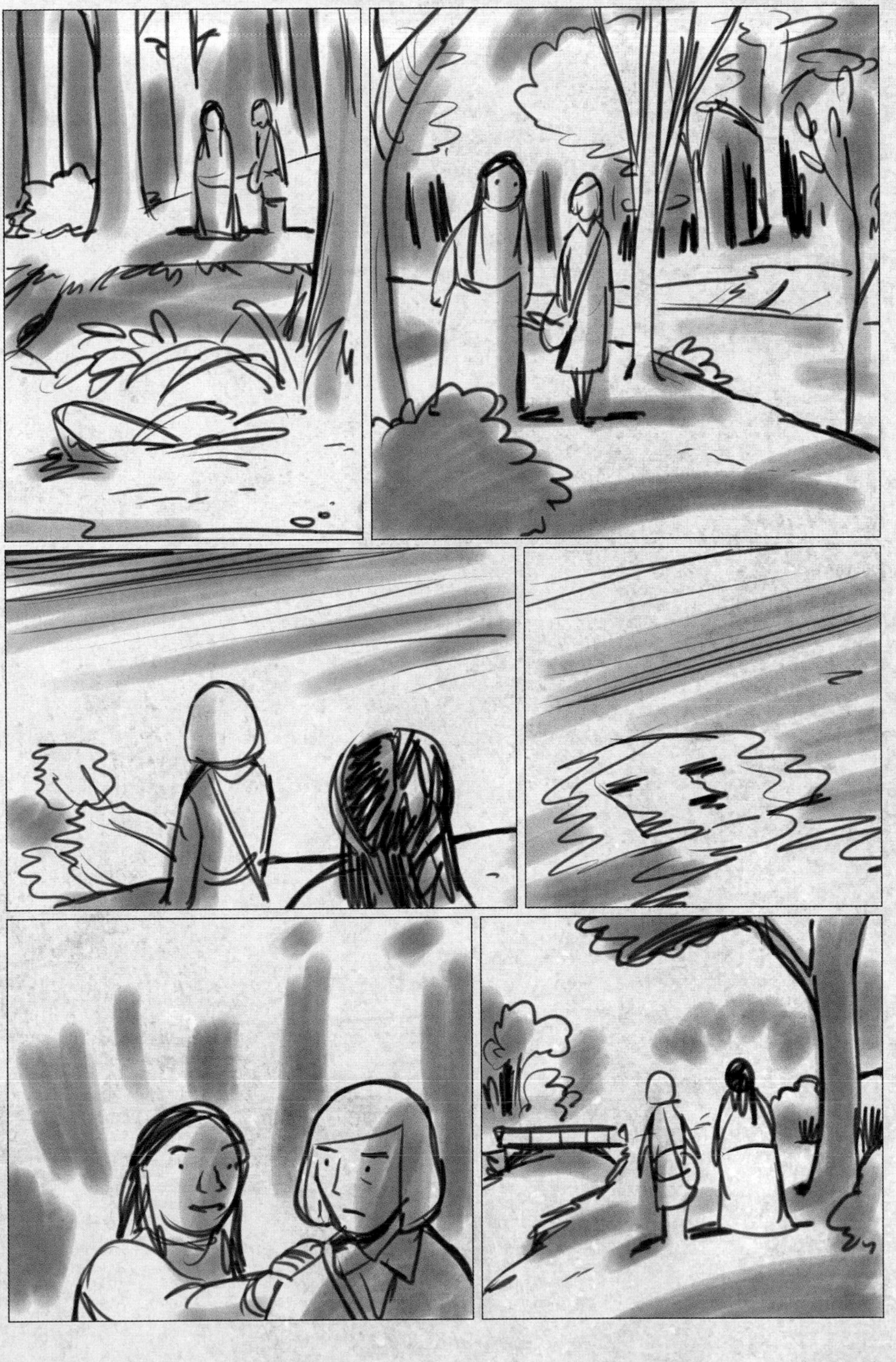

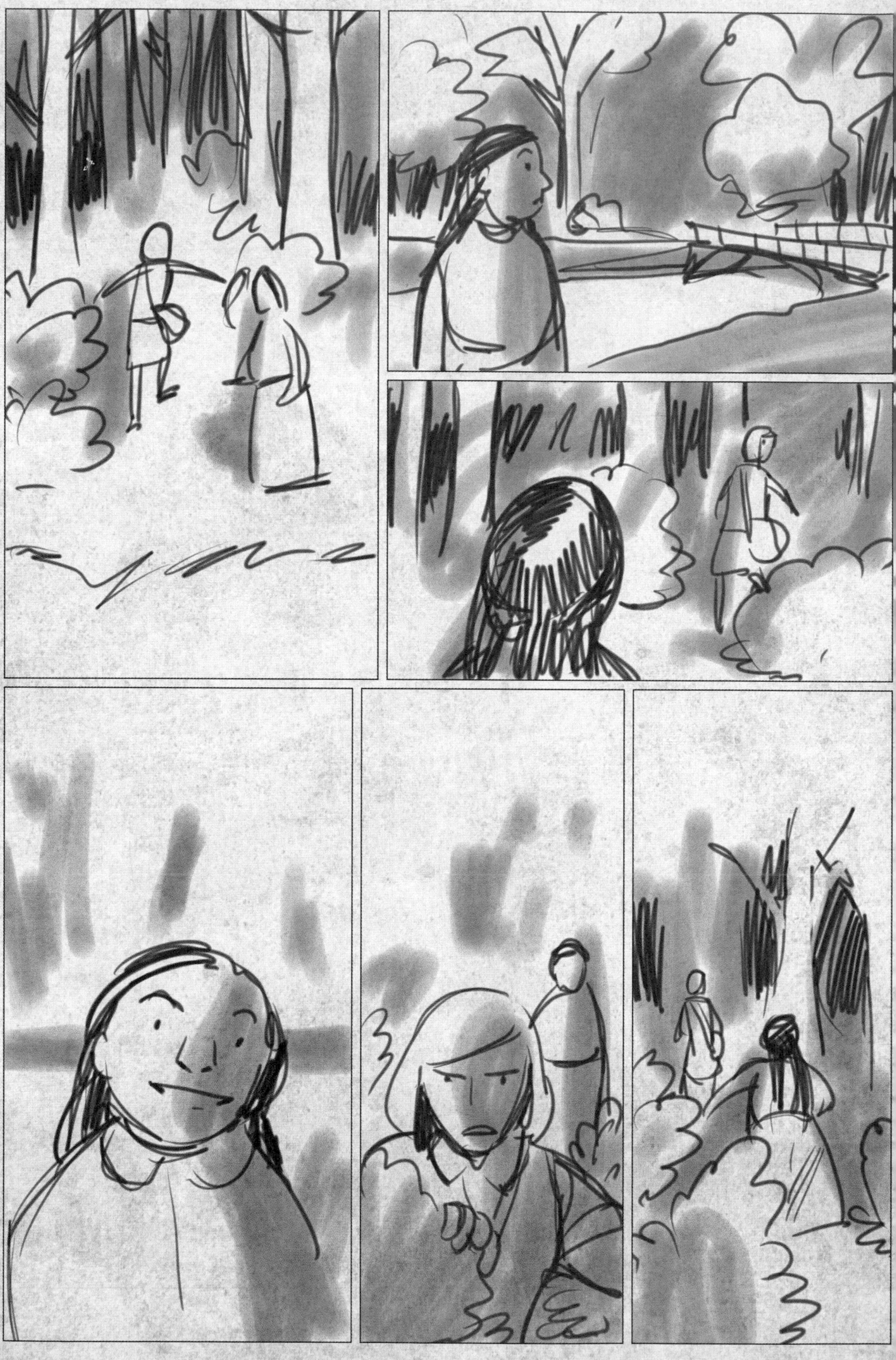

PANEL 1
Emmy turns, going in a different direction. She is pushing through brush. Odessa stands in the background, watching her.

EMMY:

I think maybe I'd like to go a different way.

PANEL 2
Odessa glances back toward the bridge.

ODESSA:

I thought you were going to show me around the county.

I already know what lies beyond yonder bridge.

PANEL 3
Angle from behind Odessa as she looks toward Emmy. Emmy, in the brush, turns, looking back at her, a slight scowl on her face.

ODESSA:

Is there a reason you don't want me to visit your home?

EMMY:

If it's all the same to you…

…I'd simply like to go this way.

PANEL 4
Close on Odessa, smiling.

ODESSA:

If that suits you.

Sooner or later, though, you'll have to trust me…

…unless you decide not to.

PANEL 5
Emmy is walking through the brush, not looking back, with Odessa following her.

EMMY:

You and yours show up out of nowhere…

…saying you're my family…

…saying you want to help me…

…but I don't guess I know **anything** about you.

PANEL 6
Close on Odessa.

ODESSA:

Well, that's why we're taking this constitutional, isn't it?

You have questions about who we are…

…where we come from…

…and I mean to remedy that as much as I can.

Pages 8 and 9 are FLASHBACKS of a sort. I kind of like the idea that they are four stacked panels...but the layout is, of course, all yours.

PANEL 1
Cut to a shot of the family, all standing together. In this shot, though, Hester (looking a little younger and innocent, maybe even dressed in a white dress) and Amaryllis are among the others. Behind them, the sky is roiling with almost volcanic colors.

CAPTION (Odessa):

"As to where we came from...

"...that's not so simple a question.

"I only know that we have near about **always** been.

PANEL 2
Odessa is walking along, maybe a walking stick in her hand.

CAPTION (Odessa):

"We're a **family**, like we've said...

"...in that we come from the same place...

PANEL 3
And now we cut to a dusty dirt road, bloody footprints appearing in the dirt.

CAPTION (Odessa):

"...but we don't none of us stay together.

"We each of us wander the world in our own way...

PANEL 4
Cut to a train rattling down the tracks, Levi in an open boxcar, legs hanging out, wind whipping past.

CAPTION (Odessa):

"Those are the first of our traditions.

"Never together.

"...and never **settling** in any one place.

PAGE 9 (Four Panels)

PANEL 1
Cut to a shot of the strange mansion we saw in the previous issue. This page is actually going to show the mansion in several different places. Here we see the house sitting on a dark beach in the middle of the night, waves lapping at its foundation. A lighthouse stands in the background, a beam flashing across the mansion. In my mind, this is Cape Hatteras Lighthouse: https://upload.wikimedia.org/wikipedia/commons/0/0c/Cape_hatteras_lighthouse_img_0529.jpg

CAPTION (Odessa):

"Only during the time of the **conclave** do we gather at the **meeting lodge**...

"...and that house, like the rest of us, has simply **always** existed...

PANEL 2
Cut to a shot of the house rising in a city, tall skyscrapers on either side of it.

CAPTION (Odessa):

"...or maybe it only ever exists when we need it...

"...and where we need to come together.

PANEL 3
Cut to a shot of the house sitting precariously on a mountainous ledge.

CAPTION (Odessa):

"The conclaves take place but once each decade...

"...but the lodge has appeared--and called us all together--on occasions of great importance.

PANEL 4
Cut to a shot of the house, we see the mansion, looking very much like it did in the last issue, rising up from the vast field.

CAPTION (Odessa):

"Those times are few and far between...

"...only a handful of instances that I recall...

"...most of them involving Hester and her antics..."

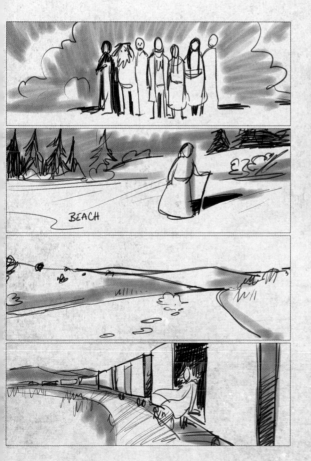

PANEL 1
Cut back to the here and now. Emmy and Odessa are walking along a paved road. We are behind them. In the distance, we see a church steeple rising from behind the trees.

ODESSA:

...and **now**, of course.

EMMY:

So you've come together for one of your special meetings...

...the kind that only ever happen during times of great significance...

...and it has something to do with **me**?

PANEL 2
Emmy and Odessa are now walking past a small community church. Sitting on the steps of the church is the preacher (we saw him way back in issue 1).

ODESSA:

Yes, dear. Yes.

Hester is **gone**.

It's long past time for us to bring **you** into the fold.

EMMY:

You said you cast Hester out...

...and you still haven't told me why...

...but wouldn't that mean I've been exiled as well?

PANEL 3
From behind Emmy. She waves at the preacher on the steps.

EMMY:

Hey there, Reverend Worley!

Good to see you!

PANEL 4
On the reverend, looking up from his Bible, smiling and waving.

REVEREND:

Good afternoon, Emmy!

Isn't it just a lovely day?

Hope to see you and your Pa at services this week!

The congregation would love for you to visit with us!

PANEL 5

Angle from behind the reverend. We see the open Bible in his hands. This is the Bible that had the letters washed off in the first issue. Here, we see the pages have no words on them, just a smear of watery ink across blank, crinkled pages. In the background, we see Odessa and Emmy walking past. Emmy is calling out.

EMMY:

Yes, sir!

See you then!

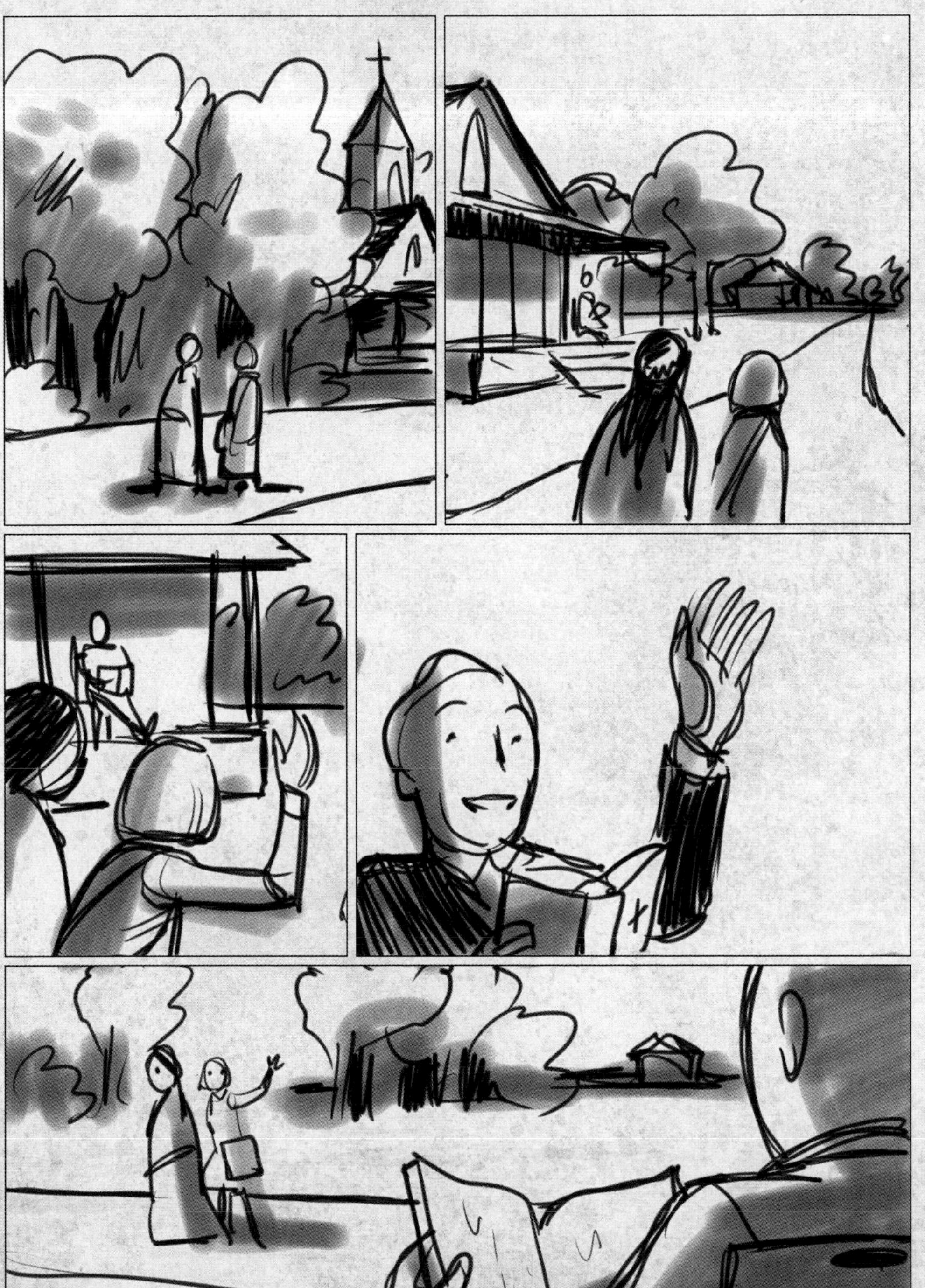

PANEL 1
Emmy and Odessa walk along the road (lined with trees). Next to the road is a white sign with hand-painted letters. It reads MAMA LOVES PAPA.

ODESSA:

We haven't turned our backs on you, child.

Over the years, we've each and every one of us looked in on you from time to time.

PANEL 2
Emmy and Odessa keep walking along. It's a different section of the road, this one running alongside some crops. Another sign is here. It reads PAPA LOVES WOMEN.

EMMY:

Doesn't that break your own rules?

I thought you didn't like to meet one another.

ODESSA:

Well, we had to be sure who you were...

...who you would become.

PANEL 3
Further along the road. Now we see a farm with a silo in the distant background. Another sign is along the road: MAMA CAUGHT PAPA WITH THREE GIRLS SWIMMING.

ODESSA:

Now that we're certain that you're one of us, there will be **changes**...

...for you and for us.

One of the family will take you under his or her wing for a short time...

...no more than a year or two...

...to learn you our ways.

PANEL 4
Still moving along the road. Another sign: HERE LIES PAPA.

EMMY:

Will it be you?

ODESSA:

Might be, but that will be your decision, really.

PANEL 5
Changing the angle, we are now behind the next sign that Emmy and Odessa are approaching.

EMMY:

How would I even begin to make a decision like that?

I don't know a thing about any of you.

PANEL 6
And now the sign is in the foreground with Emmy and Odessa walking past and into the background. We can read the sign now. The letters are much more scratchy and creepy looking now. The sign reads: GOD SAVE US.

ODESSA:

Should I tell you about your brothers and sisters, then?

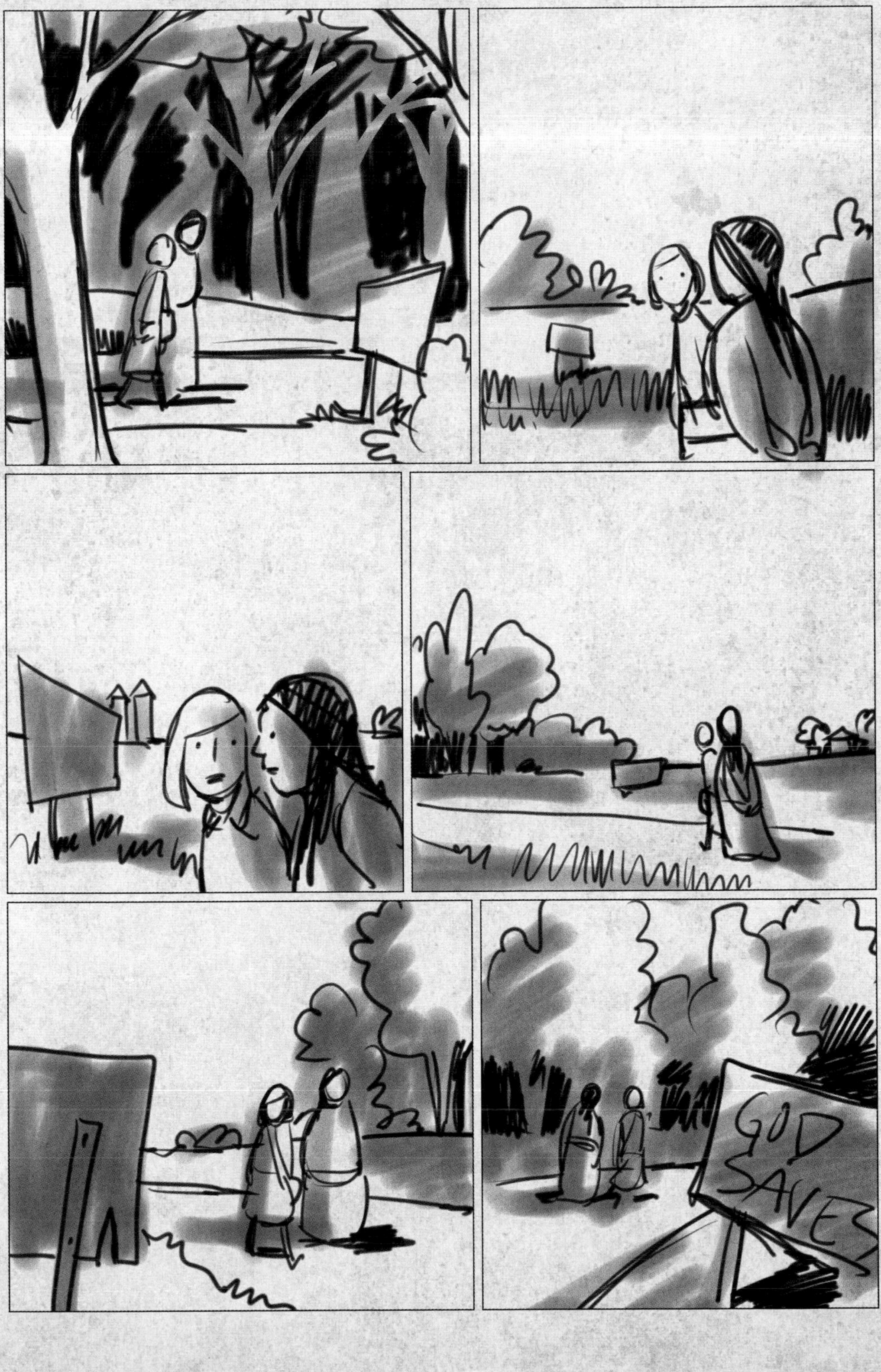
GOD
SAVE

Pages 12 and 13 comprise FLASHBACKS. Each panel focuses on a different member of the family.

PANEL 1
Cut to a shot of Odessa in the middle of the woods. The brush grows wild. It is night, and there are animals all around--birds, possums, deer, rabbits, all looking at Odessa, who stands among them, sort of a slightly more creepy Disney Princess moment.

CAPTION (Odessa):

"We're each of us **different**.

"We each have our own **gifts**.

"Take me, for instance.

"I have a connection to the woods and all the creatures that live thereabouts.

PANEL 2
Cut to a shot of Levi, sitting around a hobo fire, playing a tune on a bird flute. All around him, ghostly, vaporous figures gather, listening.

CAPTION (Odessa):

"**Levi**, on the other hand, is a **psychopomp**...

"...and he guides the dead to the afterlife...

"...and the living from one stage of life to the next.

SFX (Musical Notes):

Musical notes

PANEL 3
Cut to a shot of Mildred--a vague outline--walking along. She is walking past a tobacco field. A swarm of locusts is swooping around behind her, flying in clouds like smoke.

CAPTION (Odessa):

"**Mildred** is quiet and only rarely seen.

"She is a force of **disorder** and **chaos**.

"Where she treads, disaster often follows.

PANEL 4
Cut to a shot of Willa, sitting in a rocking chair in a dusty old house. She is knitting away, and the cloth she knits is bunched around her on the floor.

CAPTION (Odessa):

"**Willa** is a **knitting witch**.

"She can stitch out the knots of fate with them needles of hers...

"...controlling **fortune** and **calamity** alike.

SFX (Knitting):

Tik-tik-t-tik-tik-tik

PANEL 1
Cut to a shot of Kaine, looming over the bed of a sleeping child, whispering to them. In the shadows behind him, hideous shade-figures take shape.

CAPTION (Odessa):

"**Kaine** is a **bogeyman**.

"No one who is sleeping will wake in his presence…and his whispers bring vivid--and **even deadly**--nightmares.

"If I were you, I wouldn't want to choose him as my guide.

PANEL 2
Cut to a shot of Corbin, a blood-dripping straight razor in his hand. A skeletal-faced phantom is appearing before him.

CAPTION (Odessa):

"The same can be said for **Corbin**.

"He's a **necromancer,** and he can call up haints to do his bidding…

"…but only those he kills himself will heed his commands.

PANEL 3
Cut to a shot of Amaryllis, standing on the beach at night, looking out toward crashing waves. She is reaching out, and the surf and the waves take on the shape of mythical creatures--dragons and unicorns. This is the same beach we saw in 9.1 (but the house is not there).

CAPTION (Odessa):

"A pity you'll never meet **Amaryllis**.

"Like you, she could bend all of reality to her will.

PANEL 4
Pull back, and we see Hester, again younger and more innocent looking. We're behind her as she looks toward Amaryllis at the beach.

CAPTION (Odessa):

"She was the **greatest** of us.

"But she took **Hester** as her student…"

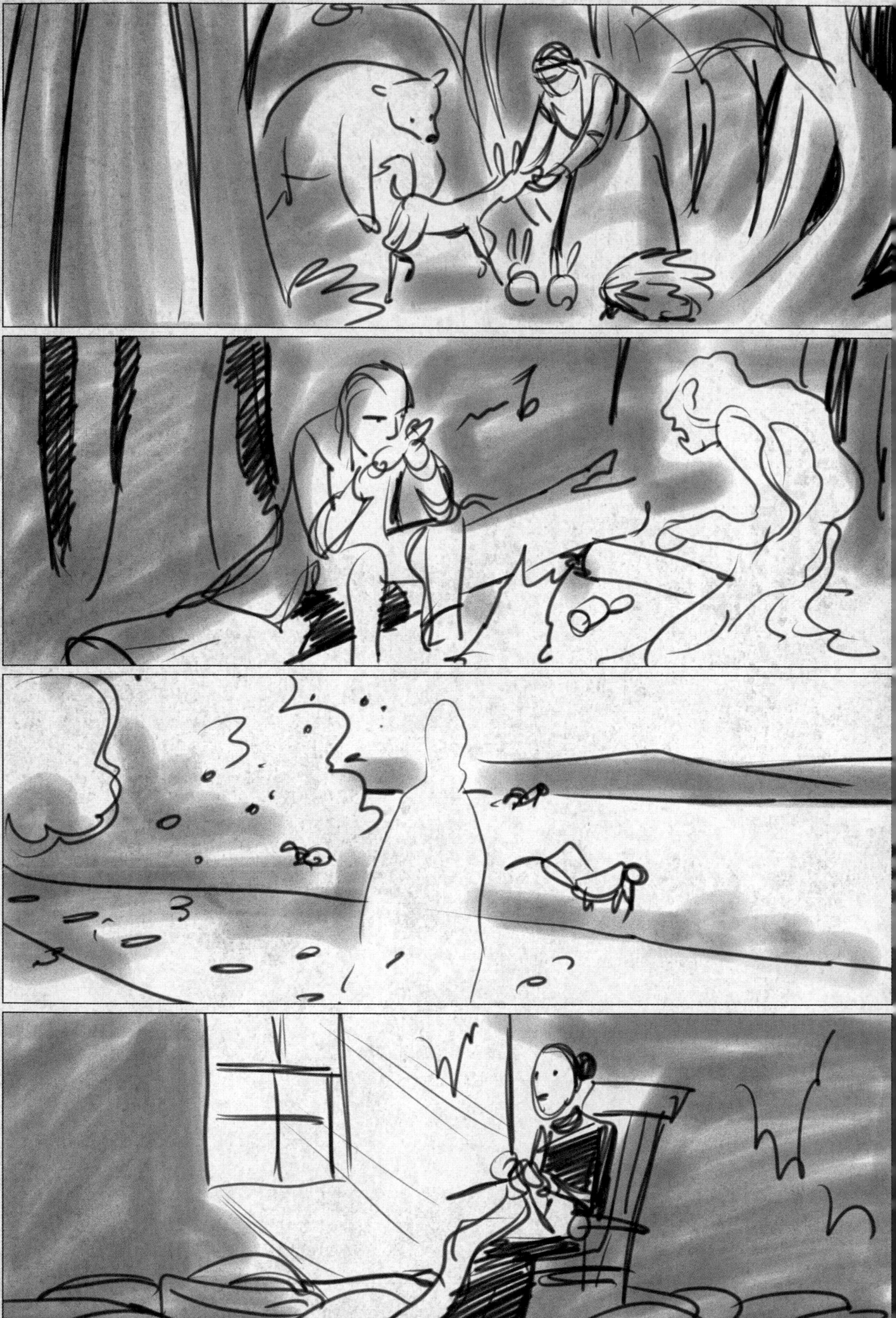

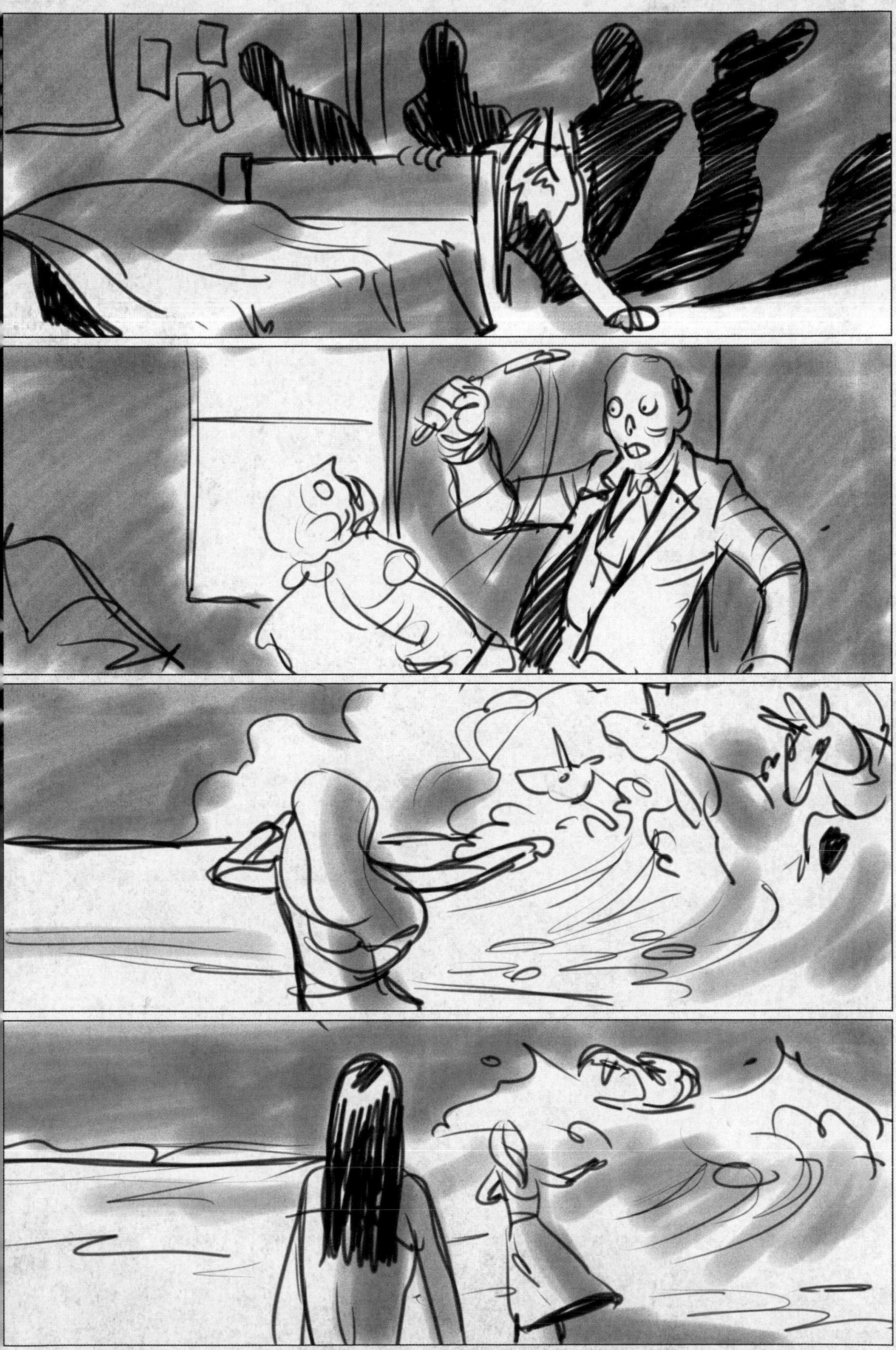

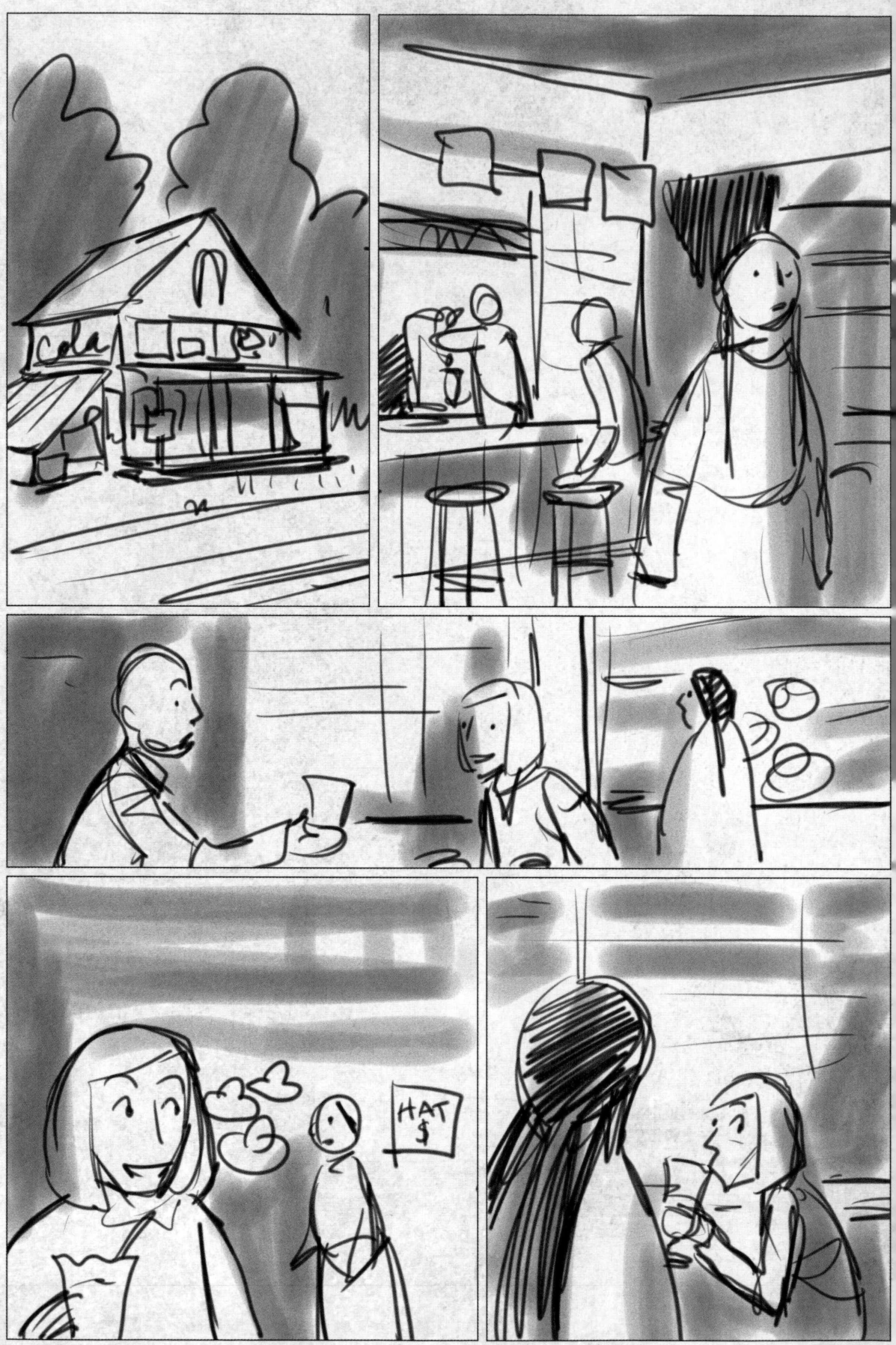
Cola
HAT
$

PANEL 1
Cut back to the HERE AND NOW. We are in downtown Harrow now. We've seen the city before, back in the second arc. Here we see a small drugstore. The window also proudly proclaims SODA FOUNTAIN.

ODESSA (OP, from drug store):

...and that was her **undoing**.

PANEL 2
Inside now, and we see Emmy and Odessa in the store. While Odessa is standing nearby, looking around, Emmy is sitting at the counter of the soda fountain (reference: http://cf.collectorsweekly.com/uploads/2014/04/1920-washington-DC-shorpy.jpg). The man behind the counter is preparing an ice cream float.

EMMY:

What happened to her?

What did Hester do?

ODESSA:

Oh, I don't know that you want to hear about that.

PANEL 3
The man behind the counter looks at Emmy and Odessa nervously as he slides a couple of ice cream floats to them. He is serving Emmy first.

SERVER:

Here you go, Ms. Emmy.

No charge.

EMMY:

Thank you kindly.

PANEL 4
Emmy has her ice cream float in front of her, but she glances back at Odessa, who is looking at a display of flowered straw hats.

EMMY:

Are you sure you don't want one?

They're **delicious**...

...maybe one of my favorite things even though I don't get them often.

ODESSA:

I'll pass, if it's all the same to you.

PANEL 5
Odessa steps closer, almost looking down her nose at Emmy as she sips from her float.

ODESSA:

Such pleasures are not for our kind.

They **bind** us...

...like food from the fair folk.

PANEL 1
Emmy turns in her seat, the glass in hand, ready to take another sip. Odessa looks at her, disappointed.

EMMY:

What do you mean?

ODESSA:

It's like Levi and those pigs' feet of his.

These are the pleasures of natural folks.

PANEL 2
Close on Odessa, looking a little sad.

ODESSA:

We should have been more vigilant.

We should have watched more carefully.

To pull you away from all this now...

...will be **painful**.

PANEL 3
Emmy, growing concerned, sets her half-finished float on the counter. She looks at Odessa, a little worried.

EMMY:

I don't understand.

PANEL 4
Odessa turns away from Emmy, waving her concerns away.

ODESSA:

It's nothing that should trouble you right now.

Finish your drink.

We should return to the lodge soon and--

PANEL 5
Emmy looks at Odessa, not necessarily stern, but urgent.

EMMY:

Tell me.

PANEL 6
Odessa looks at Emmy, struggling to find the right words, trying to change the subject.

ODESSA:

You asked about Amaryllis.

EMMY:

You're changing the subject.

ODESSA:

Why don't I tell you about her, hmm?

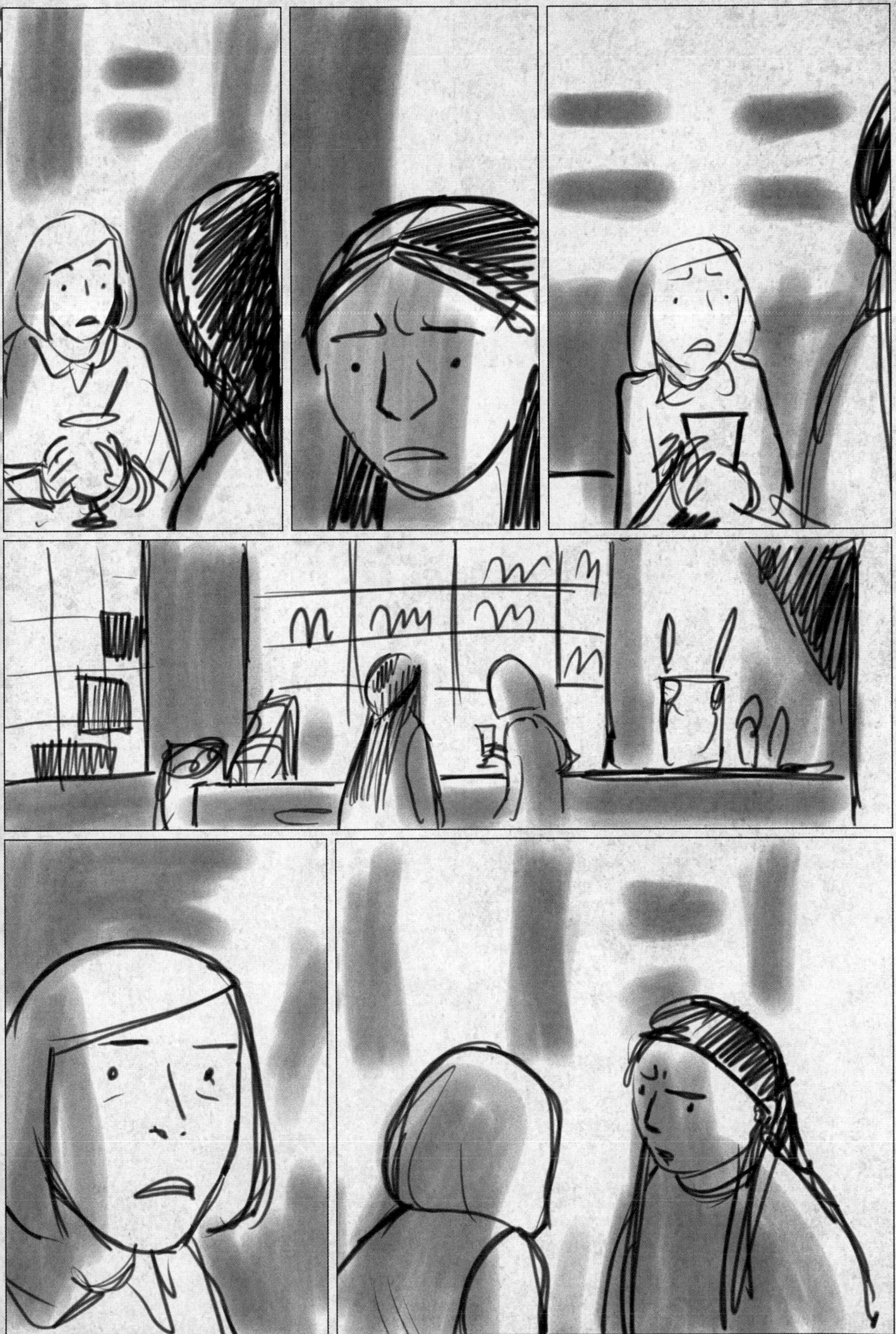

PAGES 16–18 are FLASHBACKS.

PANEL 1
Cut to the FLASHBACK. We are back at the beach, the same scene we saw on 13.3. Amaryllis stands at the water's edge, reaching out. Hester is behind her. The lighthouse is in the background, casting its glow across the beach.

CAPTION (Odessa):

"Once…long ago…our numbers were **plentiful**. We were spread out across the world.

"Over time, some of us simply **vanished**…faded like old memories…

"…or left this realm in search of others.

PANEL 2
Close on Amaryllis.

CAPTION (Odessa):

"But others were **killed**.

"Even though we are long lived, we can die.

"Even the most powerful of us can be **stricken** from this world.

PANEL 3
Past Hester. Amaryllis stands at the shore, looking back at her.

CAPTION (Odessa):

"There was even a time when we **warred** against one another…"

AMARYLLIS:

Come here, Hester.

Look out across the waves with me.

CAPTION (Odessa):

"…sibling killing sibling out of **greed** and **jealousy** and even **boredom**.

PANEL 4
Hester is walking up to the shore with Amaryllis. The glow of the lighthouse washes over them both.

CAPTION (Odessa):

"Amaryllis helped to put an end to the conflict among us."

AMARYLLIS:

Tell me what you see out there.

CAPTION (Odessa):

"She helped establish the law…the tradition…that no member of our family would **ever** kill another.

PANEL 5
Close on Hester, troubled.

CAPTION (Odessa):

"She saw in Hester gifts almost equal to her own."

HESTER:

Nothing.

I don't see anything.

CAPTION (Odessa):

"It was a power that Hester herself could not see…

PANEL 6
Looking toward the beach from across the surf, where mythical shapes take shape in the foamy waves. Amaryllis and Hester stand on the beach, the flashing lighthouse behind them.

CAPTION (Odessa):

"And it **maddened** her."

AMARYLLIS:

But you can see anything you want.

You can shape the water in any way you can imagine.

That is the **talent** you and I share.

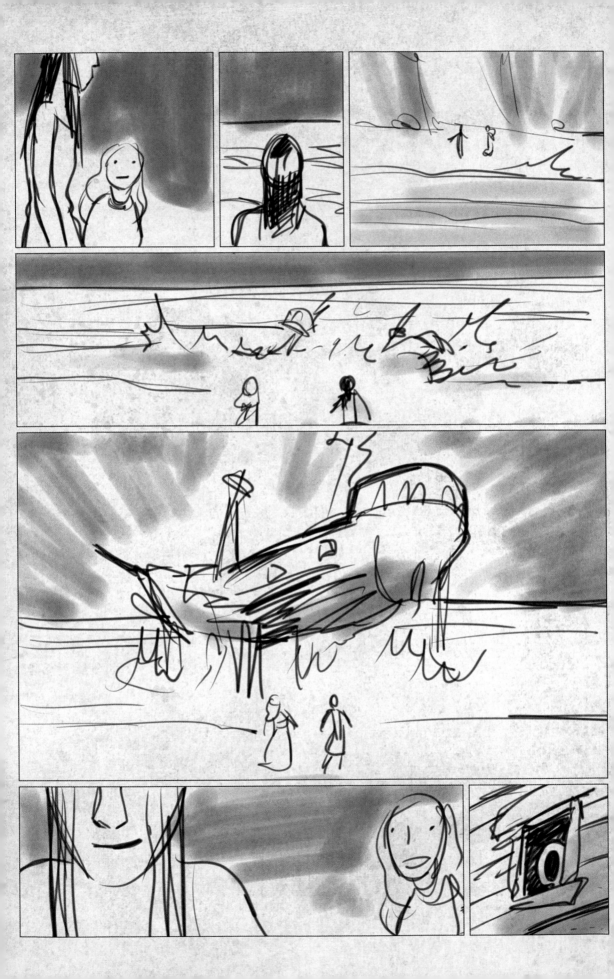

PANEL 1
Close on Amaryllis and Hester. Amaryllis looks down at the younger woman, who is staring out across the waves.

HESTER:

What if I wanted to call something up from **below**--from **beneath** the water?

AMARYLLIS:

Try.

Try and see what happens.

PANEL 2
Close on Hester, concentrating.

NO COPY.

PANEL 3
On the water (similar angle to 17.1), a spray erupting across the surface.

NO COPY.

PANEL 4
Bigger panel, as the bow of an ancient pirate ship erupts from the water in a splash. The ship is old and waterlogged and rotted.

SFX (Ship):

Sploosh!

PANEL 5
The ship is now floating blackly on the surface, its sails in wet tatters, the light of the lighthouse flashing across it.

NO COPY.

PANEL 6
Close on Hester and Amaryllis. Amaryllis looks at the younger woman, pleased.

AMARYLLIS:

See?

Look at what you've done.

Look at what you've created, just by--

PANEL 1
Big panel as a CANNONBALL speeds through the night, blasting through Amaryllis, tearing her in half. She wears an expression of horrible shock on her face. Hester stands by the side, spattered in blood, but unfazed. In the background, we see the pirate ship, a plume of smoke rising from it as the cannon fires.

SFX (Cannon):

Wa-Boom!

PANEL 2
Hester, blood spattered, kneels before Amaryllis's ripped-up body. Blood is soaking into the sand. Hester reaches down, touching the gruesome scene.

CAPTION (Odessa):

"Hester **coveted** the power Amaryllis possessed…

"…and so she broke our traditions for the first time…

PANEL 3
Close on Hester, putting a piece of bloody flesh in her mouth. Her fingers are stained with blood. Blood dribbles down her chin.

CAPTION (Odessa):

"…and she **claimed** that power for **her own**.

PANEL 4
From behind Hester now, turning, looking inland. She is looking toward the scene we saw on 9.1. The meeting lodge has appeared on the beach.

CAPTION (Odessa):

"That is why we banished her…

"…because we weren't willing to go against the laws ourselves…"

PANEL 1
Cut back to the HERE AND NOW. Emmy and Odessa are walking along another forested path.

ODESSA:

...because we were **unwilling** to kill her.

PANEL 2
Angling past Odessa in profile. Emmy looks at her, the shadows from the trees giving her a slightly sinister look.

EMMY:

Unwilling?

Or afraid to try?

PANEL 3
Emmy and Odessa continue down the path. Odessa raises an eyebrow at Emmy.

ODESSA:

Just then...

...you sounded a bit like her.

PANEL 4
Close on Odessa.

ODESSA:

We always hoped she would simply vanish...

...like so many of our kind who came before...

PANEL 5
Odessa and Emmy continue along the forest path.

ODESSA:

...but she settled here...

...and it was here she broke another of our commandments.

PANEL 6
Odessa looks to Emmy, her face taking on a serious cast.

ODESSA:

We are not **gods**, Emmy.

We cannot establish **churches**.

We cannot take on **worshipers**.

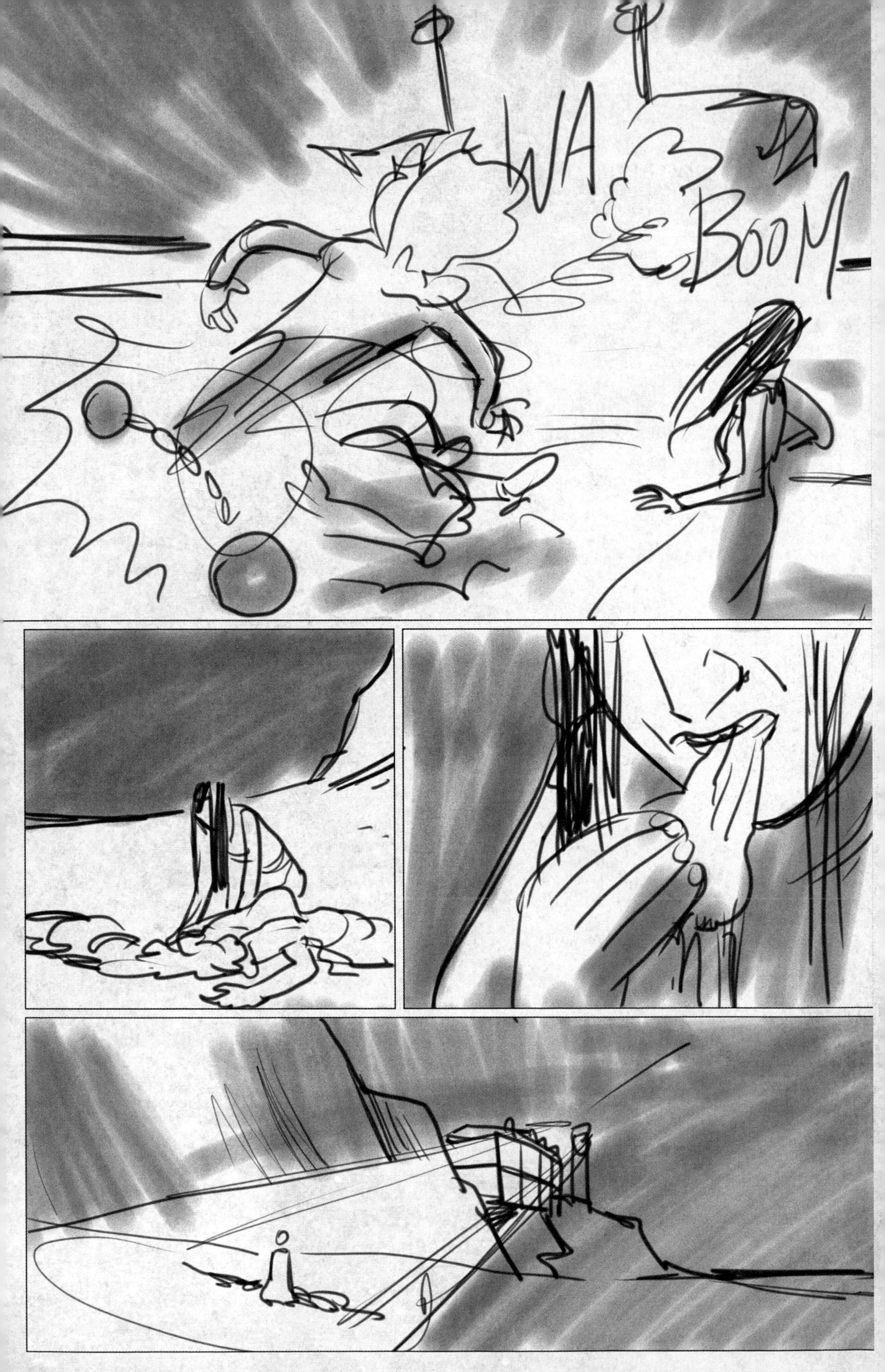
WA
BOOM

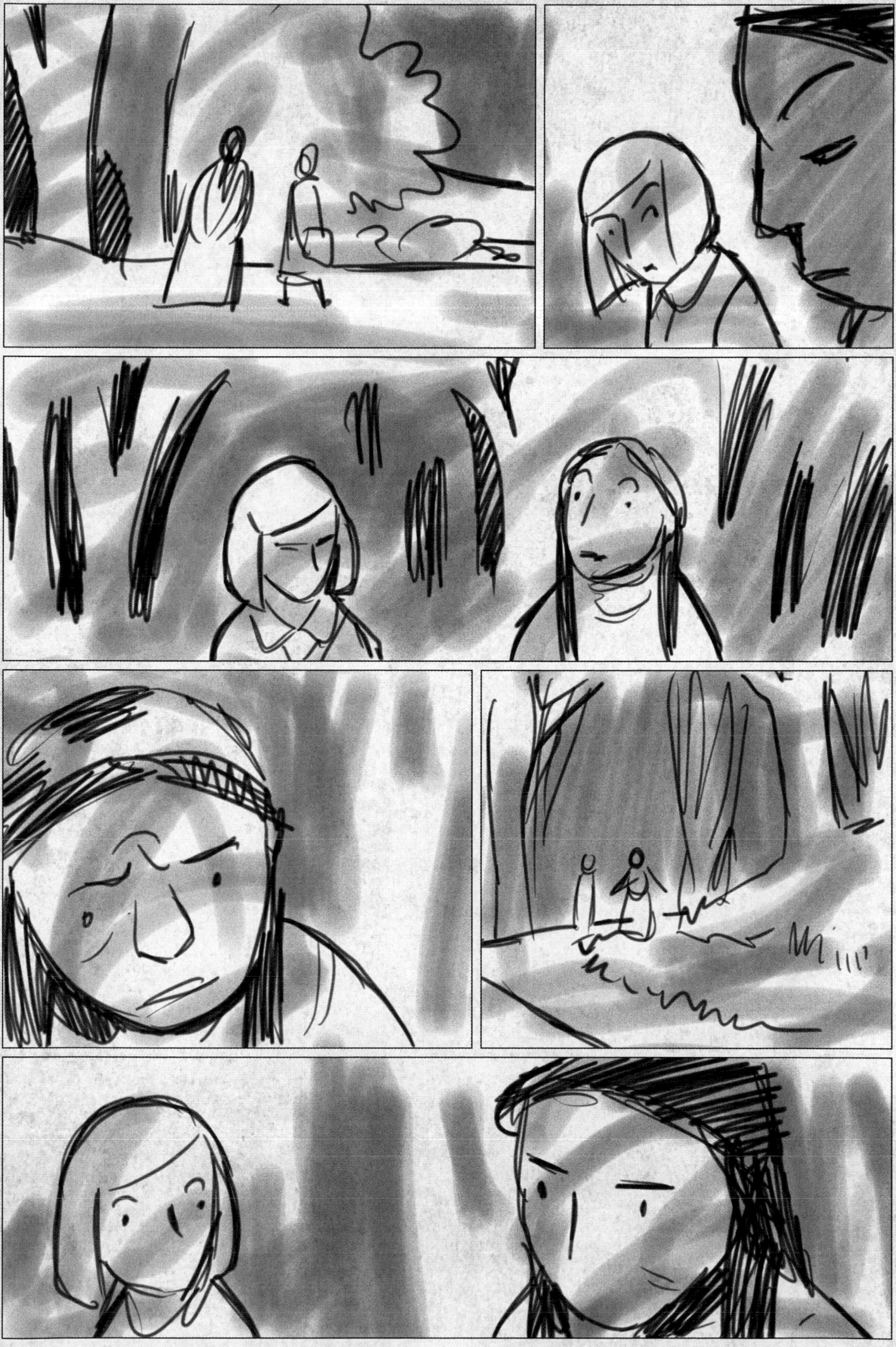

PANEL 1
Emmy looks at Odessa, a slight expression of confusion.

EMMY:

You talk like I've done that.

I don't--

PANEL 2
Odessa looks at Emmy.

ODESSA:

Not intentionally, no.

But you roam the county as if surveying your domain.

The people here, they look to you for protection and guidance.

They **love** and **fear** you.

PANEL 3
Close on Odessa.

ODESSA:

If that's not a god…

…then what is?

PANEL 4
Odessa and Emmy walk along. Emmy looks down.

ODESSA:

Don't fret, child.

You didn't know our ways.

We've only just come to you to help you discover who you really are.

PANEL 5
Emmy looks at Odessa, hopeful.

EMMY:

And you can help me understand this power I have inside me?

PANEL 6
Odessa and Emmy are emerging from the forest, into the light.

ODESSA:

The **power**…

…and the **darkness**.

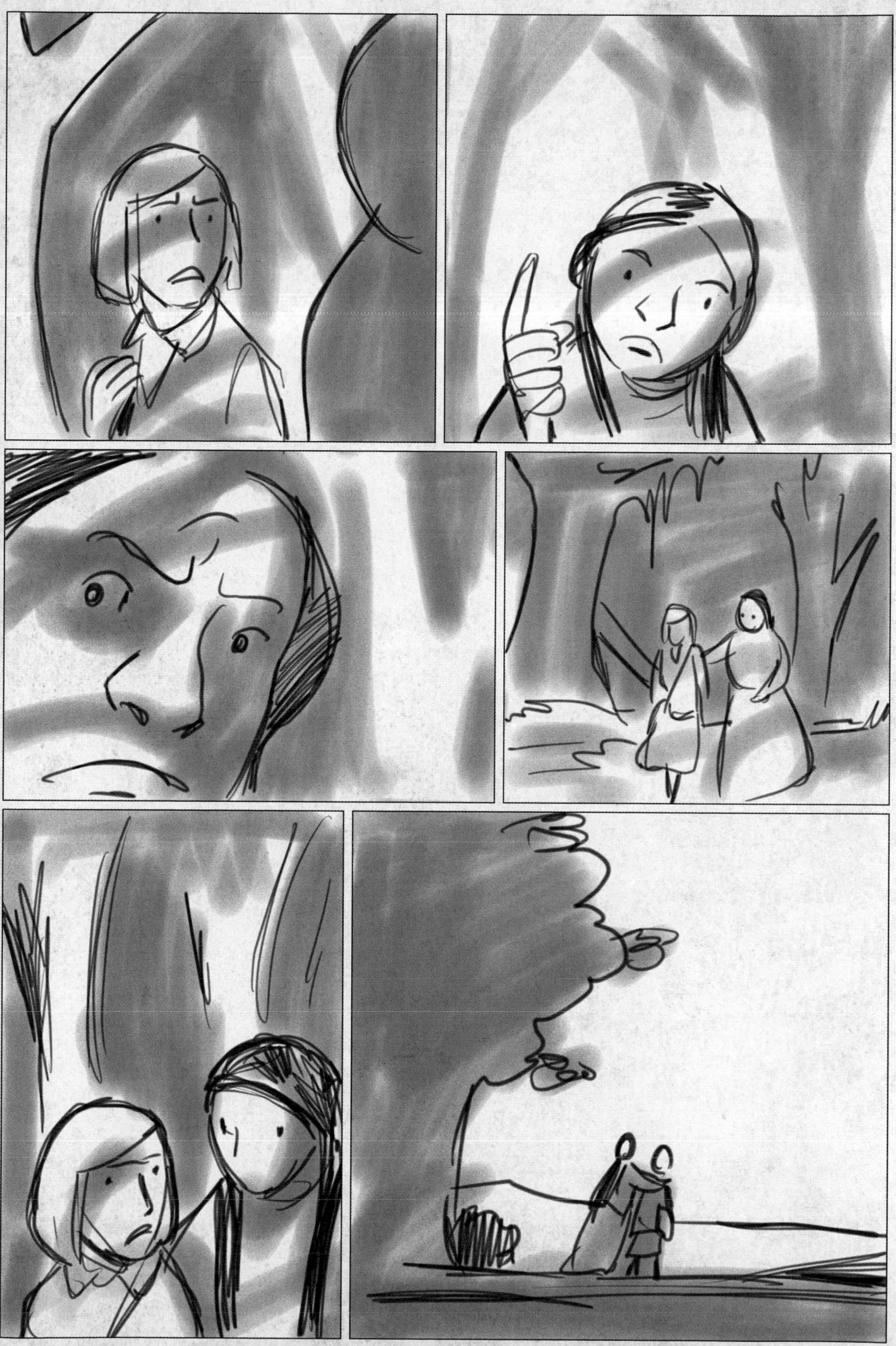

PAGE 21 (Five Panels)

PANEL 1
Emmy and Odessa now approach the meeting lodge, standing in the clearing.

ODESSA:

You only need to **accept** our guidance.

PANEL 2
Emmy and Odessa are crossing the clearing toward the lodge. Emmy looks at Odessa, a little sad.

EMMY:

But that would mean leaving Harrow County…

…leaving all my friends…

…my Pa…

PANEL 3
Angle past Emmy. Odessa, climbing the steps, looks back and down at her, sadly.

NO COPY.

PANEL 4
Emmy and Odessa enter the house, Odessa leading the way.

EMMY:

I suppose I could come back, though, right?

I could visit?

PANEL 5
Odessa looks back at Emmy sadly as she pushes open a doorway.

ODESSA:

No, child.

I'm afraid not.

PAGE 22 (Six Panels)

PANEL 1
Odessa and Emmy step into the room where the other members of the Family await.

EMMY:

But--

PANEL 2
Odessa (with the other members of the family behind her) turns to face Emmy.

ODESSA:

Much of Harrow County was **created** by Hester.

That's how she built her own steps to **divinity**.

Even what she didn't create, she **influenced**.

The very soil is **rich** with her **blood**.

And it can bind you the way it bound her.

PANEL 3
Close on Emmy, eyes wide and afraid.

ODESSA (OP):

You'll never be able to come with us…

…to truly become one of us…

…to truly understand **your** place in the world…

…until **this** place is destroyed.

PANEL 4
Angle past Odessa and some of the family members. Emmy is growing afraid and frightened.

EMMY:

You want me to **destroy** Harrow County?

I won't do that!

I can't!

PANEL 5
Past Emmy. On the family. Levi is stepping up beside Odessa. He offers a creepy smile.

LEVI:

Don't you worry none, little sister.

We wouldn't **never** ask you to shoulder such a burden.

And that's why…

PANEL 6
Extreme close-up on Levi's smile.

LEVI:

…**we're** going to do it for you.

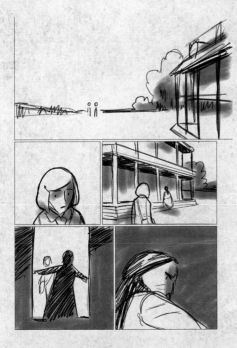

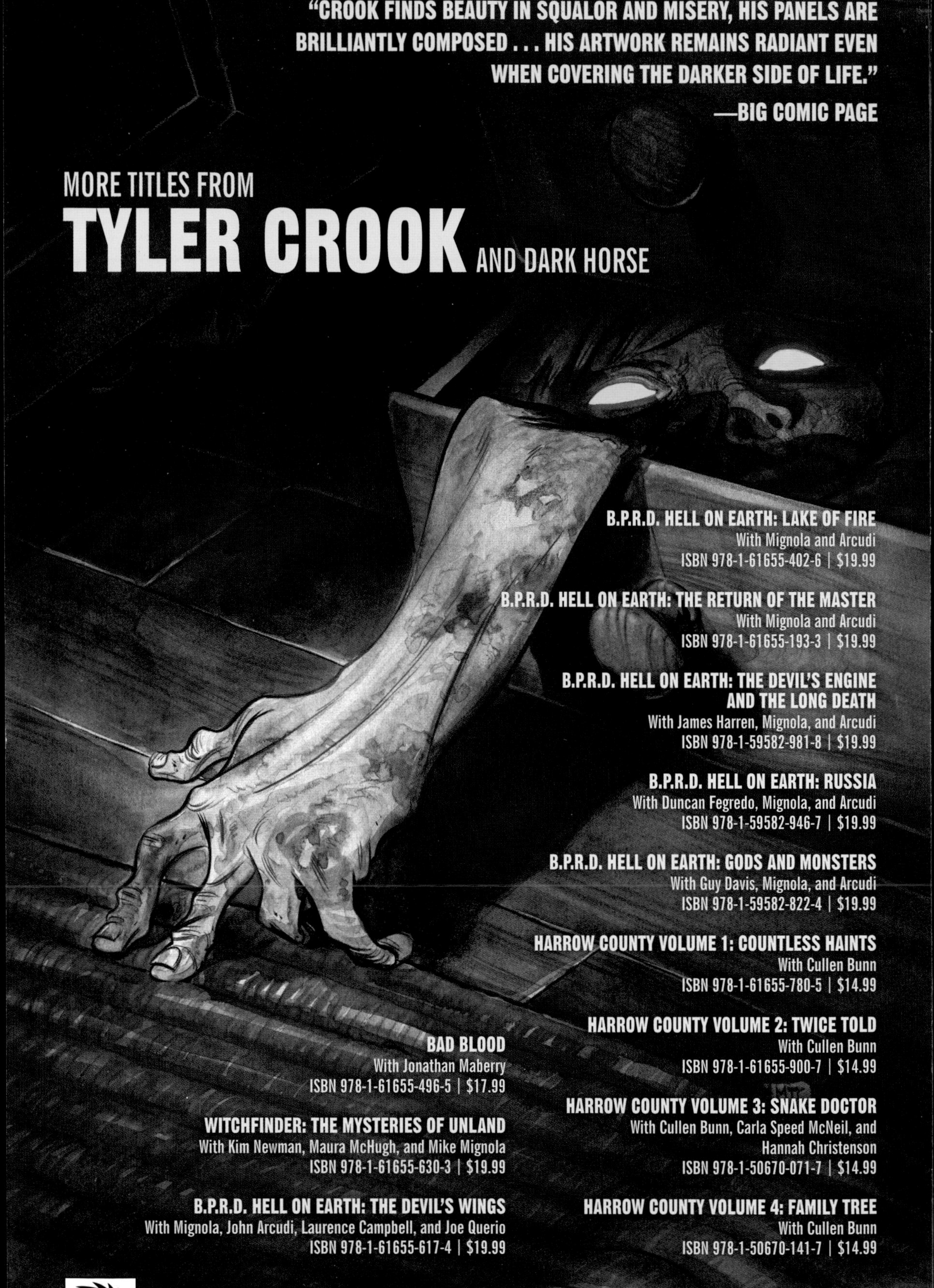

"CROOK FINDS BEAUTY IN SQUALOR AND MISERY, HIS PANELS ARE BRILLIANTLY COMPOSED . . . HIS ARTWORK REMAINS RADIANT EVEN WHEN COVERING THE DARKER SIDE OF LIFE."

—BIG COMIC PAGE

MORE TITLES FROM

TYLER CROOK AND DARK HORSE

BAD BLOOD
With Jonathan Maberry
ISBN 978-1-61655-496-5 | $17.99

WITCHFINDER: THE MYSTERIES OF UNLAND
With Kim Newman, Maura McHugh, and Mike Mignola
ISBN 978-1-61655-630-3 | $19.99

B.P.R.D. HELL ON EARTH: THE DEVIL'S WINGS
With Mignola, John Arcudi, Laurence Campbell, and Joe Querio
ISBN 978-1-61655-617-4 | $19.99

B.P.R.D. HELL ON EARTH: LAKE OF FIRE
With Mignola and Arcudi
ISBN 978-1-61655-402-6 | $19.99

B.P.R.D. HELL ON EARTH: THE RETURN OF THE MASTER
With Mignola and Arcudi
ISBN 978-1-61655-193-3 | $19.99

B.P.R.D. HELL ON EARTH: THE DEVIL'S ENGINE AND THE LONG DEATH
With James Harren, Mignola, and Arcudi
ISBN 978-1-59582-981-8 | $19.99

B.P.R.D. HELL ON EARTH: RUSSIA
With Duncan Fegredo, Mignola, and Arcudi
ISBN 978-1-59582-946-7 | $19.99

B.P.R.D. HELL ON EARTH: GODS AND MONSTERS
With Guy Davis, Mignola, and Arcudi
ISBN 978-1-59582-822-4 | $19.99

HARROW COUNTY VOLUME 1: COUNTLESS HAINTS
With Cullen Bunn
ISBN 978-1-61655-780-5 | $14.99

HARROW COUNTY VOLUME 2: TWICE TOLD
With Cullen Bunn
ISBN 978-1-61655-900-7 | $14.99

HARROW COUNTY VOLUME 3: SNAKE DOCTOR
With Cullen Bunn, Carla Speed McNeil, and Hannah Christenson
ISBN 978-1-50670-071-7 | $14.99

HARROW COUNTY VOLUME 4: FAMILY TREE
With Cullen Bunn
ISBN 978-1-50670-141-7 | $14.99

DARK HORSE BOOKS

AVAILABLE AT YOUR LOCAL COMICS SHOP OR BOOKSTORE! • To find a comics shop in your area, call 1-888-266-4226.
For more information or to order direct visit DarkHorse.com or call 1-800-862-0052 Mon.–Fri. 9 a.m. to 5 p.m. Pacific Time. Prices and availability subject to change without notice.